MIRACLE IN SLOW MOTION:
From autism diagnosis to an exciting future

Part One – Tim from birth to 11 years old

by

Sally Wagter

Published by Autism Development Publishing

Some names and identifying details
have been changed to protect the
privacy of individuals.

ISBN: 978-1-8380563-1-5

Cover art by germancreative

Autism Development Publishing

www.autismdevelopmentconsultancy.com
www.releasingmychildspotential.com

DEDICATION

For Tim, whose love, commitment
and perseverance amazes me more
each day…

Contents

Foreword

You have picked up one of those rare books that can alter the trajectory of your life. And, if you have a child on the autism spectrum, this book can *certainly* enable you to change the life of that special person.

What you are about to read is a very moving story of a family's journey through autism – but it isn't *only* that. It is a practical and inspirational blueprint for how you can approach a child or adult who has special challenges. There is a lot to take from this book, and I am very excited for you to take it. The messages we receive and the advice we are often given when our children are diagnosed with autism or a related challenge can be incredibly unhelpful, counterproductive, and even unkind. Without question, this was true for Sally.

The difference with her is that, after weathering an incredible array of challenges with her son, with herself, and with the people trying to help her son, Sally breaks free. And, in so doing, she is able to help her son in the most profound way.

I feel a special kinship with Sally, her husband Erik, and Tim, their amazing son. I used to be where Tim was. I crossed the bridge that Tim has crossed.

When I was a young boy, I was diagnosed with severe autism, registering a tested I.Q. below 30. I didn't respond to my name or any other attempts at communication. I made no eye contact with others. I was mute, with no language or any verbal indication of wants whatsoever. I seemed completely shut off to the world, often appearing to be deaf. Although I displayed no interest in other people, I remained fascinated with inanimate objects, such as kitchen plates. In fact, I would often sit on the floor and spin a kitchen plate on its edge for hours and hours on end. Other repetitive behaviors, such as rocking back and forth or flapping my hands in front of my face, would continue throughout each day. I didn't want to be held and would often recoil from human touch.

After receiving the diagnosis, my parents raced from specialist to specialist, trying to find solutions. Instead, they received only the grimmest of prognoses.

I would be as I was for the rest of my life. I would never speak, certainly not in sentences. I would never have the capability to make friends and form meaningful relationships. I would always prefer objects to people.

And the predictions mounted. I would never go to a regular school, have a girlfriend or a job, a first love or a last day of summer camp. For me, there would be no high school or college graduation, no buying my first car or moving into my first home, no marriage, no career.

I would, always and forever, be encapsulated within my own world. The recommendation: lifelong institutionalization.

The only reason that this future did not become *my* future was because my parents (authors and teachers Barry Neil Kaufman and Samahria Lyte Kaufman) had the guts to venture in an entirely new direction. Discarding the pessimism and behavior-modification focus of traditional autism treatment, my parents developed a program to reach me. They called it The Son-Rise Program®.

Rather than trying to force me to conform to a world that I did not yet understand, they began by joining me in my world. This led to the development of the first signature technique of The Son-Rise Program: joining. When I would spin a plate, my mother would get a plate of her own and spin with me. When I would rock back and forth, my mother would rock with me.

Although many professionals vociferously criticized my parents at the time, my parents proved incredibly prescient. As they joined me, I began to trust them, bond with them, and let them into my world. For the first time, I started looking at them and *smiling* at them. They were valuing my world, my experience, and my interests.

And as I let them in, they encouraged me to come out, inviting me to engage with them, communicate with them, and play with them. They slowly built up my social interaction by designing games and activities centered around interests and motivations that I already had, such as animals and airplanes.

After my parents worked with me every day for three and a half years, I emerged from my autism without any trace of my former condition. All of those futures that I was never supposed to have – friends, girlfriends, first loves and last days of summer camp, sports teams, graduating college (I graduated from the Ivy League's Brown University with a degree in Biomedical Ethics), a fulfilling career, a wonderfully loving marriage – I went on to experience all of them.

After my autism journey, my father recounted our story in the bestselling book *Son-Rise: The Miracle Continues,* which was made into an award-winning NBC-TV movie called *Son-Rise: A Miracle of Love.* In 1983, my parents founded the Autism Treatment Center of America®, part of a charitable non-profit organization in Sheffield, Massachusetts. The ATCA serves as the worldwide teaching center for The Son-Rise Program. Parents and professionals from all over the world attend our training programs so that they can help their children in a loving, respectful, and open-hearted way to grow beyond their original prognoses.

Now, I am the former CEO and current Director of Global Education at the ATCA, and I've spent the past twenty-five years working to get the techniques of The Son-Rise Program into the hands of families who can use them, whether by helping families individually, working with professionals, or conducting lectures and seminars across the globe (and online). It warms my heart that my book, *Autism Breakthrough: The Groundbreaking Method That Has Helped Families All Over the World,* has changed the autism conversation in the many countries in which it was published and translated.

In fact, it was at a lecture I did in London in January of 2008 where I first met Sally. She took The Son-Rise Program strategies and techniques I outlined in the lecture right home with her to help her son. How incredible that my journey served as the catalyst – and then the roadmap – for Tim's magnificent transformation!

This book you've cracked open is a testament to the power of the parent. I am living proof of the fact that nothing has a bigger impact on any child's growth and flowering than the parent. No one loves their child like a parent. No one has the long-term commitment and dedication that a parent has. And, in truth, no 4-hour evaluation can possibly match the day in, day out experience that a parent has with their own child. It is the leveraging of this – rather than the dismissing of it – that holds the key to the fruition of our children's potential.

One thing I know for sure is that change comes from being willing to do something different. *You've got to do something different to get something different.*

Change doesn't come from wishing for it or begging for it, nor from railing against how things are. And it usually doesn't come from doing what everyone else is doing. It comes from being willing to step outside the box – to *leap* outside the box – and take a route that is not only different but often *opposite* to what everyone says you're supposed to do.

And that is exactly what Sally did. (And that's what Erik did, too!) Sally had the daring to listen to her own voice…and then follow it. And that rebounded directly to the benefit of her son and, ultimately, to her entire family.

Sally's son Tim had a lot of enormous challenges – from his inability to communicate (in a way that others could understand) to his difficulty with just getting through the day to his full-throttle meltdowns. These issues did not just get in Tim's way; they dominated a lot of the whole family's daily experience.

Like any caring mother, Sally searched for ways to help him. Unlike most, when she saw things that didn't work and didn't feel right to her, she didn't just go along. She changed course. She had the courage to value what she saw and felt above what she was told. She put her son's future over the avoidance of being judged by others.

That's what made the difference.

She could have forced Tim to remain in a cookie-cutter educational system that wasn't working for him. She didn't. She could have done as she was told and tried to stamp out Tim's differentness and uniqueness. She didn't. Instead, she took the first step in any successful Son-Rise Program: She prioritized what Tim loved, valued, and needed above adhering to artificial benchmarks. Above what experts preached. And above what the world demanded.

When Sally tried Son-Rise Program techniques, and Tim responded powerfully from within himself, she went with what worked for Tim. She chose something that felt honoring of her son and right for her.

And, wow, did Tim ever blossom. Explosively! Spectacularly! Social, friendly, funny, thoughtful, caring, and incredibly creative, Tim is an exceptional human being. He has unbelievable musical talent, but he doesn't exhibit those talents (writing songs, playing the piano) in a solitary way but rather in a social way. (On YouTube, I recently watched a hilarious and musical take on Robin Hood (all written by Tim) starring Tim and his (neurotypical) friends. It was awesome.)

Read this book, and let it inspire you and guide you. Just as Sally, Erik, and Tim did great things, so can you, and so can your family.

Our kids are capable of more.

We are capable of more.

As Sally and I had dinner together at the restaurant of the London hotel I was staying at while doing a lecture in London several years after that first lecture at which we met, I was bowled over. This woman, who years ago was (understandably) lost and scared, was a beaming powerhouse! Confident, strong, enthusiastic, and justifiably proud of what she and her son had accomplished, she thanked me – tearfully – and told me how excited she was about an idea she had: to write a book about her family's journey. I said that I thought the idea was absolutely wonderful and could help a lot of other families out there. And she did it!

And I will tell you: Sally's sincerity, honesty (she doesn't shy away from discussing her own difficulties and stumbles), and, ultimately, her growth come bursting through the pages. Wherever you are in your own journey, I am 100% certain that the reading of this book in your hands will be a very awakening and transformative experience. I stand with you and celebrate you as you embark upon this most amazing adventure.

Raun K. Kaufman
Author, *Autism Breakthrough*
Director of Global Education, Autism Treatment Center of America
Facebook: https://m.facebook.com/Raun.K.Kaufman
Web: www.RaunKKaufman.com

WANT HELP?
The Autism Treatment Center of America can help you!
Facebook: https://m.facebook.com/AutismTreatment
Web: www.AutismTreatment.org
Phone: +1-413-229-2100

Chapter One – The Beginning

'I feel a bit bored and in need of an adventure,' Tim said as he sauntered into the kitchen yesterday morning.

'Why don't you get the bus to Worthing and wander around. Are you OK with the bus to get there?'

'Yeah, sure.'

'Oh, and can you try to be back by five so you can eat before the party tonight?'

'Of course!'

As he left the house I called out, 'Love you.'

He called back, 'Love you forever Mum, see you later!' and he was gone.

But it wasn't always this way. Tim's freedom and independence had been a long time coming…

I will begin at the beginning. Erik, my gorgeous Dutch husband, and I met in Holland and after a year and a half of dating, back and forth between countries, he came to live in England and on the day he arrived, I agreed to marry him. We would sit and talk for hours. Going to cafes and putting the world to rights felt like such a special treat with him. He was so easy to talk to and very switched on emotionally, and he seemed to get me just by looking at me. He was an amazing songwriter and a real people person. He fitted straight into my lovely circle of friends and we ended up spending many evenings discussing 'life, the universe and everything' around dinner party tables.

He was also funny. His spoken English was amazing but also became a source of amusement between us. On one of his first visits to England, before we were going out, a friend asked where he was staying and Erik called out to them across the pub, 'I'm sleeping with Steve tonight!' We all fell about laughing.

At the time, I was teaching full-time in a local school and spent many hours sitting on the floor after a long day, marking work and preparing lessons. My life was full of school concerts, shows, fairs, projects and report-writing. Erik was a social worker and had found a job in a residential school nearby. He worked with children with varying challenges and spent his time playing sport with the children and putting on talent shows in order to raise their self-esteem. We both shared a love of music. I had a music degree and he had spent years in a band and as a worship leader in his church. I was a pianist, while he was a guitar player and singer. Music, for both of us, was our emotional outlet and a huge part of our identity. Little did we know how precious this was and how soon these opportunities would be taken from us.

Our wedding day was perfect – a beautiful lazy summer day, laughing with family and friends, with children running about in the beautiful grounds at the reception. The guests were mostly my friends and family, so that Erik had to welcome many people he had never met before. His best man, however, had travelled through many countries to be by his side and his closest family were with us.

As Erik and I both worked with children and loved children, it was an automatic assumption that we would have children one day. My sister once said that there was never a right time and we made a decision after a year of marriage to go for it. I became pregnant immediately and we were suddenly thrown into the world of expectant parents. Excited? Yes. Nervous? Yes, especially me. We moved, as we had been living in a tiny flat and on moving day, a whole team of friends came to help us out. That was one amazing thing about our life at that point – we had a lovely network of friends.

The birth… now what can I say? Doctors called it normal. For me, it was the most physically painful and terrifying time of my life. They kept sending me home because I wasn't dilated enough and when I begged for them to let me stay, they said I could stay but Erik couldn't stay with me. Well, I couldn't go through that on my own, so I had to hobble back home and cope with the agonising contractions without any help, only to rush back and be told I was 10cm dilated and about to have my baby. I was in too much pain to be relieved that something was finally happening at that point.

Three hours later and I was still writhing in agony. The gas and air made me dizzy and I felt drunk, but it did nothing to reduce the pain.

If you could bottle that moment when the pain leaves and your baby arrives, I think you would never be unhappy again. The euphoria of seeing for the first time the tiny little human being that has been a part of you for so long is overwhelming. I was in love instantly. He was perfect, beautiful. He bonded with me and breastfed immediately. I phoned my Mum at four in the morning and she was so excited she couldn't sleep. She and Dad came to see us first thing.

A whole little person and he was ours. I kept staring at him. I marvelled at him. I loved him so much. How can you describe how much you love your newborn baby? Words are hard to find.

The Early Days

When we took Tim home, we were immediately immersed in caring for him, feeding him, changing him, loving him. We noticed that he cried a lot – quite excessively in fact, as he had colic for the first three months of his life. However hard we tried, he could not be pacified. At one point in the first two weeks he cried so much that Erik's parents, who were staying, cried too. They couldn't help themselves – it was heart-breaking to see him in such pain and distress. What was wrong? We tried every colic treatment in the book. We walked around with him, burped him, jiggled him, soothed him… his pain and cries were excruciating to hear and he seemed so unsettled.

Immediately my Mum, who was a nutritional therapist, suggested we try sacro-cranial osteopathy. I had never heard of it, but my baby was crying and my Mum was suggesting something, so I decided it was best to try it. It helped a little. The osteopath explained that sometimes a baby's skull gets pushed and pulled out of shape during birth and the pressure on particular nerves can cause severe pain. Well, he would often sleep quite peacefully after treatments which we took as a good sign, but his erratic pain and crying would return quite unexpectedly.

When we were in the car and driving along, he seemed fine, but when we stopped or had to wait at lights, his screaming would start up. I remember on the way to his Dedication, we had to wait at the level crossing and the screaming started. We then had to wait outside a friend's house and it started again. When we got to the church, he had finally calmed down and I carried him in in his car seat. When the time came to go to the front, the pastor asked me to take him out and I remember a strong feeling of panic – would it start up the screaming and crying all over again? We were lucky – for the short time he was the centre of attention, he stayed calm.

Unfortunately, I had to go back to work when he was three months old and it meant the beginning of dividing myself between my child and the reality of having to earn money. If I could go back and change anything about that time, I would have found any other way to bring in money so I didn't have to leave him. I found myself writing school reports with one hand and feeding him with the other.

The first time we had to leave him was one of my most heart-breaking memories. I had sorted my work so I was running music clubs after school, bringing in quite good money and working only for that hour at the end of the school day. I thought this was clever, as I wouldn't have to leave him for so long. Because this particular school was a thirty-minute-drive away, I figured if I found someone near the school I wouldn't have to leave him for so long. However, I didn't know this lady very well and he didn't know her at all. I ridiculously trusted her out of necessity and when I returned ninety minutes later, I found him still strapped in his car seat and, according to the lady, he had been crying non-stop since we left. She hadn't been able to soothe him at all. Feeling angry, I wondered if she'd even bothered to take him out and walk around with him. I cuddled him and soothed him and cried all the way home, vowing I would never take him there again.

That's when my friend, Sarah, came to the rescue. Sarah saw Tim as we did. She fell in love with him straight away. In her words he was 'a beautiful baby with a smile to melt your heart and a keen sense of humour, who always wanted a cuddle'. She was a mother herself with lots of experience of other babies. She looked after Tim for two days a week during the first few years of his life while I worked and I felt safe leaving him with her as she really bonded with him and genuinely loved him, as he did her.

Sarah found him easy to play with and she genuinely adored the hours she spent with him. They would play with clothes pegs, sponges, stacking pots, they would sing songs and he would indicate animals to be included in the songs she was singing. There was such a bond of love and happiness between them. For me, that was the best gift ever. However, she was shocked at Tim's total sense of terror on waking up in the cot upstairs on his own at her house. When she saw this happen, she broke all her own rules and acted on her instinct with Tim, rocking him to sleep in her arms and always making sure he was never far away from her when asleep so she could immediately comfort him as he awoke.

At about a year old, he would point and clap with Sarah and wave goodbye. Tim would make eye contact with us – he was interested in being around us and would play alongside other babies. He smiled at us, gurgled and made happy noises. He started at one point to say 'Ma' for Mama and 'Pa' for papa and he even created a name for Sarah. He showed obvious delight in us and our attentions. He started walking at eleven months and would career around the room, full of enthusiasm. A friend and I would meet up with our babies and discuss their developmental stages – whose teeth were coming through first and who was eating what etc. I enjoyed these get-togethers and loved talking with my friend about all the developmental changes we could see in our babies.

We have photo albums full of Tim's bright, happy face, eyes smiling cheekily right into ours, sharing fun. He was quite exceptionally connected, reaching out for other babies and engaging with us in play and laughter. At my parents' house he would kick a football around the garden and Erik, who had played in the Dutch Under-Thirteen football team, was excited by his love for it and his great dribbling skills. He would run around the park and we would lift him into the air, gazing into his beautiful smiling face and spin him around with the sun on our faces while he laughed and then reached up for more. We would take picnics to the beach and Erik and I would walk along the sand with him, laughing and chasing him. He ate big, chunky cakes, which I always made with gluten-free flour and sweetened with dates and apples – and he had no problem chewing on a raw carrot or crunching on a crispy apple. Erik, Tim and I created some great memories and enjoyed all the moments the three of us shared.

Mum and Dad – Tim aged just two

Mum and Dad would sometimes come down to babysit and my Mum writes about how adorable he was and what a 'darling'. She notes that he loved playing with his trains, his cars, rolling them back and forth to her, playing with bubbles, looking at books etc. He would let her bath him and though he didn't want to pour water himself, he would let her pour it. He had been suspicious and a little afraid of my Dad up until this point too, but Mum notes that he was just starting to play with Dad a little – fiddling with his fingers and letting him blow bubbles for him.

However, we were finding that Tim was becoming increasingly wary of anyone outside his immediate circle – basically me, Erik, my Mum and Sarah. Mum noted in one of her diaries that she didn't think we should leave Tim for more than three hours in anyone else's care as he really couldn't cope. She felt he needed a few trusted people around him and that was enough. She also felt that we should respect his need to be kept away from other people – but that was so hard in the issue of real life and having to earn money – and also, should we?

She noted that he seemed increasingly vulnerable and unable to comfort himself and also that he was starting to really struggle with understanding that he could play the same game but in a different place. For example, he would become really upset if a game was moved into a different room, which we later learnt was known as difficulty with transitions. Later, I found in one of Mum's diaries that she felt as though his development had stalled at the age one and a half and that his progression was beginning to change.

It's funny. When things veer off track with your child's development you don't notice straight away. Because it is such a constantly moving and evolving process you never know quite where you are, what's expected or whether or not things will just come right. You live with and love your child all the time, reading to him, playing with him, looking after him and your identities are totally entangled in such a way that you hardly know where you end and he begins. Nothing stops still for long enough for you to be able to easily identify specific problems and even if these problems are identified you never know if they are just phases or part of something more complex.

Issues were not obvious, but crept up on us over a period of time. It was only pointed out to me later on that Tim was no longer pointing and that the few words he had started to say weren't developing.

Eating

As Tim went through the weaning process and through the first year of his life, he started to eat all sorts of foods – waffles, mushed vegetables, eggs, fruit, yoghurts and progressed to eating whole apples and healthy cakes.

Then at about the age of one and a half, his eating patterns changed. It was very gradual. He didn't want a meal for a few days – fair enough – lots of toddlers go off their food for a while if they are a little under the weather, but it continued. He gradually began to eat less and less and become really angry if we tried to persuade him. It was like he was exercising his right to say no.

He suddenly would not allow any meat, fish, vegetables, or fruit to pass his lips and refused to try anything new. How were we going to provide him with a balanced diet? He occasionally had a *tiny* bit of egg – but that also soon stopped. The only way we could get protein into him was by putting more eggs in his waffles, which we made with buckwheat flour.

Something happens to you as a mother when your child refuses to eat proper food. You panic a little, ask advice and panic some more when it makes no difference. Experts tell you that no child has ever starved themselves and that he will definitely choose to eat eventually. We were sent to a dietary therapist at the hospital but she could only tell me what he *should* be eating, which we already knew. The problem was that he was refusing almost everything. As a result, he went almost a year with only eggs in his waffles as protein and seemed to have no interest in food at all. Instead of a happy, pleasurable event, eating was clearly an ordeal for him.

Due to the fact that Tim was so unsettled, couldn't sit still and couldn't yet speak, Mum had contacted a local support group for hyperactive children, who had found that early nutritional intervention could really help. Under their guidance, we started giving Tim vitamin and mineral drops, zinc drops and fish oil. The oils were mixed into the very limited food that he would eat, while the drops were put into his drinks. Luckily, they were tasteless.

We found these made a difference to his tantrums and behaviour and he seemed a little more settled. However, he wouldn't eat anything without us sitting with him, encouraging every painstaking mouthful and the only food that he would eat independently was his waffles and occasional Pom Bear crisps.

Patterns Of Behaviour

Now when I took him to the park, instead of running and playing, he tended to head straight for the bandstand, delighting in walking up and down the steps. But he wouldn't just do it a few times and then move on to something else. He would walk up and down those bandstand steps over and over again. I noted in one of my diaries that he was very much a child of repetition.

Sarah noted that after the summer holidays, she was shaken at how our gorgeous, formerly outgoing little boy, who had always responded to strangers, was suddenly frightened when anyone approached or spoke. Tim had always loved going out with her and on one sunny afternoon, they were walking back to the house together when he stopped at the sight of a raven on the grass. Sarah knelt beside him, talking to him about the bird – but when she looked at his face, she immediately scooped him up in her arms, because the look of utter terror on his face horrified her. As she held him to her, talking softly and trying to reassure him, she felt his whole body shaking against her.

He also started to run away really fast wherever we went. He wouldn't stay close to me anymore, which became such a fixture that, on the odd occasion it wasn't like this, it became a diary moment, as I was so elated:

'For the first time ever in his life today I turned round, called him and reached for his hand and he reached up, took my hand and walked along with me. It was the nicest feeling – like we were there together…but it only lasted a few seconds, then he was off again, running unpredictably everywhere'.

He would hardly ever stop still and I so longed for those 'together' moments as they were so elusive. If he ever stayed in my arms for a moment and didn't struggle, I held that moment so close. The feeling was the reason I became a mum – being close to my child and him wanting to be close to me. Those episodes, however fleeting, were gold-dust.

Sarah was worried that because of Tim's now obvious fear of people, he was becoming increasingly isolated so she and her husband would take Tim to the local garden centre, getting there just after they opened at 9am when it was really quiet. They would wander round together and finish the visit in the café, though often, Tim would get overwhelmed and Sarah would end up carrying him out as he wailed, promising they would return. They sat at the same table every week – until the time they got there to find someone else sitting in their place and once more, Tim became inconsolable as no other table would do.

Tim refused to sit in his pushchair and yet often got upset if we wanted him to walk. Getting from one place to another was becoming very complex. Once after a lovely outing to the park, playing again on the bandstand steps, it was time to go and Tim desperately didn't want to. He had a massive meltdown and it took all my strength to calm him before taking him to the car. It could often take upwards of twenty minutes of just holding him in his distress while he struggled, trying to comfort him until he came to terms with leaving and was okay to move on. If other people were about, I had to steel myself to ignore their stares and mutters, focusing instead, on Tim's wellbeing.

Church was no easier. My diary input says it best:

'Tim and church just don't work. They don't fit together. It causes stress for him and for me – there's no point me being there for my own sake and there's nothing there for Tim. At the moment he physically reacts when we approach in the car and he resists when we walk into the building. He doesn't like crowds – he clings to me most of the time or runs away and plays in the courtyard. I sense fear in him like he thinks I'm going to leave him. I can't bear to sense that fear anymore. His stress makes me stressed and I'm sure it's vice versa.'

I have since learnt a lot about the flight or fight mode. I can see in hindsight that he was in this mode most of the time. He was either running away or battling us. I had known there was a lot of fear in him, but I'd thought it was in my power to comfort him by holding him, talking to him, trying to play with and distract him. However, it was getting harder to comfort him and I was having to be increasingly strong to keep him from running away during his episodes of distress.

While it sounds overwhelming, there were many times when Tim showed his cute and happy side. He was cosy, thoughtful and very gentle. When we went to the park, he would sometimes squat patiently for ages holding out a peanut until a squirrel became brave enough to take it out of his hand. From my point of view there were hundreds of similar gorgeous moments with him. I loved him and delighted in every moment I spent with him. We would play little singing games when he would spontaneously giggle. Erik would chase him round the garden on all fours, making him shriek with hilarity, sometimes giggling so much that he could barely breathe. When he was curled up in bed, he would become snuggly and relaxed. As parents we had these lovely interludes but other people rarely saw them.

Simply because someone else was there, Tim would revert to flight or fight mode, behaving in anti-social ways and becoming seriously distressed. I would try to convince my friends that he could be sweet and fun, though they didn't seem to believe me. Once I commented to a friend about our 'happy chaps' and she came back with, 'but your chap isn't happy, is he?'. His behaviour depended on where we were and what we were doing. It also was influenced by timing – we had to be very precise on how long we let him do something, so we were constantly managing the variables around him to try to prevent his meltdowns and keep him on an even keel.

Was his blood sugar too low? Did he need more oils or vitamins? Was his behaviour badly affected when we ran out of his supplements? These sorts of questions were endless as we regulated everything around him as much as possible.

It was hard to notice, but subtly things were shifting even further. Regulating the variables was getting harder and the happy times were becoming fewer. Because Tim became so distressed when with people, Erik and I sometimes fantasised about going to live on a desert island with no one else! Maybe we could all find peace that way.

However, even in our little family, life became more challenging. Tim needed to have me to himself or Erik to himself, but couldn't cope with the dynamic of Erik and me as a couple. He would pull us apart if we started talking to each other, or scream in distress. His difficulties were dominating our family unit and bulldozing Erik and me apart – and these things weren't negotiable. We couldn't say, 'Come on Tim, let's lighten things up a little around here – you know we love you and only want the best for you. Let's play some games together and have some fun'.

He was unable to process what we said to him and did not seem to feel our unconditional love for him. Consequently, he was becoming increasingly insecure and strong-willed as he attempted to make sense of a world around him that he was now struggling to understand.

Panic and Tantrums

His behaviour cycle became a bit of a pattern. On a holiday in Holland when he was two, my diary says:

'For some reason he cannot be told to stay with us at any place – on a vast beach, on a large farm, in a park… so how can we *possibly* take him into town? It's almost impossible… With this behaviour cycle continuing it just won't work. We can force him in his pushchair but he screams, shouts and causes a huge fuss. I take him out and carry him but he wants to get down. I can restrict him with reins but he screams, sits down, refuses to move and arches his back if I carry him… it's like there *is* no way through…'

Tim became overwhelmed, seeing every person as such a threat that he was driven to try to escape. However I held onto the belief that if he would just *let* me in to comfort him, he would be able to integrate and even enjoy being with people instead of fearing them so much. Visiting friends was turning into a nightmare because Tim would treat them as an enemy, while in reality the opposite was true – they were delighted to see him and just wanted to love him. What was forcing him to push everyone away?

At this point, since losing his initial words, language wasn't developing, so he still couldn't say 'Mama' or 'Papa' and I remember thinking during a massive meltdown that if he could at least call out my name, I'd be able to comfort him. My heart yearned for that sense of acknowledgement and belonging with him. Maybe if he could say my name, he would be opening up a part of himself to be close to me.

I Need a Vice!

At one point, I decided to visit a new Mum and Toddler Group, looking forward to meeting new mums for much-needed companionship and to talk about our children. However, when I walked in the door and saw happy mums chatting with cups of tea while their children socialised easily with each other nearby, panic set in.

What had I been expecting? I remember a sinking feeling in my gut that we could totally wreck this peace. I didn't know anyone, so I walked in politely and started to say hello.

Two minutes later, I found myself right at the end of this lady's garden with Tim lying on my knees, back arched and screaming, beside himself. Other children approached to help and try to be friends, but their mere presence made Tim scream louder and tense up more. It was when alone at the end of the garden with Tim screaming on my lap, socially isolated and lonely, that I felt I needed a vice. But what? I didn't smoke, I didn't drink, I didn't take drugs – though right at that moment I needed all three.

Someone suggested that I take him back to the car, calm him down and try again. Following this advice, I managed to bring him back in for a short while, while he ran around the house amongst the other children. I didn't manage a cup of tea, but I did spend a couple of minutes feeling more like a normal mum while talking to the others. My concern that he was not speaking yet came up in conversation and one lady lent me a book on how to encourage your child to talk. Later, at home, Tim ripped the cover during a meltdown and however hard I tried, I couldn't relate to it in any way. The concerns it was dealing with simply didn't apply to our experience. In fact, none of the advice in any of the baby books seemed relevant to us. They were full of what your baby should be doing at what age alongside helpful hints, none of which touched on anything we were going through. They all just made me feel further from any answers.

The Three Hearing Tests

So, Tim couldn't talk – maybe he couldn't hear properly. Wouldn't that be great if that was all it was? If he just couldn't hear us, then of course he couldn't reiterate sounds properly and would be frightened when out and about. It all made total sense. I really hoped this was the reason, because it was something we could put right. It would at least make *sense* of some of his difficulties.

We took him to the first hearing test. The kind, patient nurse tried really hard, waving teddy bears about behind him and making noises, but he would just not respond. They could not complete the tests in order to get any clear results. So we were sent to the next hospital. Well, his appointment was forty-five minutes late and that delay meant Tim just couldn't cope any more. He struggled and fought any attempt to keep him still in the examination room. He just wanted out. No amount of coercing could keep him there, let alone make him cooperate. The doctor became impatient. We were sent to a third hospital – a specialist one this time with a device set up that could register what someone was hearing without being dependent on their responses.

I was actually disappointed to learn that his hearing was fine. Looking back, I know this sounds extreme but the sense of not knowing what was wrong was making me a little crazy. We had to tick hearing off the list and look down other avenues to see what could be going on with him.

Can't Cope? Fall Asleep…

All through his toddler months I took him to a mixture of playgroups and activities, thinking that maybe his social and speech difficulties had their foundation in the fact that he was alone too much and if he could just get used to the company of other children more, he would be okay. However, taking him to any group set off the same anxiety within him. Tim would ignore other children, becoming engrossed in his own play and if any group activity began he would refuse to be part of it, squirming to get away. More often than not, I'd have to leave amidst an upsetting struggle. I just couldn't understand why he was so distressed all the time. There were no reasons that I could clearly see and all the other children in the same circumstances were fine.

At church, friends were pushing me to leave him in the crèche so I could have a semblance of normal life for a while, but why would I leave him if I didn't have to? He was distressed enough when I had to leave him to go to work. His attachment to me meant he would cling to me as if his security rested with me alone. Only when I was becoming ill with the strain did I let them persuade me, but I worried all through the service. When I rushed back to the creche, I learnt that he'd cried so hard he had fallen asleep with exhaustion. There was no happy playing or bonding with any other adult or child. He just seemed to need me or Erik to make his world right and no one else would suffice. What broke my heart was that he couldn't even *say* that he wanted us. He could only cry and hope that people would understand him.

The falling asleep thing became a pattern. When I spontaneously took him to a friend's house one day, who had a child his age, he started clinging to me and crying, which escalated to screaming and struggling to get away. Being so highly distressed and anxious wore him out so that he fell asleep from his exhaustive crying.

On his second birthday, when I invited a few close friends to celebrate with him, he cried so much that I had to take him to another room to try to calm him and when I brought him back in, he fell asleep on my lap, sweaty and tear-stained. The other children's expectations for a 'birthday moment' were so high that it was only fair to let them go ahead. So they blew his candles out for him, ate his cake and the other parents took photos of their children round the cake, singing Happy Birthday. I cuddled my sleeping birthday boy on the sofa, unable to stop my own tears from falling.

What was happening? Where was the happiness and communication from my beautiful child? Why couldn't he enjoy a birthday party? Why couldn't he go to playgroups? What was making him so highly anxious? Why wasn't he talking? I was exhausted from trying to manage him, and confused and heartbroken at his evident unhappiness. All I wanted was for him to be okay, but I couldn't make it happen for him.

The stress he experienced whenever other people were near was palpable. If a friend popped in to say hello, his body would tense and he would run to the furthest corner of the house in obvious fear. I was caught between my need for friendship and my need to protect Tim. It was very socially isolating.

There were already theories flying around as to why Tim couldn't yet talk. I was told I talked too fast, while Erik and I were criticized for our lifestyle which I never understood as we were working and living normally. Mum felt that our sporadic work hours were not helping Tim's well-being. I was teaching part-time and running clubs. Erik was working as a social worker and running children's parties on the side. Fair enough, but we knew many families who had far more hectic lives and their children were fine. Surely that couldn't be it, could it? Besides, we weren't working from choice – we needed the money to live.

Interestingly, it didn't once cross my mind that Tim's issues might be the beginning of something permanent. Honestly not. I don't know why. I knew there was a delay in his speech, but delays are acceptable. Everyone develops at different paces, right? He'd get there. I knew he was scared and that a lot of his fear was expressed in angry outbursts, but it was a fear I thought at some point I'd be able to help him with.

Because I was a new mother, I didn't have any experience of other children's early development. I didn't realise that Tim's lack of communication was more than just a delay with his speech. Tim was not responding or initiating connections and resisted any interaction at all costs.

Sarah had recently been blessed with a granddaughter and she had been totally willing to incorporate looking after Tim with her new-found grandparent role. But she had discovered that Tim was unable to cope with her dividing her attention between him and the baby, as he had highly charged meltdowns whenever she picked her up. At this time, despite totally loving Tim, his inability to cope with the baby forced her to stop looking after him. She was heart-broken and I was crushed as Sarah was one of the only people who knew how to look after him.

'I Can't Look After Him For You'

Unfortunately, I still had to leave him for a few hours, three days a week, while I worked. As Sarah was sadly now unavailable, I needed to find someone new. I was recommended a lovely childminder, Jenny, who lived just around the corner. She was the textbook childminder – warm and friendly, with a fantastic attitude towards children. She had two sons of her own and looked after other children after school. She was happy to have Tim and seemed unworried when I explained how frightened Tim could be. Relieved to find such a safe pair of hands, I started to leave him with her. Often he cried heartbreakingly when I left, but she had a fantastic track record and on meeting her, I felt that if anyone could cope with his insecurity, she could. A few weeks later she met me at the door and told me that something was seriously wrong and she couldn't manage him anymore.

A textbook child-minder could not look after my child.

The sick feeling in my stomach was growing. He couldn't function. He couldn't relate. He couldn't make attachments to other people or play with them. He could only scream and show distress. He couldn't have 'any' child minder, even someone experienced and trustworthy – he needed someone who knew him, loved him and could devote their time to him and who wouldn't be distracted by anyone else. That's why Sarah had been such a Godsend – she knew him, loved him and they'd had fun together – giggling, playing, communicating and he obviously felt safe with her. She loved him. Why couldn't other people develop a relationship with him in the same way?

Another friend, after a visit, mentioned that he hadn't looked at her once. I comforted myself with the thought that maybe he didn't like her and didn't want to look at her! I felt the need to defend him. To me he was perfect and I didn't like how people were picking up on complications in his development. He and I were a team and I was totally on his side – his number one ally. It didn't stop me crying myself to sleep though and agonising over what I could do to help him.

One of my colleagues once told me that having a child is like having your heart walking around outside your body – it felt just like that. And my heart couldn't feel happy if his didn't – we were intrinsically linked.

Where Are My Coping Mechanisms?

Up until having Tim, when things got emotionally tough or complex in my life, I would do one of two things – I would seek out a friend or I would sit at my piano and play my heart out. So I found it particularly hard at this point that even Erik's guitar playing, our singing and my piano playing made Tim cry and scream. I couldn't even hum quietly in his ear. If I played a note on the piano he would shriek as if in pain until I stopped. I chose to stop playing. How can you continue to do something that causes such distress to your child? Piano playing had been a release for me. Now it just created stress.

Erik so wanted me to continue playing the piano that he would try to occupy Tim in his bedroom so I could play for a couple of minutes. We tried it once or twice but his pitiful screaming rang through the house while I played. How could I possibly continue? I gave my piano to a friend. You would think that headphones and an electric piano would solve this problem – we thought so too and my lovely Dad bought me a second-hand one as a present. But Tim became unsettled and distressed by the virtually silent tapping of the keys – even without the music.

The thing was, that caused *me* distress. All my coping mechanisms were being taken away – friends, music, me-time… I wasn't the only one – Erik's music-making was equally important to him and being denied this outlet also caused him distress and frustration. Surely this wasn't right? We felt so trapped. We couldn't go out, we couldn't play music, we couldn't chat together in front of him, we couldn't ever relax when anyone visited the house and we could hardly leave him with anyone. We were also on constant alert for major meltdowns and distress reactions from Tim. What *was* this? Still, it didn't cross my mind that this wasn't something we could solve.

Chapter Two – Autism – is it, isn't it?

In all the autism biographies I have read, they come to the point where they get close to finding out – it might be through a film, a book, a conversation, the internet or just a sudden realisation. With me it was a phone call.

Bizarrely, a couple had approached us at church, having seen the continuous stress we were going through and offered to pray with us. I had been very used to praying with people before Tim came along but right now being prayed for was a very unusual experience for me because I was usually in the throes of running round after Tim who was constantly in escape mode. It was a very kind, understanding prayer and I felt quite a high level of empathy for what we were going through. It touched me and later I chose to phone them to tell them I appreciated their thoughts. Little did I know that this conversation was going to trigger a possibility that would pervade my heart for the rest of my life.

We chatted for a while and then she asked me quite casually whether I had considered that Tim might have Aspergers or autism. What? You mean his difficulties might be permanent? She then asked me if anyone in my family had problems like these. Well, my brother had a few processing difficulties, but was definitely not diagnosed with anything. Hang on, are you saying that there might be something permanently *wrong* here?

Please no. A dawning black realisation washed through me. Erik took over the conversation while I sank to the floor, in my own version of a meltdown. I was trying to block out my inner world where my mind had ratcheted into overdrive, processing thoughts that were taking me in a direction where I didn't want to go. I knew about processing difficulties. I knew they brought pain. I didn't want them in my little boy's life – and definitely not permanently.

Please, please God no. Not my precious, beautiful, smiling child. He's adorable. I love him. It's a *delay* – there's nothing wrong – you *can't* tell me otherwise. I was trapped in some painful twilight zone. Please someone stop this from happening.

This woman had just finished a degree on Asperger's syndrome and it seemed to me that she felt excited to have noticed Tim's difficulties and be able to identify them. For her it was *interesting*, while I felt my world implode.

In every story I've read, there's a turning point where people realise there's something more than a delay in their child's development. Sometimes there's relief – but not for me. The moment before, my heart was intact. Now it was shocked and broken. Although this was the first time this had been mentioned and there was no confirmation, something in me realised. It was a sharp-edged, painful knowledge. The kind you go to sleep with, wake up with and live with throughout the day as a shadow on your horizon, a weight in your gut and a hurt with every breath. Always.

In my head it had just been a delay. I believed all his issues would just melt away with time and we would have the future we were hoping for and expecting. I felt angry with the whole concept of autism. The only images I had in my mind were of seriously disabled people, unusual behaviours, violence and difficulty in communicating. Was this going to happen to Tim? *Why?* Why couldn't *my* child have the golden ticket? Why couldn't *he* be the one without difficulties? This conversation had changed my perception in a heartbeat. It was like a car crash. One minute I didn't know and the next minute I did and that knowledge would pervade the rest of my life. It has. One minute Tim's entire life was one way and the next it was another.

It wasn't that I could only picture *Rain Man* – where he was depicted as a pain, weird, odd and socially retarded, I also envisaged Tim as the random guy who had lashed out at me in a care home I'd worked in. I'd had experience of processing difficulties and this is what I believed was ahead of us. I'd had personal experience of emotional processing, after living with my Mum's depression, so knew how internal problems could affect people. It looked like we might be heading into a lifetime of further difficulties with my perfect and beautiful child. He was so new to this world. His life was already complex enough – and now I was being told there was a possibility of this never easing up.

I knew of people with autism who, from a distance, looked as though they had to be managed and herded through town accompanied by carers. People who couldn't ever be independent. People who seemed angry and were cut off from society.

I'd also had a child for two years in my class – he had called out continuously; been unable to make any connections or learn anything new; he'd on occasion had tried to climb out of the windows and crawled around under the tables while I was teaching and he kept running away. I'd had to support him through numerous epileptic fits during the day and he'd regressed in his development during this two-year period. He had also recently been diagnosed with autism.

No, no, NO… I looked at Tim and saw how perfect he was. Perhaps it's not true… Sometimes, I could imagine that it wasn't true – that it had all been a bad dream and the relief was huge. But somehow, the knowing crept back in and the sickness I felt was like a deep and pervading grief.

This feeling was overwhelming. I remember three days later, I had to run a Music Inset Training Day in a school an hour away. My emotions were very shaky and I desperately didn't want to do it, but our finances meant I had to. My Dad offered to drive me – travelling an hour and a half to my house, then an hour to and from the school – just so I didn't have to face the drive on my own. My parents were so supportive, but of course they were sharing our confusion. Dad and I agreed not to mention it on the way, but only to talk constantly about positive things to keep me going – I could break down again on the way home. I just had to make it through the day. That was one of the hardest days I've ever had to get through. I had to play games with teachers, talk about children and how to find creative ways to enhance their development, consciously filing the thoughts of my own son's development in a place in my head, far enough away so as not to distract my performance.

Over the next few weeks I spent so many hours trying to work my thoughts out. We were still managing Tim daily. Difficult behaviour and developmental difficulties plagued my mind. Sarah joined me. She loved Tim like we did and was equally devastated by this possibility. Erik didn't know if he believed it and was reserving judgement. He wanted to wait to know more. Later he told me that if he had broken down too, there would have been no one to hold our family together. He may have been right. He needed to be strong. He also felt powerless to make me feel better. He was at the beginning of a long period of denial. Sometimes this came across to me as insensitivity. I felt as if my heart was broken and yet here he was – apparently okay. It's interesting how grief can divide people – I was desperately needing to talk and Erik was holding all his thoughts and feelings inside him, trying to conserve his strength. He was right. We'd had no confirmation. And although we were divided in our feelings and responses, we were actually supportive of each other, willing to do whatever was necessary to help Tim.

Is It Autism or Not?

The next few months were full of questions. I would oscillate between hope and despair. He was affectionate – didn't that count in his favour? The way he looked at me sometimes and crinkled up his little eyes in excitement was adorable. Every day was filled with such a mixture of emotions – delight in just being with him but overwhelmed with his struggles. I couldn't begin to count the number of times people told us that Einstein hadn't spoken until he was four and talked about other children with language delays, who'd suddenly come out with whole sentences like, 'Can you pass the salt please?'

That was nice but had these children also had meltdowns every time people approached?

When he was alone with Erik and me in the moments when he was completely comfortable, he would still often laugh and giggle and cosy up with us. I so longed for other people to see him like this. It was our privilege alone to know him in this way. Some moments just felt so *normal*. In fact, the whole thing was normal to us. If we could have stayed in our own bubble without ever interacting with the outside world, we may have been fine. Leaving the bubble of our own normality was when the problems started.

I remember realising the enormity of what we were potentially facing. Usually if we had problems we would share them. But I was actually afraid to let even the idea of the 'autism' word out of the bag. What did it mean? It seemed loaded with rejection to me – separation, isolation, pain... Currently Tim was seen as a cute and gorgeous child who had major wobblies from time to time and was a bit slow in speaking. Immediately if the autism word came out of the bag, the 'cute' and 'gorgeous' could well disappear and all people would see and hear would be 'autism', each loaded with their own perceptions. People's judgements could be so inhuman. I was afraid he would be labelled and dumbed down and that attitudes towards him would change in an instant. A disability can change people's attitudes and perceptions in a heartbeat. I didn't want Tim to be seen through the label of a disability. On a recent TV programme I had heard of autism described as a brain abnormality. I didn't want my child to have a brain abnormality. With all of my being I didn't want it.

Erik felt differently about children with issues. He had worked with children and adults with disabilities for much of his life. He had even said to God that if a child with special needs were to be born, let him be born to him. In our many deep conversations about such things later on in life, I emphasised that though he had asked for such a thing, I seriously hadn't. In all of Tim's short years he had experienced so much suffering. Why would anyone choose that?

With all these wonderings flying about, we needed a practical way forward. Our health visitor suggested we contact the Child Development Centre in Chichester, which we did. A few weeks later we all went along for an appointment.

Testing

I don't know what I was expecting. They asked us questions while observing Tim playing on all the equipment around the room. I was kind of expecting a resolution one way or another – weren't these people the experts on such things? But we were asked to come again for a full day of tests and observations.

At the end of the day of testing, which involved Tim being taken to lots of different rooms with various therapists, we were told that there was a possibility of him having autism, but it would take longer for them to know for sure. It was nothing that could be diagnosed with a blood test or a cat scan, but only by observing Tim's behaviour. Why was something so serious so *vague*?

They asked us to bring him to thera-play every week for two hours where he would receive speech and language therapy and occupational therapy as well as take part in some group activities with them. I felt frustrated by the vagueness and the length of time all this would take, but I also felt a spark of hope that if they couldn't see autism straight away, maybe his difficulties couldn't be that serious.

I was allowed to stay for the first two sessions as Tim's attachment to me was so strong. On the third week of taking him, however, they asked me to leave him. They thought they would be able to test his abilities more accurately if I was out of the way. It was time for the separation. I remember stepping through those big double hospital doors, having had Tim prised off me and into the clinical waiting room, hearing him desperately cry for me.

I sat on a chair within earshot and cried too. Why were we in a hospital being forced to separate? Friends of mine would be in playgroups right now, drinking tea and chatting while their children played. I could have left and gone shopping or wandered about the hospital grounds on my own but at this point I couldn't see any reason why I would. I just wanted to be with Tim and wasn't in the mood to pretend our life was normal. Other parents joined me in the waiting area. It was awkward and polite. None of us knew the direction in which our children's lives would go and it seemed that it was all being decided in the room behind the closed doors. Not an environment conducive to easy banter.

We all wanted to watch, but because we kept trying to see through the tiny window so much, one day we came to find they had blacked it out, as they said our faces at the door were distracting the children. We had to sit and wonder what was happening when all we wanted to know was how our children were doing without us. I can see why so many places now have two-way mirrors – I would have adored to sit and watch how he was doing. It seemed strange that I was being ostracised from these vital elements of his life and development when the outcome would affect the rest of my life.

Occasionally I was invited along to the speech therapy sessions and watched Tim involved in lots of bubble-blowing and games where he said occasional words on cue and received rewards. With the occupational therapist he was given special pegs to help his pincer grip and balancing games for his gross motor skills. Often I was given things to take home with him and try. Sometimes it felt like a drop in the ocean.

Will He Talk?

Throughout this time, Tim's speech was hardly developing. He could say a few occasional words, but nothing that could gain the attention or proper understanding of another human being. Without knowing the context, these words would be hard to decipher. He also found transitioning from one activity to another really challenging. To help him with communication, they decided to start him on PECS (Picture Exchange Communication System), handing over a picture as a request for something to eat or something to play with. I could see it working as a transitioning activity. If you can't say what you want you can recognise a picture and hand it over. I know many people communicate their whole lives this way and it can work well for them. I, however, was longing to hear Tim's voice and to be able to interact with him verbally.

I remember where I was standing when I was told that Tim wouldn't need PECS permanently because his speech was developing. Seriously? My relief was immense. So much possibility opened up. Brilliant! What I didn't really take on board at the time was that being able to talk is different from being able to communicate. Tim could learn words by rote and say them again and again while playing with various toys. He could sit in a corner and chatter endlessly, but it would be just to himself and not used for communication at all.

As time went on, Tim was able to name a few objects, colours and numbers. He would only cooperate sporadically but he seemed to enjoy odd moments of this. It was something he could do. However, Tim couldn't reach out to show me something he had seen or tell me how he was feeling, unable to connect with me verbally. He did not know how. He also didn't seem to have a desire to do so. Initially I was really excited when he started to repeat sentences that he had heard on some of his favourite TV shows, but as this development didn't progress, I came to realise that this was again using speech as a kind of stimming behaviour and not as a means to communicate.

Tim had echolalia – a way of talking where you repeat what's just been said to you or phrases you remember that you have heard (delayed echolalia). Echolalia does not seem to involve independent thought – it is taken from the sound heard around you rather than the thoughts and ideas inside you. This is my understanding at least. I have also learned that it can be a building block on which to build independent thought and speech. So it is still something to be celebrated as it is the beginning of a process. Naoki Higashida, the Japanese boy with autism who, at thirteen years old, wrote the best-seller, *The Reason I Jump*, explains it as a comfort, being able to repeat familiar words and phrases, even though they may not make sense to anyone else. Maybe Tim was using his few repeated words as a kind of inner comfort rather than a means to communicate.

As Tim could not yet make himself understood with speech, he used to take our hands and pull us to whatever he wanted. We became expert at reading his prompts. However, we were still encouraged to use PECS with him until his speech improved.

Tim also showed no sense of right or wrong, no awareness of danger and generally no understanding of concepts. I could not read him stories because he could not focus or understand and he was unable to answer any of my questions about what he wanted –

even if it was apparent that the issue was important to him. It seemed that he could not process the sounds that entered his head and therefore he could not think or produce sounds back that made sense.

Amidst all these obvious difficulties it became increasingly impossible to imagine that it could all just come right. However, I clung onto a relieved and happy place of denial in my mind, where the pressure and weight was lifted. In this place, delay was still a possibility. I would sometimes tell people there was a chance we were wrong about autism, without waiting for their reactions. I needed to believe this.

Unfortunately, throughout all the thera-play sessions, speech therapy, occupational therapy and talks with Education Psychologists it was becoming more apparent that Tim was experiencing some kind of disorder rather than a delay. They were coming close to being able to tell us for sure what was going on in his development.

When it came to Diagnosis Day, Erik and I comforted each other with the fact that we knew they were going to tell us it was autism. We'd had enough talks leading up to this and we told each other that the meeting would merely confirm what we knew. Therefore it couldn't hurt. Yes, well…

Diagnosis

When the paediatrician finally said, 'Yes, this is autism', it was such a normal conversation. We were just sitting in her office as we had done many times before, discussing Tim's issues and it was said in such a normal, friendly tone of voice, as if we were talking about the weather. But how can such a normal conversation set your child's future on such a totally different path?

Tim was perfect and yet I had read books that described autism as a lifelong brain disorder and today autism was clarified. Simple as that. The concept of 'defining moment' just doesn't start to put a perspective on it. This diagnosis and the preciousness of his existence just didn't go together. What IS autism? A disability? A difference? In what way? Are the books right? Is what they say true for all children? Do some have heavier forms of autism than others? What's going on? Why do some people just call it a difference if your child can't actually talk to you or tell you what he wants? That's not different – that's *difficult* – difficult for him – and what does it mean for his future? I had heard people speak of savant skills and amazing gifts, but this meant nothing to me. How could that compensate, when all I wanted was a natural, interactive relationship with him? And I desperately didn't want his developmental issues to take away the potential we'd already seen of how loving, happy and responsive we'd known he could be.

The way I viewed him and the way I knew the world would now view him would forever be opposed. Erik and I *really* knew him. The world could put whatever label they wanted on him but they would never know him like we did. I couldn't relate what I had read about autism to the child I knew so well. He wasn't just a mixture of cans and can'ts listed in a textbook, he was an entity – a person, a soul, an existence, a child of God – and we loved him.

I didn't want my child to be locked in a box and for society to throw away the key. Nobody gave me any hope. They didn't have any. They gave me books. But after reading the first few lines I felt so despairing that Erik insisted I stop reading them. In fact he took them away and hid them. They were so very graphic about how complex it is to deal with a growing child who can't communicate, struggles to understand and who lashes out continuously in anger and frustration. So the heaviness and heartbreak only deepens, does it? For the child *and* the parent?

Tim's entire life and future – and therefore our entire life and future – was being sucked into a black hole with no way out. I'd lost my happy place. The weight in my heart was now permanent and the grief was unbearable.

If only ranting or smashing windows could have taken this diagnosis away, because that's what I felt like doing. Erik and I loved Tim with such intensity – how could that level of love not be enough to rescue him?

Erik had to go back to work straight after the meeting and I had to wait for Tim. I stumbled into an empty room and burst into tears. The paediatrician followed me, but I was so blinded by grief and confusion I can't recall anything of our conversation. It was only then that I realised the extent to which I had been holding on to the hope that this was just some farcical mistake. However this *was* autism. No chance of it being just a delay. It was a disorder – a supposed life-long disorder – in the very heart of my child.

I pulled myself together of course. Tim came out of his theraplay. I wiped my eyes and hugged him so tightly. What a phenomenally beautiful child and what a bloody stupid diagnosis hanging over him. I couldn't connect the two. I felt angry, like some invisible being was trying to take my child away from me. I held his soft little hand – how the hell could I make life right for him? I wanted to know that there was hope I would be able to share his thoughts and feelings in the future – that he could *tell* me them – that he would *want* to tell me them. I wanted to know it would get *better*. I *needed* to know that.

It was around this time that somebody told me the well-known 'Italy/Holland' story. It was meant to be a parallel of what we were going through, to help me understand and feel better. This is a version of the story:

You are in the airport with lots of friends and you are about to get on a flight to Italy. You have all been looking forward to going on this amazing holiday for months and can't wait for all the surprises and treats that await you all. But when the plane lands and you get off, you find you are not in Italy after all. While your friends are all there together – you find that your plane has landed you in Holland, alone. With all your being you don't want to be there and you hate it. However, as time goes by, you start to adjust to your new environment, gradually getting to know different people and find that new opportunities occur.

My immediate reaction was that I didn't have a *choice* – I couldn't imagine how I could accept such a situation in those circumstances. Furthermore, I didn't believe I was in a different country, anyway. If I was, I wouldn't have been able to see my friends in Italy, living the life I'd wanted, while being banished to an existence I hadn't chosen or planned. What I took away from this story was that I was actually in the *same* country as my friends, but in a parallel universe – seeing and longing for things I desperately wanted around me, while Tim and I couldn't be part of it.

Different country or parallel universe, this was the wrong place for me and I hated it. Knowing your child struggles to talk and handle everyday life is painful. Being told its permanent puts a different light on it. I suddenly wanted to get out of that clinical hospital building with all my being. I didn't belong here. Nor did Tim.

Intervention: 'You Can't Do This by Yourself'

Following the diagnosis, people started telling us that we needed services and giving us leaflets. Okay, 'services'. The beginning of interventions. We were offered support from an organisation called Portage – a local service helping children with disabilities. They would come and visit us to play with Tim and to help me for an hour a week.

Erik and I were also encouraged to attend a course once a week called Early Bird, all about autism – as we were told it would help us.

They explained about the triad of impairments and specifically how autism affected different children. We found it to be a frustrating course. It took a lot to get there in terms of organising childcare and making sure Tim was in a good state, and we felt we were having all the problems and issues of autism laid out in front of us without being offered any solutions. A lady with a whiteboard had a list of the symptoms, recited them for us and then spoke about the 'interesting traits' of the children with autism in her school. I remember thinking that it's all very well for someone who doesn't have a personal connection to autism to find it *interesting*. Tim's meltdowns and difficulties were overwhelming our everyday life. What we really needed was to talk about our own experience and discover what could help. We had grasped the facts as to what autism supposedly was – we lived with it every day. We wanted to talk about Tim. But there was only a five-minute slot at the end for such things, divided between all the parents.

A lady called Maureen came to visit us once a week through the organisation Portage. It was interesting to talk to someone about the specific difficulties I was facing with Tim and it was also a relief to have company as I was becoming more isolated daily. However, when she played with him, she often pushed him so far, he would cry and become really distressed. She wanted him to sit still and be attentive but he just couldn't do it. It felt like she was trying to bend his leg backwards – but she kept telling me he needed to be pushed, because these skills weren't coming naturally. She insisted that from now on I had to play with him in this forceful and directed way.

When she spoke to him, he wouldn't respond, which was normal for anyone he didn't know. During one of the games she was making him play, she scowled as she snapped, "No!" which made him especially anxious. When I questioned her, she replied, 'Oh, don't worry – they don't get facial expressions.'

'They? Who's 'they'? I stood up in fury. Is Tim now a part of a whole species of children who can all be put under the same umbrella and collectively be called 'they'? Where the hell has my child gone? And who are you to hold him down with all your insinuations? Where is his own sense of dignity and identity? Tim was perfect and beautiful and just needed a little extra help – which I was going to give him – end of.

I found that already I was having to work hard to protect the close and personal relationship I had with Tim against the well-meaning views and experiences of people sent to help him. When someone pops into your home for one hour then pops out again, it's hard for them to see what your relationship with your child is really like and it's easy for them to jump to conclusions based on one or two moments of difficult behaviour.

Soon after this, we were offered a higher level of help, under the title Portage Plus. This involved someone coming into our home for ten hours a week to help Tim with his development and to support us as a family. To receive this, we had to have Tim Statemented – a massive roller-coaster process of tests, assessments, reports, meetings… and he wasn't even three years old.

I knew it would be invasive to have people in and out of my home, but I would never say no to anything that might potentially help Tim. West Sussex had never offered this service before – we were the first family to receive it. Therefore, they had to start from scratch. They asked me if I'd like to attend the interviews. Of course. If someone is going to be in and out of my house and closely associated with my child for the next year, of course I want to talk to them, see what kind of person they are and how they would specifically help Tim.

However, despite the fact that the interviewee was going to work for a year with Tim in our home, I was only allowed to state my preference at the end. One of my closest friends was an Educational Psychologist and was on this panel sitting right next to me but I wasn't even allowed to discuss my thoughts with *her*. It felt bizarre that people were being interviewed on how they would interact with my son – and being forbidden to say a word. I was powerless. It seemed like my child now belonged to a system that was going to manage him and I was just an inconsequential bystander.

Chapter Three – Is my love not enough?

We now knew it was autism. But what exactly is autism? We were told constantly about the *triad of impairments* – social communication, social interaction and social imagination. The first two were quite easy for me to understand. Social imagination – as far as I understood – was about being flexible; seeing and responding to other people's perspectives; and being aware of the constantly moving unwritten social rules. I also read that it was a mental condition, present from early childhood, characterised by great difficulty in communicating and forming relationships and in forming language and abstract concepts. I also learnt that it's considered to be a lifelong disability that affects how people perceive the world. One post I read stated that it is the most severe of the developmental disabilities. Another post stated that the primary problem with autism is the way the brain processes and integrates information, resulting in problems of social interaction, communication and behaviour. Argh! I hear you! Stop! It's too much! My child is three. Please can he begin to enjoy his childhood?

Speaking in hindsight, I now know the neuro-diverse view of autism, written by Nick Walker, explains that autism is a developmental phenomenon and has a pervasive influence on development throughout the person's lifespan. He explains that autism produces distinctive, atypical ways of thinking, moving, interacting and sensory and cognitive processing and he sees that autistic individuals simply have a different neurological operating system. He doesn't see it as wrong or bad or even as an impairment but as a 'human neurological variant'. He also explains, however and I quote, 'The realm of social interaction is one context where autistic individuals tend to consistently be disabled'. How can the word *disabled* not be a difficult thing? I find this a lot to get my head around.

However, from all the points of view of what autism is, I could see a theme developing in that autism is about the whole social element of a human being. All the social issues were exactly what we had experienced continually throughout the three short years of Tim's life. Do you just accept this or is there something you can do to help your child? What also ended up as being really important in hindsight, is that the triad of impairments did not include all the sensory issues and these, I later discovered, were triggering so many of Tim's fears and reactions. These were largely overlooked at the time because of their invisibility.

For all our confusion about what autism was, we just needed to know what to do. I was still working in between looking after Tim, so had very little time to read. I listened a lot to what people said and tried to take the best ideas from all of the advice I was being given, but I was confused. If I had known there was serious hope for Tim's development and knew what to do, I would have got started straight away. But at this time I was given to understand there was little I could do, however much I wanted to help him.

Maureen from Portage made a big point of telling me that I could no longer use my natural mothering instincts with Tim and I found myself believing her. I was so new at all this. She told me I would now have learn a whole host of new ways to manage him, telling me that I was too soft with him, adding how manipulative he was. I had a strong feeling that I would need to change everything about myself in order to do the things that were asked of me. I was a spontaneous person, used to responding instinctively to Tim's needs. I felt lost. But I took it all in, determined to try hard to do all the things I needed to do to help my little boy as best I could.

The thing was, autism was so new to me. Even motherhood was still relatively new. I honestly felt overwhelmed. Up until that point, Tim and I had managed to have lots of cosy play times together. It only worked if I went along with exactly what he wanted and didn't force him into anything, but we could have some very happy, good-natured times in this way. We could be close and connected for periods of time, which was important to both him and me. And Maureen was insisting that I overlay our few happy moments by playing in a fully directed way, only allowing him to do what was on a given agenda to train him. He had to learn to follow instructions and take turns. If he wanted to do his own thing for too long, I would have to stop him and draw him into my activity, and not care about his level of distress at having to pull away from what comforted him and gave him pleasure. I could see her reasons – I had to teach a lot of these things to him specifically and repetitively as they weren't coming naturally. It was hard. Spontaneity had been the only way Tim and I had always had the most fun. Now I was becoming one of the people trying to bend his leg backwards. Our playtimes lost their fun. I started to panic that if I didn't do this enough, he may never grasp these skills. I was caught between what I understood I ought to do with him and wanting to do what made him happy.

Soon after the interview process for Portage Plus, Tina came into our lives. She was upbeat, full of energy and came with lots of ideas and advice on how to help Tim. Sometimes her presence felt like a relief and sometimes it felt like an invasion. Having someone in our house three mornings a week to help Tim divided my feelings. It was helpful to have someone else in the mix to share the burden, but I was aware that it was only because Tim had so many serious developmental difficulties that she was there at all. It was all happening so fast. I hadn't wanted Tim to be diagnosed with anything and therefore I also didn't want her there. I was very much in the middle of a grieving process and her presence only emphasised the enormity of our situation.

It felt like she was a relief worker after a disaster and I sometimes found it hard to be glad that she came so often. After all, she was only experimenting with ways that might work with him. Like everyone else, she had no definitive answers. At the end of the day she could go back home to a normal life.

I likened the situation to us living on a ship on a permanently stormy sea with her and the other therapists visiting, before departing in their motorboats back to the shore and leaving us to fend for ourselves in the middle of the storm. Cynical maybe, but I found it hard not to be cynical with our life and whole future in such a constant state of uncertainty and tension.

For Tina, working with Tim was her job and I was her client – the mother who had a child with autism, who didn't know what to do. She often swept into the house exuding so much positivity and joy that I was almost jealous. I think I struggled with her taking over and found that needing someone to help made me feel inadequate. We talked a lot about Tim and his responses and reactions and she came up with ideas from various courses she had been on and things we could try. Everything was an experiment and no therapy or process ever had a direct outcome. Often, we would have to try one idea for weeks before we could see if it worked at all. With lots of strategies we never knew.

Tina and I talked about where Tim was and set goals – like realising he didn't use the words yes or no and he didn't nod or shake his head yet. We worked out ways to attempt to teach him these things.

As well as home visits, Tina accompanied him to Nursery when he started, liaised sometimes with his speech and occupational therapists and the thera-play staff and also accompanied him as a special teaching assistant in his first term at infant school when he had just turned four. She was with us for over a year and became a link between us and the outside world for him.

We worked together with him on potty training, academic learning (letters, numbers, puzzles), and social connections (attempting to help him share and accept other children in his space at Nursery). When he behaved in ways that others found inappropriate, she discovered that timers and PECS cards worked well to help him to stop his 'inappropriate behaviours' and help ease him from one activity to another.

I was very low at this point and now realise how much my feelings and emotions were affecting Tim. I so wish I had known more about this then. I would often cry in front of him (there was hardly any time when I was not with him) and I was desperately unhappy in the year or two that followed his diagnosis. That is another thing I would change if I could go back – I would find the hope and way forward I learnt when Tim was five and would work on myself so that I could be happy, positive and fun with him. It's only in hindsight that I realise what a difference that would have made.

The thing was, I was in despair. Everything I had read and all the people I had spoken to depressed me so much that I spent a lot of my energy trying to shut it out. We were trying to help him cope with elements of life on such a limited level. He still could not talk to another child – or even to an adult, other than a few words that were difficult to decipher. He was constantly overwhelmed and distressed and all anyone could do was to try to manage him throughout the day. Meanwhile he was smiling less and less, hardly ever laughed and screamed a lot more. Despite all this effort, we were losing him and time was running out as we were told that if his behaviour hadn't improved by the time he was five, his development could stay stuck in this place.

Nutritional Crisis

Tim's physical health and eating issues were still a major concern. Tim would oscillate between hyper-energy and a spaced-out state, when he would loll on the settee for ages – very sad looking and weak.

He was becoming weaker daily, as his brain was being starved – he became hyper and would stare vacantly into space – the kind of state you can get into with very low blood sugar. He lay around looking a bit haunted and far away. It was so obvious he needed good nutritious food to calm down and be more grounded. But despite trying every technique in the book, he still wouldn't eat enough nutritious food. He squirmed and just angrily pushed everything away that we put in front of him. Dieticians couldn't help. They discussed what he should eat – but I knew what he should eat. It was about the fact that he simply wouldn't eat.

Tim showed no signs of being hungry and rarely asked for food. We had to feed him as a matter of discipline, but it was never something he wanted. He seemed to have no interest in food at all or to want to go through the process of bothering to eat.

My Mum, with her nutritional therapist hat on, wanted him to have a Live Blood Analysis test to find out about the state of his body and immune system. We went to a clinic in Horsham and following a tiny little prick test on his finger, they showed us his blood under a microscope. They explained that his red blood cells were normal but some cells were what they called 'sticky' which could indicate leaky gut, allergy and inflammation. They commented in a report that followed, on his verbal development delay, his leaky gut, candida and oxidative stress.

A lot of this was new to me. I needed to ask for leaky gut to be explained to me. This is how I understand it. The purpose of the small and large intestines is to absorb nutrients from the food. The bad bacteria and rubbish go out through the urine and the stools and the good bacteria, vitamins and minerals are absorbed into the bloodstream, which then supplies the whole body including the brain. What you don't want is the bad bits getting through to the blood, as they will inevitably reach the brain, causing all sorts of brain issues and consequent neurological complications. If the gut linings had holes, this is exactly what would happen. Tim's gut lining had holes. I also understood that too much bad bacteria getting through would lower the immune system, making you vulnerable to lots of infections and also lowering brain function and general health. The results they gave us showed that Tim's immune system levels were a 12, whereas normal immune system levels were between 40 and 204. I had never known you could measure immune systems so this, too, was new to me.

I also needed to learn about candida. I learnt that candida is a yeast that lives in the body, including the gut lining – that although the presence of yeast in our bodies can be fine to certain levels, it can go beyond these levels and start to spread and become out of control. When out of control, it can develop long threads which can break through the gut lining, creating and exacerbating leaky gut and all the problems that go with it. It was important to kill off this yeast overgrowth. I knew that sugar fed the yeast and that it was important to stay off sugary foods in order to prevent further growth.

Following the Live Blood Analysis test, Tim was given further nutritional supplements, a stronger form of IQ oil and it was recommended that he take Nystatin for the candida. While he was able to take the supplements and oils, we never managed to get the Nystatin into him and so we didn't do very well in nipping the candida in the bud at this point.

When Tim was three years and six months, we made an appointment with Jonathon Tommey. He had become a nutritionist since his own son had been diagnosed with autism and he and his wife, Polly, ran *The Autism File*, a magazine created to provide help and support to parents of children diagnosed with autism, looking at stories and the latest research etc. He organised a stool test which confirmed that there were no good bacteria to build up a good immune system within Tim and that he had a very high level of candida overgrowth and leaky gut. He gave him lots of probiotics and also suggested he try something called Ultracare Food Mix, a drink full of vitamins and minerals, specifically designed for children with allergy related conditions. It was chock-a-block full of proteins, carbohydrates, sodium, potassium, vitamins A,D,E and C, Vit B12, calcium, iron, zinc, selenium, iodine, copper…and on and on it went. It was vital that with his extremely limited food intake that he receive these nutrients.

Force-Feeding Nightmare

Of course he wouldn't accept this willingly and so began one of the most torturous processes for any child (especially a sensitive and scared child) – force feeding.

We had to get this nutrition into him. If we couldn't do this he would need to go into hospital and be fed through a drip.

He was so depleted, we had to hold him on the floor against his will, squirming and screaming. We had to hold his hands down by his sides so he couldn't move and squirt this mixture into him, trying to make sure it stayed in his mouth and didn't dribble out the sides. It felt like we were torturing him. I hadn't had a child in order to torture him. I had had a child to love and nurture. What was happening?

Incredibly, in just a few days he calmed right down. The nutritional content had reached his brain, just as Jonathon Tommey had said it would. He stood still in the corridor looking at me and there was a peacefulness in his face. He didn't seem so on edge. Despite his determination to resist, nutrition had had a relieving effect. It had felt like a vicious circle to me as I could see his state wouldn't allow him to take it willingly, but once it was in his system, he would calm down and being in a calmer state, he might eventually be able to take it without resistance. That was the plan. I suppose I can relate it to the feeling of very low blood sugar – when you feel starving with no energy but back to normal after a healthy meal. His brain responded and he wasn't so desperate all the time. It makes sense. I was learning that you can starve your brain in the same way you can starve your body.

Soon after this visit my Mum went up to Cambridge to meet with Natasha Campbell McBride who wrote the book *Gut and Psychology Syndrome*. Natasha didn't do tests but took an extensive case history of us, his grandparents, his development and his eating habits. Because Natasha was very much about diet, she prescribed home-made soups with vegetables in a home-made meat stock. She explained that 90% of the immune system is in the gut and that meat stock heals a leaky gut, making it strong, which will ultimately protect his body more.

This led on to meat stock soups that Tim still eats to this day because he still gets the benefit from them. It was the beginning of what I termed 'the mental breakdown soups'. Because they were so complicated and time-consuming to make, my Mum volunteered to make them at this point and ensure Tim always had a good supply of them. This is how invested she was in Tim's health and development.

Every week my Mum went to a local biodynamic farm for meat bones, brewed them up to make stock, brought organic and biodynamic vegetables and once a week had a mammoth soup-making session. She then divided it into portions, froze it and as we live a ninety-minute-drive away from my parents, we often met halfway on the 'soup run'.

The good news from all this hard work and investment into Tim's health was that he became willing for us to feed him in small spoonfuls. We could only use a plastic spoon, which we had to turn over so the food never touched his top lip, but if we went along with his rules and engaged in elements of high-level distraction, he would take the food. Though force-feeding had been horrible, it was clearly necessary for a short while to break the cycle – but what a relief to know we'd never have to do it again.

Two months after the Ultracare food mix and the chicken soups, Mum's diary says: 'Since the special food mixes and soups he is showing great changes – he is easier to cope with, calmer, more peaceful, speaking more, playing a little creatively with some toys with other people – we are optimistic'.

I had heard that many children with autism struggled with food and often got stuck on just one or two foods for many years, such as jam sandwiches or cheesy puffs. While Tim also got stuck in this way and would only accept very limited foods, the good thing was that they were healthy foods he became stuck on. He would eat meat stock soups three times a day for protein input, Ultracare Food Mix which we called 'red yoghurt' for other major nutritional input and waffles made from buckwheat flour as his other mainstay. If he was going to get stuck in this way, better that it be with nutritious foods!

As a teenager, I had discovered I was intolerant to dairy and gluten and had chosen to live free of it, which I still do to this day. Dizziness and headaches had gone away, digestion issues had massively cleared up and I found I had more clarity of mind as well as high levels of energy. As it was quite prevalent in my family, I had decided to keep Tim off dairy and wheat from the beginning. This was deemed very controversial at that time. The reactions of others were sometimes critical but it just felt like the right thing to do

Now I understand that the when the proteins gluten and casein within wheat and dairy don't get digested properly, they turn into substances with similar chemical structures to opiates, like morphine and heroin. These opiates are thought to get through the blood/brain barrier and block certain areas of the brain just like morphine or heroin would do. So therefore, wheat and dairy products, if someone can't digest them properly, can have quite serious effects on the brain.

Nursery

Despite seeing small benefits to Tim's state and general well-being within the home environment, the outside world still held a massive sense of threat for him. At three, he started nursery and he was so overwhelmed on the first day that he fell asleep on Tina, in the middle of all the noise and hubbub.

Sometimes he would kick chairs and bins over if someone said 'no' to him, or he would refuse to do what was asked of him. Either that or he didn't understand what was being asked of him. His sensitivities were so high that he would automatically resist when faced with playdoh or having his hands washed.

He was completely unprepared to be part of such a big group. Other than saying 'yes' to his name, Tim could not follow what was happening in the group, so therefore couldn't participate meaningfully. There was no way he could understand what one adult in front of a group of children was saying and he still couldn't talk in a way that others could understand him.

He found being in the close proximity of other children highly stressful. Sometimes he would sit on the floor and play by himself. If other children came to join him he would put his head down, look out between his fingers and stay still until they had gone. Then he would raise his head and carry on. If Tina attempted to interact with another child while she was spending time with him at playgroup, he would become aggressive towards her. If another adult tried to engage him in a book he was looking at, he would pull away.

The tiny moments when he would allow another child into his world, even for a few seconds became red-letter days. Tina would text me from nursery and I would jump for joy! Once, Tina asked a little girl if she would ask Tim to come with her to the singing circle. He actually took her hand and went with her and stayed there for twenty whole minutes. I don't know how much he joined in but the fact that he was there was amazing. There was a lot of celebration on that day!

With Tim, everything had to be on his terms. When reading he would take a book, find a place by himself and turn the pages as and when he pleased without interference. Only very occasionally would he relax sufficiently to allow Tina to talk to him, point things out or ask him questions and these, too, were red-letter moments.

His interest in numbers continued and he would sometimes enjoy counting objects with Tina. He would often copy her when she counted and occasionally, he would add the next number to hers – for instance, if she said thirteen, he would say fourteen and if she said fourteen, he would say fifteen! I found it encouraging that although a lot of what he should be learning didn't get through, certain things did – just odd, occasional little things – but the fact that they happened gave me hope that he could learn – that he could somehow take in information and use it.

Occasionally he would do something amazing that totally shocked us – like wash his hands without being prompted or say the name of a toy he had. We would be elated, thinking that he had mastered something new – but it could be months before he washed his hands or said that word again. It was all very sporadic. It was as if all the information he processed had to run through a very blocked sieve and only little tiny bits got through. There seemed to be no rhyme or reason as to why he would say something one day and not the next.

At one point I was told that where you may have to teach something to a typical child about ten times for them to learn it, you may have to teach something to a child with autism 100 times in order for them to get it. Everything just takes longer as it has a slower and more complex filter. But why? What's wrong with the filter? Can we not change the filter? Surely if we could, information would get through and he would learn. It was all about the way he processed. I allowed myself a tiny bit of hope that he *could* learn – that it was possible, even if it was sporadic.

However the pathways to emotional connection and response seemed to be even more blocked and the desire to connect on a friendship level with other children was non-existent. How do you create an element of desire in a child who has none? Tim could be around other children but still showed signs of serious distress if another person tried to interact with him. This anxiety was not easing up for him at all. How could we work on this and where was the hope for such an issue? As soon as someone showed a tiny level of interest in him, he would either lash out or shut down. I think this is the part of his autism that I hated the most. I longed for Tim to let down his guard, to soften, to stop fighting, to let others in and to start to open up to us.

I did know that other children liked Tim and that if he would *let* them get close he would be able to have friends. I wondered, however, how long other children would go on liking him if he kept pushing them away. The fact that he was likeable to others though, was another tiny spark of hope.

Tim's default place of safety at nursery was looking at books with no one to disturb him, but Tina, rightly or wrongly, continuously made sure that he moved on to try new things. When he was having a bad day, she would sometimes let him stay in his isolation, but mostly she moved him on. She found that a three-minute timer worked and that if she told him he had to stop when the timer finished, he would often accept this and move to the next activity. She also used PECS in the form of a strip of pictures that Tim could take and hand to her as a way of choosing what he wanted to do. Pictures supposedly helped to reduce his anxiety levels about what was going to happen next. It also allowed other adults to be able to work with him for short periods of time. Tina had learnt to read Tim but others hadn't, so they found that this communication could temporarily bridge the gap.

His speech continued to be very slow to develop. Occasionally he would copy words Tina said, but very rarely spoke from his own initiative. When he said something independently we would break out metaphorical bottles of champagne! It was possible! Again, little tiny moments of hope that I sometimes felt were cruel because of how rare they were and how much we wanted them.

When Tim was with Tina at the house and I didn't go out, it put Tim in a place of conflict. Who should he listen to and take instruction from? He seemed to need one person all the time to be with him. I found it confusing too, when I was there with him but he took all his instructions from Tina. Once, he was totally beside himself and I was just about to pick him up and comfort him when Tina jumped in there, scooped him up and took him outside for a walk. I had been wanting to calm him in a completely different way but was too late. He was *my* child, wasn't he? Was I wrong in the ways I wanted to look after him? He was *my* child but he was *her* job. That felt so wrong on so many levels.

Tearing Paper – Why Not?

Sometimes Tim had intense needs to do unusual things, which we discovered was called stimming or self-stimulatory behaviours. At the time he went to nursery, his main stim was tearing up paper in long thin strips and watching it fall to the ground. He loved this activity, which was deemed inappropriate at the nursery, so Tina would often jump in there to stop him before he entered his exciting world of paper tearing. If he'd found some paper and had already started, she found that showing him the timer would help him stop and she would then give him a dustpan and brush to encourage him to help clear up the mess afterwards.

I wish I knew then what I know now – because I can see that if we had taken the Son-Rise Program® approach, we could have used these activities to reach him. This could have paved the way for people to build relationships with him more easily. Why couldn't we see at this point that we should jump in and do what he was doing with him rather than always trying to force him to do things he had no interest in? We could have torn lots of different coloured bits of paper with him and taught him colours… we could have counted the bits of paper as they fell to the ground and worked on his number skills... we could have shared and enjoyed his love of paper tearing with him and made a connection that might have made him feel better! Maybe people could change their ideas of what *inappropriate* is. Painting creates a massive mess which needs clearing up, so why can't paper tearing become a new nursery activity?

At this particular point in Tim's life, we were trying to get him to participate in all the things little children generally do, but he wasn't ready and couldn't manage.

We were putting sticking plasters over his issues in order to get by, but were doing nothing to help him with his core issues. We didn't know there *was* a way to help him. I can see now that we were trying to prepare him with life skills before he was able to connect happily one-to-one. His unwillingness to have other children or adults in his space was his way of telling us that it was all too much, but we didn't receive that message. We didn't know what we know now. He could hardly process what one person close to him was saying, so how could he process what someone talking to a large group was saying or intending for him to do? We also desperately wanted him to be with other children and have fun. Except that he wasn't having that much fun.

Overview – Looking Back Already

Reading back over this so far, I can see something has clearly happened to me. I have left the wider world behind. I no longer talk about friends or my work – even my husband. Tim's autism is totally consuming my life. When a friend once told me everyone with children felt the same, I couldn't agree and at one point I made a list of all the things we did because of Tim – there were twenty-five things on the list and twenty were specifically because of autism.

I would sometimes bump into old colleagues and it would give me a total wake-up call as to how my life had changed. What could I say? I got married, changed my job, had a gorgeous baby…and now my life is swallowed up by his autism. I was still working hard in three different schools, but even that wasn't noteworthy in comparison. Tim and his development was my only priority in everything I did.

Grief

The Christmas after Tim's diagnosis, I found myself singing 'Silent night' unaccompanied and in harmony with a small group of school staff at the front of a full church. It was one of our Christmas concerts. You know when your voice catches and you have to cry but it is totally inappropriate to do so? Well, the congregation were so warm and kind and the harmonies of 'Silent Night' were so nostalgic that time seemed to stand still around me. The emotions around Christmas had always held great significance for me, but that year I realised these beautiful emotions of warmth, closeness and connectedness were far too painful. The words caught in my throat. I stopped singing and just stared out at the people, feeling paralysed by my grief. Later, sitting amongst everybody, my need to cry was welling up. I told myself this was impossible – after all, I had to lead a group of children later in the service. I was actually working. But even so in the middle of a carol, I slipped out of the church and just let go, crying and crying into the darkness. Fortunately, no one could hear me over the singing. When the song came to an end, I composed myself, resumed my seat and carried on – trying not to catch anybody's eye and hoping nobody would notice my tear-stained face.

Grief hits you in strange places and at strange times. It comes when you least need it, when you are not in an appropriate place to express it and it becomes all you can feel and experience. My child hadn't died, but there were so many aspects of him that felt lost to me, that I believed I'd never know or see – that was what I was grieving for.

If your child is ill, there's a lot of sympathy and understanding. But if your child has a developmental disorder, there seems to be none. It's just hard work and lonely and you have to get on with it. I remember standing in the staffroom at another of my schools. I'd stepped out for a moment because I was teaching nativity songs to beautifully interactive and responsive five-year-olds and the grief had overtaken my emotions in the same way. I was gathering myself, when the secretary came in and asked what was wrong. I stupidly told her, and she said, 'Well, at least his life isn't in danger

– my son has a hole in the heart,' and walked out. Where did that leave me? Was I not supposed to feel sad?

On top of my grief, I was now spending very little time with Erik because if we weren't working we were trying to support Tim, which involved a lot of turn-taking. We were the proverbial ships that passed in the night and it was really hard to find moments where we could listen to each other and feel close.

Good Time Friends?

I had to pick my friends carefully at this time. Long-term friends were always supportive but busy and unavailable on a daily basis. Friends with young children had become my new social group. Many were keen to tell me all the amazing things their children were saying or doing – they just couldn't help themselves. Some would make comments like, 'Oh, I thought so,' when I told them my news about Tim's diagnosis. Only a handful could actually see my heartbreak and had the sensitivity and capacity to be my friend through all this.

On top of my sadness as to what was happening to Tim, we had to cope with weird attitudes and judgemental looks from other people. Friends had long since stopped asking us out. So many times I had tried to join friends on outings and both Tim and I had ended up leaving amidst highly charged states of stress. Who would want that disturbance on a fun day out?

One friend kept trying though – 'We're going on a nice, relaxing day out with the children – nothing much – join us if you'd like to'. *If I'd like to?* I couldn't think of anything nicer, but there was no point trying. Tim's anxiety would be sky-high, others would talk, I would feel hurt and we would have to leave. It was a cycle that happened so many times. They would still be sitting on their picnic blankets chatting animatedly and with the expectations of a lovely sunny afternoon ahead, while I battled to get a screaming Tim into the car to go home – on our own. I was being isolated from two of my biggest needs – to enjoy being with my friends and for Tim to be fine.

I would sometimes watch families chatting and relaxing – even laughing together as their children were actually talking to them and to each other. That world was a million miles away – I wondered what it felt like… Meanwhile, I very much needed places to go with Tim where we would be happily welcomed. Such places were rare. Some people were polite but I could sense their awkwardness and judgement as Tim struggled to function, which I found so harsh. We were already struggling – just a little extra understanding would have gone such a long way for me. The hard thing was that I could rarely access even my closest friends. I so wished my family lived nearer. These are the times you need people around you who love you no matter what and the fact that my sister lived in Holland and my brother lived in Germany didn't help at this point.

Really?

It's interesting isn't it, how when something happens to your child, everyone thinks they have the right to tell you what to do and how to deal with it. They also seem to feel that you have full rights to their opinion.

One lady who knew a little of our story, stopped me in the street outside our house around this time, looked at Tim and said directly to me, 'There are some good homes around here for when he's older'.

For goodness sake, he is only three. Give us a chance! You know how sometimes comments fuel you in the opposite direction. This comment fuelled my determination that such a thing would never happen. I would do everything in my power to stop it from happening – to help him develop – to keep him with me. I just wished I knew how.

Reports – Tim aged four

Reports about Tim around this time were saying:

Severe speech and language and social communication disorder
Reliant on routines
No awareness of danger

Not able to eat independently
No interest in interacting with peers
Finds it very difficult to change from one activity to another
Finds it very hard to accept adult direction in 1-1 activities
Almost impossible to cajole him into participating in a task he does not like, over which he has no control
Behaviour unpredictable
Very little tolerance of people being in close proximity
Can't cope with too much noise
Can't access activities if surrounded by too many people or too much noise
Can become very fixated on one particular aspect of an object or activity
Becomes upset when too closely surrounded by adults or children
Very limited eating habits
High frustration levels and tendency towards temper tantrums
Can be very inflexible and very focused on his own routines
Never been seen engaging in imaginative play

I already knew that environments stressed him but the muddle and stress was also coming from his own brain – he couldn't make sense of life from the inside out or the outside in.

The Future? Try Not to Think About It…

Although he was only four, I had to actively stop myself thinking about the future. I had seen grown men with severe autism walking through town in groups, grunting, shouting out and being pushed along in wheelchairs or herded by carers. I had worked in a home for adults with autism as a teenager and one day a particularly violent client had suddenly lashed out at me. It had made me feel so insecure that I'd stopped working there.

Surely each of these adults had once been gorgeous little children like Tim, born to and cherished by doting parents. Would this be how Tim would turn out? How much of this *thing* was in our control and how much was going to happen to him, no matter what we did?

I would watch parents when they were out with their disabled adult children in town and wonder if they had known how life would turn out when their child was little. It seems inconceivable to love a child and have no control at all over how their future will pan out.

'A little boy with autism becomes a grown man with autism,' I read in a book somewhere. The person who wrote this book also told the story of a much-loved son with autism growing up and killing his own mother in the kitchen at the age of eighteen.

Where were the people who could help me at this point? Where were the people with realistic hope? With plausible positive stories? With genuine encouragement? Where were the people who could really help me? If there is no cure, which the National Autistic Society tells us, what can be done to make sure the outcome is okay? Anything?

I had to take all these thoughts and feelings and put them in a metaphorical box – not to be opened yet – if ever – and placed as far away from my real life as possible. I had to imagine this box wasn't there in order to focus my attention on the here and now – and my cute little four-year-old who I loved with all my heart and who liked to stare at books for hours and talk to his hand.

A Place to Escape

With everyday life being so hectic, every couple of months or so I would treat myself to a few hours at a local spa. This was a hotel with a small health suite – sauna, jacuzzi, steam room, pool… it was tiny, but I liked it because it was so private and often there was nobody else around. On this particular occasion, I went there to have a few hours away from stress and worry, to recuperate and regain new energy.

It was totally deserted. I found myself a place in the steaming sauna, felt my body begin to relax and let my mind aimlessly wander…This was the place where my stresses could be relieved and creativity could re-enter my thinking. In my reverie I heard some grunting noises from outside and looked out of the sauna window to see some adults walking in. I immediately realised that these men had autism and were here with their carers. In my private space – the space where I escape from autism. I looked through the window closely at the face of one of the men lashing about in the pool. He couldn't talk, appearing to be very disconnected and frightening to me, and I could see that it would be impossible to have a conversation with him. What had he been like as a child? The dark, gnawing question reappeared, 'Is this how Tim will inevitably turn out, despite what we do?'

My space had been invaded with the one thing I was trying to escape from – and had opened Pandora's box which I'd determined to keep tightly shut.

I left.

Chapter Four – Should we try the behaviour route?

ABA (Applied Behaviour Analysis)

At this point, we were advised to look at Applied Behaviour Analysis and as it was specifically designed for children with autism, I felt I should know about it and see if it would help Tim. I knew that many of Tim's behaviours and distress were beyond my understanding and I hoped that if someone knew more about autism than I did and was able to actually implement this with Tim, we ought to give it a try.

Applied Behavioural Analysis is a way of teaching complex tasks by breaking them down into small pieces that could be learnt more easily, building on logical steps. Rewards (or reinforcers) are given for correct responses or behaviours and inappropriate responses are corrected, ignored or redirected. Each learning trial is recorded with specific data and by analysing this, adjustments are made for the next stages of the educational programme. It supposedly targets many skills such as attention, imitation, language, self-help skills and academic skills as well as behaviour. It is based on techniques for increasing useful behaviours and decreasing behaviours that may cause harm or interfere with learning.

We already had Tina, speech therapy, occupational therapy, thera-play, nursery and biomedical interventions going on. Also, school was about to start for three mornings a week. Could we really implement something *new*? However, as we started to research, we found out that for many children it had taken them so much further in their development and some children were happily functioning with friends and a great future. Wow. I almost felt we owed it to Tim to try.

Being ultimately behaviour-based, it seemed quite alien to me, but I had already been told I couldn't use my natural mothering instincts any more so maybe this was just an extension of that. Maybe I had to toughen up and realise that the natural side of nurturing and teaching Tim had no place anymore.

Tim still spent his days lining up cars and making sculptures of his toys but not really playing with them. He would jump and flap his hands when happy or excited, but was still unable to naturally respond to us. He was very rigid in his expectations and his behaviour was erratic. The ABA made me a little nervous that yet more people would try to force him more and more into boxes where he just didn't fit. It could be an intensely painful process for him. I remembered how Maureen's insistence on very directed games had created so much anxiety within him.

However, as it was explained to me, ABA focused on the positives of the child's behaviour and broke tasks down into tiny steps in order to teach them. Tiny steps seemed like a good idea. In learning, the child would be asked to perform tasks and be rewarded if he got it right and reprimanded or corrected if he got it wrong. I can't imagine any parent liking the idea of aversives or reprimands, but I knew that lots of versions of ABA now chose not to use aversives. We would ask for that kind. I envisaged Tim sitting at a table working constantly on little tasks in tiny steps and gradually piecing together the gaps in his understanding and abilities. That vision was okay.

But the one thing I'd forgotten was that Tim was a mover. He couldn't sit at a table for more than a minute. We had never been able to persuade Tim to sit anywhere against his will and I worried that he would not do any of these tasks willingly. He was often in a heightened state of fight/flight and seemed unable to calm himself, or be calmed by others. How could he take instruction in this state? He also had a great need to be in control. Would the ABA method be able to change that in him?

We would have to make sure that people didn't keep telling Tim off, giving him punishments if he didn't cooperate. Surely we would have a say in that? I felt a rising panic about the lack of control I would have – yet again – about how other people would treat my child. This lack of control on my part was really starting to eat me. It was my place to love and protect him, and it seemed others had taken over for too long – but now I was once more giving away yet more power. It was all in a desperate attempt to help him, but it wasn't an easy feeling.

I had many questions, but as I had read stories of children really moving on with ABA, I felt we had no choice but to try it. I knew that my knowledge was very limited at this point and we needed a plan. Nothing else was bringing him closer to us and something had to.

Nothing so far had awakened in Tim the ability to relate – interacting, sharing, learning naturally, developing curiosity…Tim's development seemed to be stuck behind a perpetually locked door. Might this process have the magic ingredient?

We had some opposition from our current therapists, mainly out of concern – Helen, from the Child Development Centre had had experience of this putting unnecessary pressure on families she had known, and Portage felt it was a bit too 'severe', but all in all, we decided that it was not actually going too far against what we had been trying to do so far. School and Tina and all his therapists were constantly trying to persuade him to follow instructions and respond to things – wouldn't this just be more of that?

Whatever my misgivings were, I knew I had to throw myself totally into Tim's ABA so he would have the very best chance. I had to be fully behind it, especially if I had to motivate others to feel the same.

Erik and I looked into the process, found an ABA case leader to be assigned to us, advertised and interviewed prospective therapists to train and carefully chose two to start with. We also had two friends, Beth and Diane, who had said they were willing to come to the training and do occasional sessions with Tim on a voluntary basis.

Making a Start on ABA

The day of the initial workshop came. I liked the fact that we were being proactive and I liked that the whole day would focus around my favourite subject. I loved talking about Tim and was sure I would learn some good tips and ideas to genuinely help him. I was eager to discover the secrets to an approach I knew nothing about yet. Anything I could learn that could help him would be a step in the right direction.

There are many more aspects to running workshops than you would imagine – organising lifts for people who don't have cars, making sure everyone's there on time, food and drink for everyone and also, most importantly, finding someone for Tim to go to while we all gathered to talk about him.

On this occasion, Julie, one of the therapists we had hired, didn't turn up at the required time and it took us ages to communicate with her and go out and pick her up. It wasted the first hour of the session – and this was costing about £100 per hour. I had to try so hard not to think of money and to focus on the subject at hand. I didn't show my frustration, because of course I wanted everyone to be happy and up-beat and in a good state for learning – there was so much at stake here.

Jackie, our Case leader, was an intelligent, upbeat person full of personality and fun. When she started talking, she spoke about the triad of impairments again in exactly the way I had read in so many books. She then spoke of autism as being a profile of deficits and excesses. Basically things your child couldn't do and things your child did too much. It reminded me of the text books that I struggled to relate to but I believed that if I could face it, I might have a clearer understanding of what the issues were so we could get to the 'how we can help him' place.

DEFICITS were considered to be things such as:
Speech and language skills
Communication skills
Attention skills
Self-help skills
Fine motor skills
Gross motor skills
Social skills
Play skills

EXCESSES were considered to be things such as:
Self-stimulatory behaviour (stims)
Tantrums/non-compliance
Aggression to self or others
Rigidity/routines

Yes, he has all these deficits and all these excesses. Yes. I could recognise them in his behaviour and his developmental issues. In hindsight I have examined what Tim's issues were and slotted them into the ABA deficit/excess mind-set. I never liked this way of viewing Tim, but I had the belief that the more I understood, the more I could help him.

Let's Examine His 'Deficits'

SPEECH AND LANGUAGE: His articulation was poor. He often couldn't make himself understood even if he did get some words out. He often didn't understand what we said and couldn't follow a single instruction or suggestion. He had echolalia, repeating words exactly as we had said them, with no relation to their meaning – eg.,

Me – 'Would you like a drink?'
Tim – 'Would you like a drink?'

It was as though he couldn't get the meaning of what he was saying and could only repeat words as a mechanical exercise. He would also endlessly repeat phrases from his favourite television programmes which I knew also to be part of his echolalia.

COMMUNICATION SKILLS: At this point these were related to basic requests only – he would never comment on things, tell us things, question things or make gestures. He didn't know how to gain someone's attention and showed no desire to draw us into his world to share anything he was thinking or feeling.

ATTENTION SKILLS: For anything an adult wanted him to do, these were mostly non-existent. He could give his full attention to his stimming behaviour, however. He could concentrate for hours then – but for him to sit and listen to a story, play with a puzzle or interact with a person was pretty limited.

SELF-HELP SKILLS: At the age of four, Tim was only just starting to feed himself. He would put the food on the spoon and turn the spoon upside down to avoid it touching his top lip. He was only intermittently willing to wash his hands. He couldn't put on or take off any of his own clothes and he certainly couldn't brush his own teeth.

FINE MOTOR SKILLS: Tim's hand was so wobbly when on the very odd occasion he put pen to paper, he had no control and could not produce anything more than a few spidery scribbles. His pincer grip was very under-developed. He would not allow us to teach him better ways to hold a pencil for example – so it was hard to know what he would be capable of.

GROSS MOTOR SKILLS: in some of these areas Tim was pretty much in the same place as his peers. However, at all his OT tests he would always resist hopping across the room or standing on one leg, so even OT's found it hard to know what he could do.

SOCIAL SKILLS: Well, Tim couldn't talk to another child, would hardly let another child near him and had very little interest in relating to another child. When he waved, his little hand even faced towards himself and not outwards towards others. I realise that this was because that's how it appears when somebody waves to him, but he didn't seem to have picked up that other people wave differently. How could Tim develop social skills if he avoided other people at all costs?

He had no awareness that other people were different entities with their own thoughts and feelings. His only awareness seemed to be of himself and what he needed.

PLAY SKILLS: Tim's play skills were extremely repetitive. He would never zoom cars around the room, on the edges of tables and sofas and make them crash. He would line them up – all very proper and organised. He did the same things over and over again – perhaps trying to create order out of chaos – but he didn't play in the conventional sense. He would make sculptures of little people hanging off lorries at peculiar angles etc but he would never enact scenes or make the people talk to each other.

Let's Examine His 'Excesses'

SELF-STIMULATORY BEHAVIOUR: Tim would stare at books on his own for hours, talking to himself, holding his hands tensely to his chest and moving backwards and forwards in an excited way. He would walk around making noises into his hand which he held right up to his face and moved jaggedly from side to side. He would tear paper for hours and leave a sea of shreds over an entire room. He would run round and round a table again and again and he would watch DVDs for as long as we would let him, re-winding short passages again and again until he was dripping with sweat. He also loved watching objects spin and reflections on the ceiling and walls.

TANTRUMS/NON-COMPLIANCE: This was the aspect of his difficulties that most worried me. He would get an idea in his head about something he wanted and woe betide anyone who got in his way. He was in that mindset a lot and to ask something of him during that state was like a red rag to a bull. He wouldn't – he couldn't. Instead he would refuse, scream and lash out if we persisted.

He was in fight/flight mode nearly all the time. Could this be addressed by discipline? I couldn't imagine Tim sitting meekly at a table attempting to perform a task anyone asked of him. If he couldn't understand why, he wouldn't do it. End of.

During this time, Erik and I would only take Tim to town with a clear 'get-out strategy'. So Erik would give him a warning and if he continued pulling in directions we weren't going in, he would pick him up over his shoulder and take him back to the car, kicking and screaming with all his might. Not much of a strategy really – a survival mechanism. But we would have to decide in advance what to do, so we didn't find ourselves in the position of arguing about it on the street while it was happening – a position we had found ourselves in many times.

Sometimes at home when Tim was having a meltdown and Erik and I were arguing over how to deal with him, I would walk out of the house, with Tim crying and Erik and I in mid-argument. I felt so passionately that I was right – that Tim needed hugs, love and connection and calming down. While Erik felt so passionately that he was right – that Tim needed boundaries and discipline. On one occasion, I remember finding myself outside the house in my night shirt, crying and sitting on the step, waiting for Tim to calm down. You would think that a teacher and a social worker would know that the state we were in would directly affect our child – but we were so desperate due to lack of sleep and never-ending battles and we each so strongly felt that our approach was the answer to his difficulties, that consequence eluded us.

For a while now, when Tim went into full meltdown mode, when he flailed, screamed and lashed out, we would give him 'time out'. I can't remember who recommended this to us but Erik and I are now both embarrassed that we ever thought this was the best thing to do. It was taken from the idea that Tim would consider his 'wrongdoings' and resolve to do better next time. It also came from the idea that he was 'acting up' to get our attention and so to remove our attention would help him to realise that acting in this way didn't actually get him what he wanted. It was taken I think from the Supernanny concept of the 'naughty step'. As he wouldn't sit on a naughty step we gave him a 'naughty room' which we then called 'the thinking room' as we honestly didn't consider he was being naughty, but just didn't know how else to help him calm down. It was a room where there was nothing he could throw about and break in his frustration. It was the little toilet by our front door. The idea was for him to 'come to his senses' and calm down and learn about the results of his actions. Please don't ask me to justify this. I still don't agree with it.

Erik says it was an attempt to remove him from the triggers and sensory overload, to help him calm down and make better decisions. Our motives were good but the reality was so not helpful for Tim. Erik and I have both since apologised to him.

However, it was assumed that the child would fully understand why he had been given time out and that he would reflect and learn and change his behaviour. Well, Tim wasn't at this stage yet. Learning didn't yet happen in this way for him.

Tim would have triggers. For instance, he had no understanding that you couldn't see something you liked in a shop and just take it. He also couldn't understand our explanations of why you couldn't just take things. He would see something and he had to have it. So far, we had never been able to reason with that level of need and desperation. Erik and I continued to fall on different sides – I felt Tim couldn't cope with his feelings and needed help – kindness and understanding and calming down (and talking things through – though I'd actually never achieved the 'talking things through' to this point). Erik felt that in order to help him and offer him security, we needed to give him firm boundaries and let him know clearly what was right and wrong. He felt part of Tim's actions showed a level of insecurity and that boundaries would bring security. At the time we debated a lot, but I can see in hindsight that we were both trying to achieve the same thing – a comforted child.

AGGRESSION TO SELF OR OTHERS

Tim never hit other children and only hit an adult who was with him if he was totally hyped up with frustration and panic. He did actually lash out at me sometimes – but I felt that was the point where he needed help and calming down and human comfort. Erik thought that was the moment he should have a warning then go into the 'thinking room' so he would know for sure that it was a wrong thing to do. Again, a divide. I was really hoping these ABA workshops would resolve this one. It sided with Erik. I continued to feel unhappy about the conflict between us.

RIGIDITY/ROUTINES
If we were driving somewhere and realised we had gone the wrong way and had to turn around, Tim would arch his back, scream and writhe in his seat. He couldn't cope with us going back on ourselves. I honestly don't know why such a thing should bother him so much. But it seriously did. If he thought something was going to happen and it turned out that it couldn't, that was very hard as he was not at a place where he could be reasoned with. However, he was never a child who needed totally strict routines, the same thing every day. Erik and I are not natural routine people and I think that other people put Tim's need for sameness on to him as something that 'children with autism need', but I never felt it was his biggest issue.

However, his rigidity was obvious. That was when he had an idea in his head and had to follow it through whatever the consequences. Could he change his mind on that? Could he get to a place where it didn't matter? No way. This also applied to his stimming behaviours – when he was in his own world, focused on his book and pacing around mumbling into his hand, there was no way we could stop him and communicate with him at this time. His rigidity was one of his greatest stumbling blocks.

The ABA Sessions

The ABA sessions started with an initial two-day workshop and following that we did two-hour ABA sessions each day. We figured we could build them up from there.

Jackie asked us lots of questions about Tim in order to get a picture and Erik and I answered them the best we could.

For all Jackie's positivity, some of the ways she talked in the first meeting I found quite chilling. She said that if we asked Tim to say something he would have to say it within three seconds as conversation moved between people so quickly – she then said they could be flexible and allow him up to five seconds to respond. What? Can you just change a processing delay by upping the pressure? She also said about Tim's sensory overloads that (and I quote) 'Life's like that and you just have to get used to it'. About the way Tim spoke, she said we were only allowed to respond to him if he asked for something accurately according the rules she was going to set for him – eg., if he spoke in a whiney voice we had to ignore him – and we could only respond if he spoke perfectly to us. There was one particular teaching point I remember – she also said that if we asked him to clap his hands for example, he would have to clap a few times. If he did it just once it would be wrong. If he looked around for a while (in thought), then clapped his hands that would also be wrong.

Jackie wanted to undo the things he had learnt 'wrongly' and build them up again in a 'correct' way – but it didn't make sense as he could already say 'would you like apple juice' but she decided she wanted him only to say 'apple juice' each time. It was like she had a plan to undo everything that he currently was and re-programme him in the way she thought he ought to be.

Following the first meeting, Jackie then went away and devised a programme for us all to follow. One part encouraged him to start saying 'no thank you' instead of screaming in resistance when someone asked him to do something he didn't want to do. In the next session, six weeks later, this turned into a great debate. We had taught him to say 'no thank you' instead of screaming, which was good, but he was then saying 'no thank you' to pretty much everything that was asked of him. Katherine, one of his therapists, felt that it was okay for him to refuse something that was a game perhaps, but not something that was a request, like 'please pass me the blue ball'. Then came the question, how was he supposed to know the difference?

We whiled away hours having debates like this – I know, because I have it all on video – and never came to clear conclusions to enable us all to sing from the same hymn sheet.

After the explanations on the second day, Tim had been around in the morning and in the afternoon the plan was for Julie and Katherine to play with him while Jackie looked on and advised. Julie and Katherine were sitting on the floor surrounded by toys and lots of musical instruments, but he gave them a fleeting look, before he retreated to the corner of the room to look at his book and doing his scripting, which was when he repeated phrases from various TV programmes and stories, while talking into his moving hand. This is an extract from the video we took:

Me: I think he's been doing his own stuff for so long that I don't think he realises that he's meant to be playing with you.

Julie: Why don't we go on the trampoline?

They wanted to engage him in an activity so that Jackie could assess how they played with him and give them tips but they couldn't. It was the 'do something fun and he'll just join in' idea but he didn't.

Julie said, 'Tim, do you want to go for a bounce?'

But Tim carried on stimming and talking to himself.

So Katherine suggested, 'I bet he'll probably follow you.'

It took Erik and I heaps of encouragement to get Tim to follow Julie but Tim didn't stay engaged, as from the moment he got on the trampoline, he just wanted to get off again. It was a very unnatural setting, as he and the therapists all had to perform in order for Jackie to give them tips and feedback on how to best deal with him – I know it from similar classroom situations as 'the observer effect'.

Tim had the ball and Erik said, 'Tim throw to Katherine,' and Tim threw it to the wall. Erik said, 'I think he's being naughty now.' But I don't think he was.

Jackie said, 'Once he realises, we're all still here and not reacting he'll be okay. Once he kind of realises we're not interested, he'll stop.'

The premise behind this, I think, was that he was doing what he was doing for attention and that when he realised he wouldn't get the attention he was looking for, he'd stop. The thing is, I look back in hindsight and can see that he wasn't doing any of this for attention. He wasn't even aware of what he was supposed to do. He was just doing what he needed to do to make himself feel better in what was, for him, a highly stressful situation.

He had spent all morning in his own head, stimming and walking about and as no one had engaged him, he had retreated further into his own thoughts. Jackie said, 'Tim is throwing things because he wants someone to say 'don't do it' or 'calm down.'

But surely that's back to the idea that he was constantly craving attention and I now know he wasn't.

Tim was ignoring everyone and walking around the room throwing the football at his toys, while Julie was encouraging him to stop. Tim started throwing balloons in Katherine's direction.

Jackie's take on the situation was, 'Look, he's just trying to get a reaction.' Whereas I now believe he wasn't doing anything of the sort.

Everyone was discussing what he was doing as if he wasn't in the room but no one was actually talking to him or trying to engage him in a way that made sense to him. They all had a plan for what they wanted to do with him and their expectations of him. Beth tried to sing a song and engage him in that. Someone else wanted him to do a puzzle and engage him in that – and he wasn't playing.

Tim was looking at a book. Julie tried to join in, but Tim resisted her presence and got cross.

Then Beth jumped in by chanting, 'Number one, tickle your tum.'

However Tim said, 'Bye bye tickle,' and as she persisted, he just got more irate.

Then Tim initiated an activity by picking up a puzzle, so Julie and Katherine immediately started to play it with him. However his response was to pick up all the pieces and bring them over to me. Jackie said he obviously wanted to do it as he was the one that got the puzzle out, but she considered his behaviour to be overly controlling by the fact that he wanted me to play with it, instead of the helpers, who at this stage he didn't know very well. So the compromise she would allow, was that I would be permitted to sit on the floor alongside Julie and Katherine as long as I didn't speak to him or join in, while the girls did the puzzle with him. Otherwise we were supposedly giving in to his need for control.

She said, 'Sally pay him minimal attention because you are in the teaching environment now'.

I felt it was actually a good thing that he'd taken down a puzzle and initiated an activity with me – but that couldn't be celebrated because of the control issue. We had to teach him that he wasn't in control.

In the middle of all this Tim turned to me and said, 'Nana come soon?' in a desperate plea. I told him Nana would come soon and tried to be as reassuring as I could. But I felt under pressure not to give him attention.

They all celebrated when he put in the correct puzzle piece. They all celebrated when he got something right. Jackie said it was all about differentiated reinforcement. We couldn't celebrate that he had come to get me because he was being controlling. However, I could celebrate him putting in a correct piece of the jigsaw puzzle because he'd done something 'right'.

When he was fully engaged, his stimming stopped and just for one or two short moments he seemed to be able to focus, so he could put a whole jigsaw puzzle together and answer questions about it, 'Where is the boy… what colour is the bus… etc'. Most of these puzzles we had done with him before and we knew he could answer these questions, so for all their praise, this wasn't a breakthrough but I was still glad they could see him engage in this way.

When he had done the puzzle, at Jackie's request everyone sang 'The Wheels on the Bus' and Tim joined in happily. When the first verse was finished Jackie gave everyone instructions, 'Let's sing the wipers on the bus now,' and everyone started to sing. Then Jackie demanded that everyone turned their attention to a new puzzle. Everyone was making over-excited exclamations of 'wow' and 'look at this,' etc. while Tim continued singing, 'The wheels on the bus'.

Jackie told everyone to ignore him, adding, 'Don't say too much – just carry on with the puzzle because that's *control*'.

Then Tim walked away.

Jackie said to me, 'Oh we've lost him – but keep going – ask Julie and Katherine to keep playing and talking loudly about the puzzle.'

Leaving me to wonder how Tim wanting to carry on singing a song that they had started with him could be considered controlling.

ABA View Of Stimming Behaviours

With regards to Tim's stimming behaviours, Jackie said she would never go over to Tim while he was looking at a book and scripting, as that would reinforce this behaviour. Instead, by ignoring him when stimming, he would learn that it was not okay.

Really? The rules of the ABA seemed wrong and unnatural to me right from the beginning. But we'd started. I was aware of my limited knowledge and I was made to understand that I was in the way if I thought like this, thus limiting the progress Tim could make. I had to be 100% on board in order to see progress in Tim. It was difficult though, because I realised quite soon that I wasn't on board. Not at all.

The Peaceful Village and the Major Meltdown

Once, after a slow dinner at home, with me trying to persuade each reluctant mouthful, I took Tim to a duck pond in a beautiful little village nearby. The day had a sunny and relaxing feel about it. Unfortunately, I didn't have bread for the ducks and kicked myself because it meant we'd have to go into the shop opposite to get some – I knew this could set off a major trigger, but I also knew I had to take him somewhere and I thought it was worth the risk.

We parked the car and he held my hand and walked with me across the road to the shop to buy bread. Waiting in queues was usually a disaster – the quicker we were in and out the better, but this was out of my hands. While waiting he saw some birthday cards on a shelf by the counter. One had a picture of Noddy on it. He started to point and pull me towards it, as I immediately realised that he wanted me to buy it.

I couldn't buy him the Noddy card. I didn't want him to think I would buy him whatever he asked for – as surely that was heading in a dangerous direction regarding his expectations. I also didn't have money for it. I panicked a little inside hoping against hope that his desire for this card would blow over. And…it did! He walked out with me and the bread towards the duck pond quite happily. I couldn't believe it – but who was I to question it when things went well? We had a lovely time feeding the ducks and enjoying the sunshine and the peace. When we had finished, I took his little hand and we started to walk in the direction of the car. What a fantastic afternoon...

No. Not the car. The shop. We are going to the shop. To get the Noddy card… Not the car…

What? It had all been going so well. But, as I later gathered, Tim had somehow got it in his head that we would be returning to the shop after feeding the ducks to get the Noddy card. Maybe there had been a hint in my words that had made him think that.

For the first ten minutes of pulling and screaming, I was seriously embarrassed. For the next ten minutes, I had forgotten the other people and was just trying to calm him. For the last ten minutes, I was honestly just trying to keep him alive. He was so strong. If I couldn't hold on to him he would run straight into the road or the water. He was screaming and writhing on the ground beside himself with anger and he had a frightening amount of strength.

Where was Erik? He might be working nearby. At one point I managed to prise my mobile from my pocket. No charge. I resigned myself just to stay with Tim and keep him alive. A proverbial English gentleman walked by, busy trying not to look, on the other side of the road.

Half an hour into this drama, along came a mum with a pushchair and some little children. My world and hers seemed light years apart. She came straight up to me and asked if I was okay. What – not walking by on the other side of the road? No, I wasn't okay. I burst into tears of relief and exhaustion and asked if she could help me. She spoke to Tim and he stilled, stopped crying and looked at her. He even sat up and allowed her to talk to him. I asked her if she would please walk to our car with us, petrified of it all starting up again. She did and she didn't leave me until he was safely buckled into his car seat. I don't know her name but she felt like a guardian angel to me that day.

If Tim had wanted an incredible new toy or a particular food he was craving, I can imagine a tiny part of such a reaction. But for a greetings card? It was so obvious to me that this was nothing to do with the greetings card, but maybe something else – a desperate need for control, perhaps? Trains of thought he had to complete? Or was it that he had recognised Noddy as a friendly, familiar face in an alien environment and wanted the safety the character represented? How could I know?

Control and Manipulation?

The ABA sessions focused a lot on control – apparently, we needed to break Tim's need for control. This was the monster we needed to defeat. Their theory was that if we kept on long enough, he would eventually relinquish his need to control us and start to cooperate with what we wanted. I wanted the same outcome, desperately, because I wanted to be able to reach him. His control was definitely a major block, but I was shocked at their assumption that we been subconsciously allowing it all this time. Could we really get him to give up his need to control by using these ABA techniques?

Manipulation was another big thing that had to be 'nipped in the bud'. I was told he was being very manipulative with me and it had to stop.

Behaviour

In the past out of desperation, when Tim lashed out or wouldn't stop screaming, we had put him for a while in the thinking room to calm down. This, as I've mentioned, had been a source of controversy between Erik and me, however Jackie had decided we should not only continue this process but take it further. It would be used as a means to make him conform.

The approach she took was that if he didn't comply with a command, we would take him to the thinking room and leave him there until he stopped crying. Then we would bring him out, to put the command to him again. This cycle would be continued until he understood that it was better to cooperate.

But in the midst of all this, had anyone considered his feelings? Did they actually think what it would feel like from his point of view, or was the only important thing here his cooperation? As for my own feelings, I had to totally put them aside, trying hard to do what I was told was the right thing. My head was filled with all the instructions I'd been given by the experts, 'You can't use your natural mothering instincts any more'…'you now just have to manage him'…'you won't be able to teach him anything until he learns to conform…'

I felt as though I had been thrown into a world where everything was upside down, but where I believed I had to follow every instruction to the letter if my child were to get through this successfully.

One thing I found particularly heart-wrenching was that we were told to leave him until he stopped crying before opening the door. If I, as a child, was really upset and crying to gain comfort, I probably wouldn't stop crying very quickly without that comfort. Then when I finally saw the person I needed and let my relief out by crying, I would be shut up in the room on my own again until I stopped. Is that what they meant by 'breaking him down'. That sounded like torture to me. Surely doing this to a child *is* torture and specially to a child that can't *tell* you how he's feeling. Were we trying to break his spirit by doing this? Was that the idea?

I, along with Jackie and the other ABA therapists, desperately wanted to see him being accessible and compliant, so if this was the suggested way, I would have to breathe in and keep trying. I would try to hold in my own desperation if this was the only way to help Tim, as they'd promised that once he had overcome this need to control, he would be able to learn and develop – and if we didn't do it this way, he could be stuck in this state and lost to us forever. The thing is, it wasn't only breaking Tim down, it was breaking all of us down and we hadn't so far seen anything of the promised breakthroughs.

Communication

We were trying to teach him yes and no. We would hold out something and ask him, 'Would you like this?' We would model, 'Yes please' and give it to him. But it led to complications. We would say, 'Would you like a crisp?' and he would say, 'Yes please' and we would give it to him – then he would come to us and say, 'I would like yes please'. He hadn't really understood the process.

When I questioned his paediatrician at one point on whether it was a delay or a disorder, she said, 'He does have a disorder and part of it might never go away.' Her words – I didn't like to believe it – and she said, 'And he does have quite a bit of delay'.

Jackie could see there was quite a bit of disorder in his expressive and receptive language skills.

Erik felt he understood more than people thought. He could pick up on how to use the battery-operated buttons on a book really easily, but if you asked him, 'How are you?' He would look blankly with no understanding. We could not explain the emotions of happy or sad in a way he could understand, although we knew he felt these things deeply. He was starting to be aware of how he felt when he hurt himself, asking for attention in the only way he knew how – 'I want ouch.'

I think meaning he wanted us to notice and pay attention to his pain – but sad, happy, no response – nothing. Though if he accidentally kicked me when we were playing he would say, 'Poor Mummy,' and come and look after me a little.

Jackie asked, 'Do you think he does that because that's what he's learnt you do?'

I said, 'Well, he learns everything in that way, then he takes it on as his own.'

'So empathy towards other people is also delayed?'

'Well, yes.'

Tim's scripting was one of the things that concerned me the most. He would go up to people and start scripting from various TV shows. While this made no sense to the person and made him look odd to others, he was obviously trying to communicate and under the impression they could understand his outpouring of odd sounds. Watching his earnestness, I was struck by how hard he was trying to make himself understood. At the same time, I was aware of the sideways glances and the 'What's wrong with your child?' looks when he launched into one of these one-sided conversations. As a mother that hurts because you want to help your child to be accepted. Even more importantly, he was trying to reach out verbally, but was unable to connect with other people because of his inability to use words correctly.

Because of this I felt it was imperative he learn to talk– but how *do* you talk? Where do you talk from? If your thoughts are muddled your speech will be muddled – if you don't grasp words or pick up on the meanings of words how can you reiterate them in a meaningful way to someone else? Furthermore, I believed there was a time limit to this.

But even when he had a few words he couldn't learn them in any context, other than to ask for a few specific things that he wanted – for instance, 'I want hand-walk,' meant, 'I want you to take my hand and come with me.'

'I want what can I see?' This meant, 'I want to go and sit on the high windowsill and look out at the world.'

'I want ouch,' meant, 'I've hurt myself and I want you to notice.'

'I want yes please'. Well, this probably meant he wanted the last thing he had when we modelled to him, 'yes please'.

He had no inbuilt understanding of his own ability to communicate or make sense to a level that others outside his inner circle could relate to. I felt an urgency to help him, afraid of where all this could lead if we didn't seriously help him. He was so precious, but something within him just wasn't functioning.

Jackie said we all learn through imitation but Tim *didn't* seem to learn through imitation or repetition, while he may have learnt a few specific things like colours but these were very surface skills. They didn't seem very relevant to the state he was continuously in.

'Never Give an Inch or He Will Take a Mile'

As mentioned earlier, a major element of the ABA was that Tim always had to do what we asked him to do – purely because we had asked him – every single time with no exception. On one occasion, our debate involved whether Tim should always eat at the table. In our normal life, he often liked to climb on top of the settee and find his way to the windowsill and sit high up, looking out of the window to eat his biscuits. I had never really thought much of this – biscuits were only a snack, after all and lots of people have special places where they like to sit.

On one occasion with Julie, she asked Tim to sit at the table with his snack which he did. The next day, she asked him to sit at the table but he climbed up to the windowsill. Julie asked him again to come to the table and because of our strict ABA training, she knew she had to follow through otherwise he would never take an instruction seriously. So, she insisted and a great upset ensued until she felt she had to walk out of the room and leave him screaming on his own. When she returned, he had managed to calm down a little and she tried to reconnect with him by taking him out on the trampoline.

The main issue was the feeling that if we let him do something once, he would think he could always do it, due to his rigid way of thinking, so we had to be really strict about what we let him do in the first place to stop him getting ideas and learning wrong habits.

I also had a growing concern that he would get himself stuck in unhelpful behaviour patterns, but I couldn't see how enforced conformity could release him from these things.

He Must Know his Letters and Numbers

We spent hours with Tim, trying to further drill numbers and letters into him, getting him to match pictures and complete jigsaw puzzles, etc. It was so hard as we were constantly asking him to do things he had little interest in doing. Still, we persevered. We were told we hadn't 'broken him down' yet and that was apparently when he would be able to start learning.

I realise in hindsight that focusing on the puzzles and numbers was putting the cart before the horse. We hardly ever managed to get him still and focused but if someone managed to get him to accurately place a puzzle piece or say the numbers 1 – 5, even if he had said them a million times before, it would be celebrated like he'd just run a marathon. However, I felt all this celebrating was too premature. If he had come to us *willingly* it would have been worth all the celebration in the world – but the only things he really did willingly were his stimming behaviours. That was where he wanted to be – should we have left him there? I knew the idea was that if he succeeded in small things and was rewarded, he would then start to conform in bigger things, but that just didn't seem to be happening.

Breaking Tasks Down for Rewards

I found the idea of breaking tasks into small steps made sense. For anyone who struggles to learn, little tasks are easier than big ones. The idea of rewarding a child with a tickle or a game when he has achieved something was fair enough. However, it was hard to find rewards for Tim that kept him motivated. It was an ongoing struggle. Food was out, while tickles and little wind-up toys soon lost their excitement for him. What had happened on many occasions was that when he did a task he would be given his favourite battery-operated book for two minutes. The thing was, that he immediately started enjoying playing with it and resisted when it had to be taken away when his time was up. He did not understand the concept of a limited reward at all and it caused him so much distress that I couldn't see its value.

Despite small moments of sitting still and cooperating with games, Tim found little enjoyment in any of the sessions and the actual drills felt as achievable as complex algebra equations, given we were also trying to keep the attention of a very disinterested child. When we were asked to get a clicker and press it every time he looked at us, Erik totally switched off. I mentioned before that I am a teacher and that Erik worked as a children's entertainer. So we were both very used to gaining and keeping children's attention in many ways and over long periods of time.

However, with our own child in this situation, it took *all* of our effort and then some just to gain fleeting moments of attention – and very little of it was willing attention. I always felt he was coerced into it. But if after many long minutes of hard work, we managed to gain his attention and he actually looked at us for a second, we then had to remember to pick up and click a clicker – by which time we could have lost his attention. What was this? In my work I regularly spent time gaining the attention of large groups of children and knew instinctively that that was the moment to immediately engage them, not to waste the prize by turning my attention elsewhere.

But I couldn't let it go – if this was the thing we had to do, we would just have to keep on trying.

Regularly from 4 am, before I had to go to work, I would spend hours carefully preparing specific work and resources for the drills and tasks he would be doing that afternoon. I was determined to keep up with the detail in order to see progress. Surely the more we did, the more progress he would make? Then when coming back from work, I would sometimes get notes from Julie saying she hadn't managed to do any of these tasks because of a meltdown and I would go back into despair mode. How was he going to get better if we didn't do this stuff with him every day? We had to get past these meltdowns. But we made no progress with alleviating their frequency.

Is This Going too Far?

One of the little games we were playing with Tim at this stage was a very simple one – rolling a dice and if it landed on a three for instance, we all had to do an action three times – like clapping our hands or tapping our head etc. None of these games were ever initiated by Tim, but he didn't always resist, at the start at least. It was very directed by what *we* thought he should learn, which is what we believed was important at the time. One evening Erik and I called Tim over to play the game. He rolled the dice and it came out on a five. He clapped five times, so did I, so did Erik. Next, he rolled a two. He refused to choose an action to do twice. Not a federal sin. But, with all that we were learning and being encouraged to do, if he did not cooperate, the plan had been made to put him in the thinking room until he *did* cooperate. We were told if we did not do this *every* time, he would *never* learn to cooperate. Erik took him to the thinking room. When he had cried and quietened down, he came back and we asked him to choose an action. He wouldn't. He was taken back to the thinking room. After another whole crying session, he came out and finally tapped his knees twice. We celebrated.

I wondered what we were really teaching him. Were we *crazy*? Was this really the way to help a child engage in a *game*? I think we were so lacking in knowledge and answers that we were desperately trying to do what we were being told – but we were totally not feeling right about it.

The Meltdown to End all Meltdowns

Then came a crisis point. It was three months into the programme and Jackie was here for a three-hour training workshop.

My lounge was full of people – Erik, myself, Katherine, Julie, Beth and Jackie – and the room was buzzing with conversation and expectation. The idea was for the therapists to play with Tim and receive feedback. I immediately sensed that this was stressing Tim. He was moving constantly, agitated, anxious, and nothing in him seemed settled. I can't remember exactly what happened but he must have been close to Jackie when something triggered him and he lashed out. He happened to hit her with his flailing arms. I don't for a minute think he did it on purpose. He then immediately ran to me for comfort.

'Stop.' Jackie barred his way. 'Sally don't let him come to you.' She was adamant. 'That was wrong. He needs to apologise. Don't let him come to you – that's control.'

I stepped back, as always, trying to do the right thing and not hinder any lessons that were being taught.

'Sally, why don't you go out the back door, so you are out of sight? That'll help.'

I left in a whirl of people almost shooing me out though the door. I walked round the garden and went into the kitchen. Tim had run to the other door, but they had shut it so he couldn't get to me. Everyone was chatting and waiting for Jackie's instructions as to what to do next. She told them to 'just wait and see' how long it would take Tim to apologise. On Jackie's instruction they were all ignoring him.

In my opinion he had no idea why I had left or what anyone wanted from him. He was still overwhelmed from all these people invading his home and all the expectation surrounding him. From my point of view, he had needed me for comfort – now I had been forced away from him because of a perceived wrong-doing. Someone was in the kitchen with me, talking it all through. To this day, I can't remember who it was – it's another of those experiences where you are so focused on the distress of your child that all peripheral things fade away. He was crying for me, calling me, begging…he was clawing at the door, for goodness sake. Honest to God, at one point they actually started talking and even laughing amongst themselves as Tim broke his heart, calling for me.

'Hold on,' said the person in the kitchen with me. 'It's all for the best. His behaviour will probably improve loads after this. It's a lesson he's got to learn – there could be a big breakthrough after this'.

'But he doesn't even know what he's got to *do.*' Ten minutes. Twenty minutes… half an hour… a whole hour… honest to God, *an hour and a half…*

Hang on. I am choosing *for* this. I can take control back. *I don't have to do this anymore.*

Enough. I opened the door. I let him come to me. I didn't care anymore. He came to me, sobbing, his little body hot from sweat and hiccupping as his sobbing made it difficult for him to breathe. If my small child could only learn through such suffering, then I would rather he didn't learn at all. This emotional torture was *wrong.*

Enough

That's when I broke it off with ABA.

I didn't have another plan. I just knew I couldn't do that one anymore. I would just love him and spend time with him. That would be enough. And I would wait for another answer to come along.

I know ABA has worked for some families and I have read *Let Me Hear Your Voice, A Life To Rescue* and *Facing Autism,* all of which advocate ABA as the saving grace for their children. However, the ABA process clearly was not a good fit for the way Tim ticked, his emerging personality or all his sensory confusion. It didn't sit right with Tim and it subsequently didn't sit right with me.

Is Behaviour Modification the Only Way?

Because his autism was so deeply engrained inside him, I couldn't see how it could be reached by behaviour modification. If your sensory system and your brain are very muddled, it may cause distress or a level of dysfunction which *leads* to difficult behaviour, but surely dealing with behaviour alone does not reach the real and actual *core* of your child's processing. And if you can't reach the *core,* how can you effect helpful changes for your child? I had the feeling we could continue endlessly dealing with behaviour but we weren't getting *anywhere* in helping him with his social difficulties or his real communication issue – which seemed to be a serious neurological mis-wiring within his brain and his processing.

His pull back to his stimming behaviours and need for control was like a strong magnetic force. I wondered how Tim could be expected to learn if he were constantly so distressed and coerced when all he wanted was to be doing what made sense to him.

Another question I asked myself: Because a child has autism, do they naturally lose their right to autonomy? Is it true that the *only* way to teach someone with autism is to take away their choices and force them into the compliance that adults want to see? Of course I wanted Tim to relate easily and for it all to look okay from the outside, but I equally wanted him to feel right on the inside, too. Something about forcing a child, causing such distress never really sat right with me – the concept of 'first do no harm' came to mind and my gut feeling told me that, for Tim, this *was* causing harm. For me it felt as though my beloved child was living behind a thick plate of glass, spinning round and round and down and down and I couldn't break the glass to reach in and save him.

Maybe there weren't any answers after all. Some people said I should accept his autism. Did they mean we should stop trying to help him? Maybe he couldn't prevent the way he felt or behaved. Maybe it wasn't in his control – or ours.

I thought of Tim's autism as being a big ball of ice that needs to melt. How to melt it? If you can find a way to melt it, you will do that all day every day because at least you are able to *do* something to bring your child closer to you. But ABA hadn't taken us there.

Chapter Five – Starting school – grasping at straws

So, we were moving on from the ABA – never to return. What was there left to help Tim? We would have to rely on the school system. When Tim had started ABA, he had also started school on a Monday, Wednesday and Friday morning every week.

Looking back, I feel embarrassed that I thought school would have the resources to ease Tim's difficulties. ABA had begun just before Tim started school in September 2006. I had been in for the Induction Day and it hadn't gone well – Tim had had a meltdown and I had cried in the Headteacher's office. Tim was not wired to cope in a school environment. All of his natural ways of functioning seemed to be in conflict with what was expected of him.

I was aware that school was probably not the best environment for Tim. I knew he couldn't interact with a single child close to him, let alone lots of children and schools are full of unpredictability and distraction. I understood this would be very hard for him to deal with, let alone to learn in, but as we had also recently started the ABA, I was hoping that the promised improvement in his behaviours would allow him to find school easier to deal with over a period of time. I just deeply wanted him to feel normal and therefore wanted him to go to school like everybody else. However, my diaries around that time are full of 'notes to self' about the fact that I was aware this wasn't necessarily the right move.

I wanted him to have a sense of community and friends more than anything, and this is where potential friends were, right? No matter that he hadn't been able to talk to another child, let alone make friends in all of his four years. I couldn't stop trying, could I? My desire told me that maybe if I just put him in an environment with lots of typically functioning children it would rub off on him. Something in me had to keep believing such things.

I visualised Tim being popular, friends gathering around him, inviting him to their parties… but when we got to the school it was obvious the other children seemed to have something he didn't. What was it? Initiative? Interest? Enjoyment? Ease? Confidence? A sense of self? A brain that worked in a straightforward way? A huge desire for friendships with each other? How could he join in? He didn't have the sense of self that the other children had. They were all talking to each other and playing and laughing. Suddenly, throwing him in the mix with typically functioning children after the summer holidays emphasised his difficulties.

He attended school on a Monday, Wednesday and Friday mornings only, for the first term with Tina and then with another one-to-one for the rest of the year. He didn't learn much, but he managed to stay in the classroom and mix a little with the other children. Was it worth it? I don't know. I just wanted to know if he would manage to cope with the routines of the day. What I didn't realise was that time was marching on and none of his issues regarding interaction and speech were being worked on.

For the first seven weeks we took him there, they always told us he was fine – that he'd done well. That seemed a bit odd, as we were expecting something to go wrong – maybe school had the magic ingredient after all?

It was only at a meeting seven weeks into the term that they told us that on some days he screamed for two hours. Why the hell hadn't they told us earlier? It was our first encounter with the weird sense of pride some schools seem to have, when they want to be seen as succeeding and therefore chose not to tell us about Tim's significant problems in settling in. But this wasn't about their pride or their success, or otherwise – this should have been all about Tim and how he was managing and feeling.

My initial concerns were that he must be overwhelmed or didn't know what to do – but the school just said he screamed, they sorted it and it was over. Come on!

A Friend – Water in the Desert

One day though, something actually good happened. Erik picked Tim up from school and when he came back he said, 'Tim has a girlfriend'. Apparently one little girl in Tim's class had taken a shine to him and they did lots of things together – oh, wow! A friend! Her name was Kylie and she was very petite with long dark hair. I introduced myself to her mum and Kylie became a regular at our house, coming round for many playdates.

Kylie was like water in a desert for me. She signified the possibility of friendship and a willingness to break down invisible barriers and make the impossible possible. Tim was obviously likeable and now it was only about him breaking down *his* barriers to allow children to be friends with him. I could see that it was mostly his inability to connect to the others that kept him at bay – usually if a child approached him, he zoned out or ran away.

But he liked Kylie – he loved her in fact – and she willingly played all the games he wanted to, actively enjoying each other's company. I felt it was good to keep their playdates short and positive and to always say goodbye on a happy note. They were very active playdates too – chasing games, bouncing on the trampoline, playing with sand – all the things Tim could manage and liked to do. I used to worry that Tim would want to disappear into his stimming behaviours when she was there, but if I kept the play sessions short and active, he didn't need to. I always over-compensated, talking to her when Tim couldn't and trying to make sure she felt comfortable. Afterwards Tim would need time on his own to process his feelings and to do that he would go into his stimming world, looking at books and processing his thoughts. It was basically his way of unwinding.

Television

Tim was totally addicted to the TV at this point – he had been since he was tiny, and his addiction was becoming stronger and stronger. He would avidly watch a section of a movie, then rewind back to the section he adored and watch it repeatedly – jumping up and down and getting all excited. Sometimes it was just a clip of a few seconds that would be watched over and over. Sometimes he would just watch the end credits again and again. If we let him watch for too long, thinking that it was the perfect time to get a particular job done, for instance, he would become drenched in sweat, as his muscles would clench in excitement, taking him to 'a place of no return'. If we left him too long and he reached this state, it was very hard to bring him back from it. To turn the telly off, even with a warning and a countdown would cause a meltdown but we had no choice, then just sit it out with him.

Having the telly on was also the only way we could get food into him and the only way he could cope with other people in the house. He seemed to need the security blanket of the familiar sights and sounds when he had to do things he couldn't cope with or while so many new things were going on around him.

Sensory Issues – What's Going On?

Tim seemed to have a really distorted sensory system. He had never been able to cope with us washing his hair or brushing his teeth. With his hair, Erik and I had to prepare him, think of a major treat for him for afterwards and we would then have to hold him down tight and just do it. Poor Tim would scream and struggle and desperately try to get away and inwardly I would cringe, desperately wanting this not to be happening. The same with brushing his teeth. It became a question of just having to hold him down and firmly hold his mouth open. It was horrendous for all of us. The other option was just never to wash his hair, brush his teeth, cut his nails or wash his face. It was tempting. I wish we had known about The Son-Rise Program® techniques at this point.

Another connection I hadn't yet made was that his sensory processing issues could be a major cause of his inability to cooperate. Who can answer a complex question if they are seriously distracted or in pain?

His issues with eating were also sensory – he couldn't cope with particular tastes or textures and would retch if something was in his mouth that he wasn't comfortable with. His reaction had been like this since he was eighteen months and he was still just as sensitive.

Sounds, too, would hurt his ears and he would scream or run away at loud noises. We had no idea how he heard things, but were starting to wonder if he was receiving noises in a distorted way and if that was affecting his speech and the way he processed information. Maybe if sounds were entering his auditory canal in a distorted way, that could cause his massive reaction when there were no apparent triggers. Maybe the pitch level of sounds were different for him, too.

New sensory issues would surface at very unexpected times too. One day a friend came round with her four-year-old son. Tim and James were only a week apart in age and his Mum and I had spent a lot of time together in their early years. It was very hot and we had opened the patio doors and were sitting in the garden. It was so hot that I persuaded Tim to come inside so I could put a short-sleeved T-shirt on him and some shorts. James came with us. I was still feeling vulnerable about Tim's condition at this point and when he made a fuss at the short sleeved T-shirt in front of James (who'd reached all his milestones with ease), I tried really hard to persuade him. I just wanted something to be easy for once. But no. He resisted to such an extent that I gave in, put his long-sleeved T-shirt back on him and realised he needed some serious and quick calming down time. The only thing that would work in such an instance was the telly. So I took him into the cool bedroom and put the telly on and gave him a bit of time on his own. That was our major way of calming him at that point. It seemed to be the only thing that worked. Tim could not cope with feeling the air on his skin and felt a desperate need to be covered up all the time.

James had gone back to his Mum and when I came into the lounge, I heard him out in the garden talking to her confidentially about it all. 'He was making such a fuss, Mum' he was saying in smooth, effortless sentences, 'He didn't even want to put his shirt on. He was going, 'Nooo, nooo!'

'Well, he doesn't understand these things and he can't talk properly – not like *you* can,' my friend replied and in my paranoia I suddenly felt a surge of anger.

They could talk all cosily about what was wrong with my child could they? From their nice safe place in the typical world? I burst into the garden and honestly shouted at a four year-old, 'Oh, so he didn't want to put his T-shirt on did he James? Are *you* perfect?'

Sometimes I had to rein in my emotions a lot. And yes, I was ashamed of myself!

Despair

At this point, I lived with permanently high stress levels, lots of arguments about how to deal with Tim (with Erik and I still often falling passionately on different sides), a deep grief which resulted in sadness spilling out at odd times, particularly when I saw little children spontaneously talking to their parents or laughing with friends. I was often consumed by jealousy and also permanently exhausted, on full alert for danger, triggers and meltdowns and Tim's continuous complex behaviours and high anxiety. Every minute of every day consumed me in this way. I could barely recognise even the memory of the person I had been before all this started.

In the book *The Thinking Mom's Revolution* the only Dad spoke of his intense frustration and I quote: 'Just tell me! Show me! What do I have to do? Even if I can't implement it, at very least I want to know what the solution is. At least then I would have a definitive plan. Do I have to move this ten-storey building by hand? Is that the answer? Great!... …At least I know what to do now and there's an end and a way to get there.' (Bytes from the Count, 2013, p.256)

I cannot say this better myself. I would move a ten-storey building. I would do *anything* – I just need to know what and I will do it.

There were fewer and fewer moments of happiness. I didn't want all these difficulties and these traumas – to be living in a parallel universe to my friends, watching Tim deal every day with such difficulties.

Someone at one point chose to say to me, 'Would you rather give Tim to someone else to look after?' My immediate response was 'No! He's mine! I want him, I love him… I just don't know what's the right thing to *do*'.

We were not free to go out to a friend's house or a park. Tim would get fixated and things *had* to go his way. Should I let things go his way? If I did, I felt I was fuelling his rigidity but if I challenged him, his behaviour became unmanageable, he would have a massive meltdown and we would both end up highly distressed and exhausted. I was constantly questioning how I should deal with him – that, too, was exhausting…

No doctor could give me an answer and no education system could help me. Everyone had different opinions and no one seemed to know what to do or take any responsibility to help me. Yet I knew I needed to find out what to do. He couldn't stay in this state.

To see someone you love being so compromised is phenomenally painful. It brought out all the seriously protective mothering instinct in me. I wanted to protect him so much, but I also felt heartbreak *for* him, that he couldn't explain himself, share his feelings, make his needs understood.

He couldn't easily make the few close people who loved him understand him, even though we really tried, so how could he make a new, large group of people in a school understand him? He wasn't aware that he was so lost but to me he seemed cast adrift, unable to be anchored enough to look around and make sense of his surroundings.

I yearned for someone to break that wall down, take his hand and play with him.

How to Talk to Tim

We had found that in order to connect with Tim, we needed to be at his level, to specifically gain his attention one-to-one, until he focused on us, and then speak just one or two words very clearly. If we talked before preparing him in this way, he wouldn't even know we were speaking to him. Our voices were being transmitted but not received.

Unless someone got to his level and spoke slowly with very few words, he could not be reached. How can you ask another child to do that? How can you ask an adult to that, unless you pay them?

He didn't seem to be desperately unhappy when left to his own devices, but in fact he was forced to be alone because of his inability to communicate in a way that others could easily understand. The fact that I believed he wanted to be understood but couldn't, caused me to agonise. How did it *feel* for him? What was *he* going through? How did he feel inside himself in amidst all this confusion?

Naoki Higashida explained in *The Reason I Jump* that his behaviour made people think he wanted to be on his own but in reality he didn't. How did I know Tim didn't feel like that?

I wished with all my heart that I could love him out of this state.

Please Engage with Him

He was so often surrounded by people who didn't make any special effort to understand him. And when no one was engaging with him in this particular way, he would just stand around, disengaged, before heading back into his stimming behaviours. I so often wanted to be a fly on the wall just to check that people were engaging with him when I wasn't there. I had no way of knowing how people treated him when my back was turned and I was entrusting him into the hands of others, as he couldn't actually talk and tell me what had happened in the day and how he was feeling. I was afraid that when I wasn't there that he might be ignored – or worse, ridiculed. Unless he was engaged with someone, he could not be developing or learning. If he were not engaged, time would just pass and nothing would be happening to help him progress.

When I saw other children chatting to their mums and asking them if their friends could come round to play, I realised yet again how far removed we were from the normalities of childhood. My heart hurt just that little bit more. I didn't know how best to relate to the other mums – should I talk about the differences or just pretend everything was normal? Most of the mums were very kind though and were willing to bring their child round for playdates with Tim if I specifically asked.

I wanted Tim to know the amazingness his life could hold if he let me and other people in. I wanted him to look at me naturally and love me and respond to me in the way that in my dreams he could do. I wanted to play silly games with him and for him to enjoy making up games with friends and hanging out together – to *feel* and *access* what I knew could be good things in life.

Being a twin, I could always closely relate to my brother, and my sister was just two years older. I was surrounded by playmates in my early years, but Tim was isolated from his peers because he kept pushing people away and zoning out. It was hard for anyone to reach him. I couldn't expect people going about their everyday lives to keep getting down to his level and speaking in the clear, defined way that he needed, but without this, he was unlikely to even begin to connect or progress.

People around us were starting to experience the relief of their child going to friends' houses and being looked after by others, as they were going to parties and even sleepovers, as Tim's peers were now aged between four and five. We'd heard that the burden of care starts to lighten up as they become more independent and can spend time in other places. Our lives weren't heading in this way. Our responsibility was becoming heavier every day and unless Tim could start to communicate and develop self-care or independence skills, no one other than a paid worker would ever be able to look after him.

On the day that I was working and couldn't pick Tim up from school, my Mum drove one and a half hours to the school to pick him up and take him back to our house to look after him. We couldn't have just anyone pick him up – and we would have had to train someone in finite detail and pay them if no one in the family could do it. There was no asking another mum to take him for a while and to reciprocate by having their child on another day.

No one cut me any slack, either. At one school where I was on contract one day a week, the Headteacher suddenly announced she wanted me to run an orchestra after school each week for no extra money which meant I would have to stay an hour later – therefore I wouldn't be able to pick Tim up. I opened my mouth to start to explain the complexities of childcare and she came back with 'everyone's in the same boat'. What? No actually, we *aren't* all in the same boat. I wish we *were*.

Other People's Reactions – the Judgemental 'Look'

I had to work hard on blocking out people's reactions. A friend of mine, Dee, once came to the local supermarket with me for moral support, as she had been visiting me and I asked her to help me. We managed to get Tim round the shop with lots of distraction techniques and little games etc but when we got to the till, Tim overloaded and started screaming and writhing around in my arms. He'd had enough. I focused on looking after him and while I was doing this one lady in the queue said to Dee, 'Does that child *always* get his own way?'

I'm glad she only told me this after our visit else I think I would have seriously not been responsible for my actions.

If I went to a supermarket and something triggered him (which was a continuous possibility) nothing I could do would stop him going through the overwhelming meltdown that would inevitably follow. To try to placate him would only make things worse. I would make a conscious choice to block out the people looking at me, focus on taking care of Tim and getting out of there as quickly as possible, back to a safe place, where he could make as much noise as he liked and gradually come out the other side. But I felt disempowered, horrible and exhausted.

My Meltdown

One day this all got too much for me. I had Tim throughout the week, taking him to school and to various people while I had to work. I even had Tim every Sunday morning as Erik was the worship leader in our church and he left at nine and didn't come back til one. I had to get Tim ready and bring him to church – as always, against his will. One week, Erik's parents were staying and we were all at church. Tim was being particularly needy and was very much in a state of just wanting to escape. I was using every ounce of my energy to keep up with him – again, outside of the main hall and in a parallel universe to the general hubbub. When I walked in at one point, in pursuit of him, everyone was still and peaceful and totally involved in worship. I had this strange sensation that even though all these people were so physically close to me, if I screamed out right there and then for help, they wouldn't hear me. I think I was losing it a bit. After the service I ended up virtually screaming at Erik that I couldn't do this anymore. His parents had to watch me melt down and cry in total desperation – but I was past caring who saw – I was pretty much burnt out!

In consequence, Erik stopped worship leading in order to support us more – but it was yet one more thing that Erik gave up that he loved. We were both losing elements of our identities in order to keep up the level of care that was required at that time to look after Tim. Sometimes I felt that if I had started crying I never would have stopped, therefore it was better not to start. Only a lot later did I realise Erik felt exactly the same.

Erik also found that, where he had previously been a social person, seeking out conversations and connections with people, whenever he had time to himself, he now always chose to be by himself – just trying to recharge his own batteries and prepare for the next round of battles.

I knew I would never stop wanting Tim to be okay and I would often end up being totally obsessed to the point that Erik and I felt we hardly had anything of our special bond any more. No time together, no date nights, just falling asleep exhausted and knowing that the hard work would start all over again as soon as we were conscious.

One day, Erik insinuated that I was not prioritising our relationship. I became incredulous – I was already giving and giving all day and not having *any* time to myself, and he wanted me to give yet *more*? How could I let go of my mission to help Tim? I couldn't. Even if I had to for the sake of my marriage I still couldn't, however much I missed my time with Erik. I can see why couples divorce when in our situation. I'm glad I realised there was a half-way house and a way to connect where we could enjoy each other and work together on a mission to help Tim. We both desperately missed the people we had been when we had first got together. He had loved how much I loved people and my spontaneous nature. I had loved his creativity and sensitivity and sense of fun. All these qualities of ours seemed to have been blown apart, replaced by stress, routines, pressure and a continued state of uncertainty. We sometimes wondered if our original selves were still there.

Severe Underlying Language Disorder

When Tim was about four and a half years old we found a new speech therapist, Anna. We knew we wanted to learn more about how to help him with his speech and there was no one-to-one speech therapy available for him anymore. What he had through school was an assessment. Instructions were then given to teaching assistants and we had no idea whether they would be carried out or not. I wanted to know more about what I could do to help him. Some comments from Anna's speech therapy report are as follows:

> Tim gave some eye contact when requesting certain toys or snacks. He found it hard to listen to verbal instructions in the Picture Test Assessment and his attention to the task became gradually impaired. Tim's attention and listening skills in a classroom are an area of concern especially when considering his language difficulties. Tim can follow verbal instructions that are part of his daily routine. However, when language is taken out of context Tim has severe difficulties.
>
> Tim's receptive language scores indicate severe difficulties in verbal comprehension for a child of his age. Tim can follow one-word level instructions but needs support with two-word level instructions. Tim's verbal comprehension is an area of concern and will severely affect his ability to access the school curriculum.

This was the problem. We wanted him in school but it wasn't only his behaviour difficulties and inability to connect that were standing in his way. It was his language – his understanding of what was said to him. His ability to first understand and then carry out instructions was so limited and took so much effort for him that it was impossible for him to understand and take on board general instructions given by a teacher at the front of a class. These were things that other children could do without thinking. Maybe that was why he would wander around the classroom and mutter to himself. He couldn't make sense of what was going on around him.

Anna also said in the report that, 'Tim is able to use long sentences with clearly articulated speech. However these sentences are either direct repetitions of an adult's language (echolalia) or he has previously learnt them by rote (delayed echolalia).'

It almost felt like Tim didn't have his own mind so he used thoughts and words from someone else. I really longed to hear his *own* thoughts.

My Overload

I questioned it a lot – are development issues health-related or education-related? Because no one was helping me! Once a doctor put a whole series of appointments on hold to talk to me for half an hour because she was concerned for my wellbeing and stress levels – which was really kind. But she had nothing to help Tim himself, which in my opinion, would have immediately reduced my stress levels.

Tim's autism difficulties were eating me away on the inside all the time. On top of this, I was teaching large classes all day, earning our money by working at two different schools, running music clubs in others and interacting with fully-functioning children most days and having to field regular demands from headteachers, further eating into my time and expertise. Argh!

I became like Tim. I was full up to the brim with too much to cope with and I began to have my own set of triggers that would tip me over the edge. Previously, as I mentioned before, I had played the piano when I felt wound up like this – get my full emotions out with dramatic renditions of Sinding's 'Rustle of Spring' or a Scott Joplin rag. I had played piano for years in cafes, restaurants and hotels in order to create a relaxing atmosphere for other people. Now I couldn't even play one note to comfort myself, because it disturbed Tim so much.

What was happening?

Siobhan – Angels do Exist!

As school was only three mornings a week, we needed more help. I phoned the Early Years tutor at our local university to ask if there might be a student who would like to work with Tim. She sent an email around to her students and that was when we met Siobhan, who was a total Godsend. She really wanted to work with Tim and when she met us for the first time, she immediately formed a great bond with him. There was something special about her. She didn't find anything about him unusual. She immediately just loved him for being him.

To start with, she told me that when she was on her own with him, she and him were separate units. He would do his thing and she would sometimes ask him to do something for her – which he would do – then he would go back to his thing. But over a period of time, he began to actually look into her eyes and ask her for things, such as to go on the trampoline and she would delightedly say, 'Yes, let's go!'. She told me that gradually the separateness turned into togetherness. It was a togetherness that lasted about two years. Erik and I came to trust Siobhan to such an extent that we could actually go away on odd occasions when necessary, as Tim and Siobhan made a great team.

Siobhan explained to me that for a long while she couldn't do anything in the background like start to sing a song as he would shut her down with a 'no thank you' but after a while of playing and being with him he would eventually actually join in with her. They could be silly together! There was a lot of giggling. Tim's anxiety reduced as his trust in her grew and I could see this was a great relationship.

Siobhan also worked with Tim on his speech and language exercises. She sometimes sat in on a session to learn what he was doing and then spent lots of time playing games with him and working on his speech, amidst lots of silliness and games. She made her own little box of treats and games to bring with her when she came.

Once, she took him into town on the bus and remembers very clearly how, when they were waiting for the bus home, Tim just couldn't understand why a bus had actually stopped in front of them, but they weren't getting on it. As he was starting to get really distressed, she knelt down with him and immediately began drawing numbers out on the pavement to distract him and also to big up the number they were waiting for. She knew that another bus might come which might still not be theirs and she needed to do something to distract him and help him understand. So she involved him in the number they were waiting for and made a big point of wondering aloud whether the next bus was the right number. It helped distract him and prevented a potential meltdown.

This is what I mean by trusting her. She knew what could happen, what to do and how to look after him. Erik and I wished the whole world was made of Siobhan's – it would make life so much happier and easier all round!

Year One at School: Tim aged five

By law, Tim had to be in school full time at the age of five. He had been allowed to stay just three mornings in his Reception year because he only turned five at the end of it. His needs and the law had not been in conflict up to this point. Now we had to be completely out, or completely in. We chose in because we had no conceivable idea of what out might look like.

When Tim entered Year 1 at St Martin's Infant School, he had a new and very formidable teacher. I could see that she was very fond of order and she liked her classes 'just so'. Tim, at this point, could not sit still during lessons and would wander around the tables of children, mumbling and singing. That wouldn't bode well. It broke my heart. He wasn't able to focus on any task and he couldn't easily sit still. A few years ago, as I had previously mentioned, I had been the teacher in the class with 29 fully functioning children and one who was constantly trying to climb under the desks and out of the window. From a teacher's point of view it can be very disruptive, but when you are the parent and it's your child, it's completely different. I so wanted to hear that everything had gone well when I picked him up at the end of the day… and for a while, that's what I was told. It was only, again, when we actually had a meeting that I discovered the extent of the difficulties he was really having.

He would become frustrated towards the end of the day and start kicking the bookshelf. I found out that to prevent this, his teacher took his shoes off. Who was looking at *why* he might be feeling frustrated? Who was connecting to him? At one point, his teacher told me that she was starting to do a lot better with him now. I instantly became excited and leaned forward eagerly in my seat in expectation, but she continued with, 'because I am learning to tune him *out* and the children are learning to *ignore* him'. Ouch – that was a slap in the face. He needed tuning *in* surely, not tuning *out*. How could he ever engage and learn and also, where was her care and compassion? She then told me that she had worked with five children with autism and had been able to reach all of them – but she could not reach Tim. Great.

The Social Communications Team

At one of our many meetings with School and County we met the Social Communications team. Their job was to liaise with the School about Tim's needs and put things in place to help. One lady gave me a book to help me called *I Am Special* all about explaining to a child with autism how different they are. It talked about how important it is for your child to have their condition explained to them. The important facts mentioned were that the child needs to know there is no cure so they don't get their hopes up for a life of work or marriage (as that is extremely unlikely) – that autism is a brain disorder – for which there is no medication and no operation – but things such as schedules, special schools and psychologists can help. Oh my goodness. Then it explained that you can't explain this to your child until they have knowledge of their body (internally and externally), a basic knowledge of the operation of the brain and an understanding of the concepts of 'illness', disorder' and 'disability'.

Seriously? So I have to get my child to a level where he can begin to understand such concepts – only to explain to him that he has a brain disorder for which there is no cure. But it's okay, because he can spend the rest of his life finding help in special places. Please God – then to top it all it says that parents shouldn't be the people to tell their child this as they are parents and not therapists and there would be in danger of role confusion. What?

For a start, Tim didn't yet understand the concepts of 'what's your favourite?' or 'how are you?' let alone the concept of how the brain works and I can't imagine it would be a nice thing for him to emerge into an awareness of himself only to be told that he has an incurable brain disorder. This is what the people *helping* me were telling me. I just wanted to run away from this world and be in a loving relationship with my child. At such times, I just wanted everyone to leave us alone.

It seemed that no one wanted to hear my child's voice or respond to his emerging ways of communicating.

Who is Helping my Child at School?

So who was working with him? Mrs Jones, a really kind dinner lady was assigned to be his one-to-one at school. I was comforted by the fact that she was warm and kind-hearted, but did she know anything about autism and the way he could learn?

The hopelessness that nothing was being done for him at school, was eating me up. Time was moving on and I had been told many times that if we hadn't given him the right input by a certain age, that his brain could set this way and he may never be able to develop further or learn to easily communicate. Was this true? My sense of urgency was growing. What could I do?

Tim's Statement and all my Questions

I mentioned that Tim had been given a Statement of Special Educational Needs at the age of two. I was told that one day I'd be grateful for it. I didn't agree but when I saw that other people I knew were fighting like crazy to get Statements for their children at school I could see what that person meant. What is written in a Statement is apparently legal and binding.

Although I pinned my hopes on the system knowing and addressing at least *some* of Tim's needs, hardly anything from the Statement was adhered to by the school. For example:

> A named person will be responsible for overseeing his objectives about developing the following: Attention and listening skills, receptive language skills, functional communication skills, social communication and play, increasing tolerance of others, fine motor skills, sensory processing, perceptual and self-help skills and reducing his levels of frustration.

Wow. If a school had all these objectives and were putting them all in place, Tim couldn't help but progress. Were they doing any of this and was there a named person? No.

There's more:

> 'The curriculum will be differentiated and modified in pace, content and delivery appropriate for a child who has difficulties on the autistic spectrum'.

Wow, that would be great too – so he can still learn similar things to the others but in his way and at his pace. Really? Of course not. There was no differentiation. They could hardly get him to engage in any work at all in fact. It didn't help that they weren't working at all on his *attention, listening* or *functional communication* as this might have helped him get to a place where he *could* start to learn.

It was also promised that he would have a *'devised and monitored programme from the speech and language therapist and the occupational therapist'*. Goodness, it just gets better and better. Did they exist? No.

We were also promised that Tim would have a *'named teacher, coordinating his overall programme and liaising with his other teachers'* and that there would be *'a teacher knowledgeable in supporting children with communication difficulties and autistic spectrum disorder.'* Though I asked many times, nobody could ever name that teacher. Tim's development was out of my hands and into theirs but they weren't doing anything.

All I can say is words on Statements mean less than nothing when they are just words on Statements and are not being acted on all through the day. The people I was dealing with were seemingly satisfied that meetings had been had and words were documented on legal paperwork, but they seemed also just as satisfied that the paperwork was filed in a cupboard. The next stage of actually administering it was almost a superfluous afterthought.

As a parent I might as well have the word *nullify* written across my forehead in large letters. I was treated by the school as if I knew nothing about my child and his needs. I know this can happen, too, from occasional conversations inside school staffrooms where parents are negated and considered a nuisance if they show too much interest. I also found that the school had very little time or inclination to discuss Tim's needs with me.

Why is Nothing Happening?

Throughout the first year I asked many times about the Occupational Therapy as Tim was not getting any stronger and his fine motor skills were really holding him back.

The statement was prescribing Occupational Therapy which was much needed but after a whole year, the school had still not implemented anything. Only after a year of failed promises did I realise that I had the power to bypass the School and go straight to the Child Development Centre myself. People promise and promise things and time is constantly passing. Why had I waited so long and relied on other people? School staff are already over-worked and over-stretched. I hated relying on them to do things that Tim needed. There was no guarantee of it happening right or even happening at all. *The Statement was no guarantee of care at all.*

The frustrating thing was, that even when I took him to the OT myself, he refused to do the tasks asked of him and the OT couldn't assess him properly anyway. From his point of view, why should he come to a strange place and hop across the room on one leg while someone with a clipboard told him what to do and made notes? It must have seemed so strange and pointless. He managed the first couple of tasks, then had a meltdown, refused to cooperate and just wanted to leave. I couldn't really blame him.

It was so hard to get a grasp on Tim's world for the first term in Year 1. He was in school full time but it was way too much. He hardly ever produced any work. Occasionally in one of his books I would see a weak pencil line across a page and a sticker saying 'achieved with help'. Surely he could achieve more than *this*? In other assessments he had been called 'bright'. Where was this brightness?

Send Someone in to See What's Really Going On

Erik and I were at our wits' end at this point. Nobody was reaching him and nothing was being done. Time was moving on and no one seemed to have a clue what to do with him. Helen, who had worked with Tim at the Child Development Centre now ran her own business observing children with autism in schools. We asked her to go in and observe how the school were dealing with Tim and how she felt he was getting on. The observations were that the School found Tim's recent behaviour difficult to manage and disruptive to the rest of the class. Tim found it hard to accept adult direction and had repeatedly had tantrums when asked to engage with staff on their terms. It was reported that one day he had been so disruptive that the whole class had to be removed from the classroom. Staff had tried 'various strategies' unsuccessfully and had now decided to 'back off'.

Tim could do the basics of lining up with the other children, saying his name for the register and sitting quietly in assembly. He also enjoyed playing chasing games with other children at playtime. The only time he seemed animated in lessons and willing to join in though was in musical activities – action songs and Christmas play rehearsals. Though he was starting to sound out short everyday words such as 'dog' and 'cat', he seemed unable to grasp real meanings of words in any kind of context. He totally failed to engage with any of the sentence-building activities the children around him were doing. He went to the toilet at one point and Mrs

Jones asked him to wash his hands. He refused and she didn't push it. In her words, she wanted to avoid a confrontation with him.

Tim went through each day not engaging or learning but somehow just 'being around'. Helen noted that staff felt frustrated and powerless to help him – despite their best efforts they had been unable to find successful strategies to engage with him and they had concerns about the impact Tim's behaviour could have on the rest of the class.

There was no 'apparent long-term strategy' in place to imaginatively find ways to meet Tim's needs and overcome the difficulties faced when persuading Tim to follow adult direction. No one had any ideas on how to motivate or engage him. Training for Mrs Jones was mentioned but all the time Tim was there this never happened, however much we requested it.

The curriculum was not being differentiated as staff were unable to engage him in any activities which kind of stopped the whole process in its tracks. Helen noted that *'because of the difficulties they are experiencing with in engaging Tim consistently in meaningful activities, staff are unable to deliver the requirements of Tim's Statement of Special Educational Needs.'*

Well, there was my answer. There was no plan in place to ensure that the wider conditions of the Statement were adhered to either. So what was he doing all day?

Bribery and Corruption!

Occasionally, because of the school's inability to cope with him, they allowed Erik to go in and work a little with Tim during lesson-time to see if *he* could get him to do anything. One day Erik went in and Tim was sitting at his desk with two tasks in front of him and the promise of something slightly better at the end if he cooperated. As usual, he was doing nothing, while Mrs Jones was trying to encourage him to engage in this activity. Erik leaned over and whispered something naughty and totally inappropriate in Tim's ear, 'I have a DVD in the car and I'll give it to you if you do these two tasks'.

Immediately Tim did them straight away – and got them right! What was *that*? And what did that *mean*? He was capable of performing the tasks – that was good – and with some kind of reward he would do them, despite being bored. But the prize had to be something he was seriously excited about and the issue with rewards is that we couldn't give him a DVD every time he did a bit of work – and nor should we. He would just keep asking for bigger and bigger things – but something had triggered a willingness or an ability inside him. Nursery, school, ABA, everyone that wanted him to follow adult direction always used rewards. In this instance it had worked, but the biggest revelation for me was that he *could* do certain things on occasions *if* he had sufficient incentive. I put the reward issue on hold for a moment, because this was more significant, because it proved he had abilities that were not being accessed. *This* was exciting and showed potential. I liked the word potential!

Praying to God

I would sometimes pray to God, 'Please, please, please restore my little man's brain connection – it's only tiny and I know you can do it. I know you love me and I'm seriously begging you – can you *see* me? You say you know me and you love me and you say I can ask *anything* in your Name. I am not merely asking, I am begging you to just link up that brain connection – just a small job – surely you would *want* to do it? I then went on to bargaining. 'God, I will do *anything*. If you heal Tim now I will spend the rest of my life telling other people about it. I'll go all over the world and tell everyone how amazing you are and what you've done – *please*!'

Erik would pray too, often by Tim's bedside, after a long and drawn-out meltdown when Tim was finally at rest. And I would wonder – were we not praying enough? Why wasn't God listening to us? Had we done something wrong? Was this a punishment? These were my thoughts, not Erik's. I thought back to the time when I was incredulously amused with my friends about the child in my class who was so unaware of himself that he defecated in the playground. I later found out he had undiagnosed autism. I had been ignorant. Was this a punishment for that? Why was this happening? I didn't ask the 'why us?' question much as I figured that good and bad things happen to everyone, but I knew if God could see right into my heart like He said he could, that He had the capacity to make me the happiest person in the entire universe. It was possible. Why would He not want to do that? It was within His capabilities.

Chapter Six – Something new to try

Around this time, two friends came to me separately with the same newspaper cutting – it was an advert with the words, 'You've heard of the *problem* of autism? Now hear a *solution*'.

A bold statement. But if the word 'solution' hadn't been in the advert I wouldn't have gone. I was tired of going to meetings about the same old things and nothing making any difference. The boldness of this statement made me curious.

A solution may be too good to be true, but I was so desperately looking for answers, I would have sold my soul if it would have helped Tim show some genuine signs of development.

The advert was about Raun Kaufman, the CEO of the Autism Treatment Center of America, who was giving talks in Brighton and London. My Mum and Dad went to the Brighton meeting and phoned me up the next day, highly recommending that we go to the one in London.

Childcare was hard as we needed to be in London from 8-10pm on a weekday, but we found a friend who was willing to sit with Tim and we decided we really wanted to find out what this was about. Actually it was fun, just being out, never mind going to London for an evening with Erik! A trip out anywhere was exciting and much needed. However, I had no idea how this evening would impact me and how it would set the stage to change the course of Tim's future.

Raun Kaufman was a highly empathetic, charismatic man. He started by explaining his story – that he had been diagnosed with severe autism as a child, with an IQ of less than 30. So his parents had embarked on an experimental, innovative, child-centred, journey, working with him for over three years at home and that because of it, he had completely recovered from his difficulties without any trace of his former condition.

In his book, *Autism Breakthrough*, he explains it like this:

> 'My parents so respected me that they focused totally on what *my* experience was – not on whether I looked strange or different to other people', and, 'As my parents began to truly understand my world, as they communicated in a thousand different ways that I was safe, that I was loved, that I was accepted, something astonishing happened. A connection began to form. Slowly, carefully, I began to peek out from behind the veil of my special world. Tentatively I began to join them in theirs'.

You'd need to read the book *Son-Rise: The Miracle Continues* by his father, Barry Neil Kaufman. As a baby, Raun began to withdraw from human contact, and would stare silently for hours, rocking endlessly. Because they were offered no hope, his parents pioneered a therapy based on unconditional love and acceptance. It's an incredible story, as Raun gradually starts to connect and communicate with the people close to him, and finally fully emerges from his condition. The book follows his amazing development all through his teenage years and even tells the story of other families who have reached their own children under the Kaufman's guidance.

I found that Raun was totally comfortable with people, highly sociable and so interesting to listen to. He'd been successfully and happily through the school system, made loads of friends, and graduated from Brown University with a degree in Biomedical Ethics. He had travelled and lived in different countries, worked in education and more recently he had been given the position of the CEO of the Autism Treatment Center of America, where his family and a group of staff were teaching the Son-Rise Program® to lots of families, all passionate to help their children. The Son-Rise Program was the name given to the process his parents had undertaken to help him and *Son-Rise: A Miracle of Love* is also the title of a film made about their journey. It was the film that spread the word and when so many families came looking for help, Raun's parents set up a centre and created a programme from all they had learned that had helped Raun.

I was as interested in observing Raun as I was interested in what he was saying. I saw no processing delays or difficulties in speaking and his empathy skills were through the roof. He spoke with respect, hope, kindness, confidence and possibility. I realised he really understood the complexities of autism – and focused very much on how life could feel for the children themselves. He was all about seeing life from the child's point of view. This was new to me, as this was the first time I had heard someone in any therapy context genuinely consider the child's point of view and putting that above purely wanting to change them.

He explained that the aim of the Son-Rise Program was first to accept our children and then to help them grow, change and connect more with us. He talked about the importance of relationship over changing behaviour. He explained that rather than forcing children into a world they don't yet understand, we start by first building a connection into *their* world that they *can* understand. My thoughts flew back to the ABA, which had all been about force and control, where the child had to do what the adult said, simply because they had requested it. So I was really interested in any approach that wasn't using force. Never again, did I want to hear Tim screaming with fear while someone was busy telling us it was for his own good.

Raun talked about parents being the experts of their children and I could see that my natural mothering instincts could find a place here. Raun believed in empowering parents to have a central, proactive role in their child's development. I was inspired. At long last, there was a possibility of a positive outcome – so different to all the negatives that I had been told continuously about Tim from his school. I wanted to know more about what Raun's parents had done for him that had helped him to get to this place. I realised it was different and unconventional but that sounded good to me. The conventional school system and therapies to date hadn't helped Tim at all, so I was really open for new ideas.

For the first time I was hearing the word autism and not feeling like it was a life sentence. I looked around the room – unlike so many other meetings I'd been to about the subject, Raun wasn't just hopelessly offering yet another pointless sticking plaster over Tim's gaping wounds, or some magic bullet. There was love, understanding and acceptance here, as he talked about autism as if it was the most normal thing in the world. Even more importantly, I could see there were lots of ways to apply what he was saying to help Tim.

Raun stated that the Son-Rise Program didn't believe in inappropriate behaviours. Wow! The word *inappropriate* was starting to grind me down. I always knew Tim was doing the best he could and for the first time I was hearing that the things he wanted to do were okay! If Tim needed to do something, he needed to do it – and that should be respected. His *reasons* were to be respected.

The more he spoke, the more I could see that the Son-Rise Program focused on relationship with each child way above any academic development. In hindsight I wonder that if autism is considered such a social disability, why more people don't try and help with the social aspect. The social element was Tim's biggest struggle. In fact, all the explanations of autism put social difficulties as the number one issue. Even the neuro-diverse view stated that autism was a social disability.

It had profoundly hurt me to hear Tim's teacher saying she chose to 'tune him out'. Maybe here, with potential new ways to view Tim and his autism and strategies to help him, I could learn how to tune him *in*? If the Son-Rise Program could seriously help me to relate better to my child and to tune him *in,* then I wanted to learn more.

I looked across at Erik, hoping he was as excited as I was. He was, but he was also concerned we make it back to the station in time. I was more concerned with meeting the guy who had once been like Tim and was now an easy-going, confident adult – I just wanted to shake his hand to make sure he was real.

Something re-ignited inside me that night. My spark of hope that had almost died on Tim's diagnosis felt like it was flickering back to life. I *wanted* to have hope of something better for Tim – and Raun Kaufman made me see that it was right to hope for something more for Tim's life. In fact, it was respectful to Tim to believe that all things were possible and not close doors on him. Yes, there were obstacles in the way – I knew the School couldn't teach him, but as the Son-Rise Program was home-based, I wanted to discover if there were other ways I *myself* could teach him, to make a difference and be part of the solution.

Raun spoke about parents attending the Son-Rise Start-Up Program – which was five consecutive days of training in London, in just a few weeks time. *What?* That's impossible – five whole days of childcare? But on the other hand if we could make it work, five whole days of focused time learning how to help our child. That's high incentive. The Caudwell Charity was also offering to pay for us both to go. What kindness and what an opportunity. It gave us a lot to think about.

Because I had insisted on meeting Raun and shaking his hand, we missed our last train and didn't arrive home until 2 am. Thank goodness for Laurie, our lovely, flexible, babysitting friend.

The Son-Rise Program Start-Up Course

The Son-Rise Program training took place in a London hotel with about 200 parents and professionals in attendance. It was an odd feeling to be in a room totally full of people all in a similar situation to us. I had always hated the thought of being part of an 'autism support group' or any such thing as I felt we would all have just sat around being sad and defeated together, or busy focusing on doing hair and nails. But this room had a different feel about it – full of interest, solution and optimism about autism.

Even though the Son-Rise Program training was conducted to a room of 200 people, I am going to talk about it as if they were training me personally. That is how it felt and so that is how I can best explain it. It turned out to be a personal process that changed the way I viewed and therefore responded to Tim and his autism and the outcome of such changes have totally turned his life around.

We had five days of training and talking – listening, learning and processing what was being said – and I probably only took in about 10%. It was all so opposite to everything I had been told.

Can I Make Friends with my Son's Autism?

This was one of the issues that made my brain hurt. I just wanted the difficulties and distress caused by Tim's autism to go away. It was pushing my life and marriage to the limit and everyday life was so complicated. Of course I didn't feel 'friends' with something that meant my little boy would be unlikely to ever connect with me or have friends of his own. He wasn't in a place to learn or take things in, to concentrate or to get a joke. He may never even live independently. I was afraid for his future. My heart didn't feel comfortable about this at all.

However, they encouraged me to see that autism was part of Tim and I loved Tim, therefore if I loved the autism in Tim, I would be loving the whole of him and not leaving any part out.

Goodness, I had not looked at it this way before! Of course, I loved Tim but I really did struggle with his autism. However if I saw autism as a bad thing, I was seeing part of Tim as bad and I had said myself I could *never* see Tim as wrong or bad. I never *wanted* to.

I desperately wanted to love all of him – I thought I already did – but I had been holding back in my own heart as I had a subconscious belief through all I had been told that a part of him was deficient. I can hear half the world calling me 'ableist' at this point and the other half the world totally getting what I'm saying. I am not proud that I felt like this but in actual fact I was not consciously aware of these feelings. At the very beginning of this training, the Son-Rise Program was unlocking some of my hidden beliefs that I didn't even know I had.

I wanted to love all of him, his complex processing, his tentative efforts at communicating, his unusual behaviours and not leave any part out.

What are my Goals for Tim?

They asked what my goals were for Tim – not the kind of goals that schools have, but my own real goals, from my heart. I thought about it and wrote 'mini conversations, conversations with a friend, beginning to 'get' stories'... He was very black and white and inwardly-focused and I so wanted him to start to show an interest in the world around him. They suggested we be unrealistic and not confined to what we thought was immediately possible. In my head I decided that I'd like to be able to sit round the table and have a conversation with him by the time he was eighteen. I envisaged a two-way conversation where he was interested in me in the same way I was interested in him.

'How much do you believe you can achieve this?' they asked? I didn't know. I wanted to believe it. They shared a quote:

> 'The doctors told me I would never walk – my mother told me I would. I believed my mother,' spoken by Wilma Rudolph, a three-times Gold Medallist in Rome.

Parent Love and Power

I certainly get the point of parent love and power. That was an easy one – I had always had a belief in Tim, and in his spirit and his abilities that was massively more ambitious than any organisation or system ever had for him. I found it impossible to believe their negative prognoses when looking into his beautiful face during those moments when he felt safe and happy with us. He had such a bright spirit with such open-heartedness, which we believed was actually who he was and who he was meant to be. We had seen him laugh, we had seen him cry. We were the ones who he snuggled up with in the evenings and who he smiled at when he found something funny. Very few other people had seen this because he was so frightened of them. He had an innate trust in us and we had a natural response to him. None of that could be documented in a school report or a Statement.

We, as parents, were also the ones who would love Tim for the rest of his life, had the commitment needed for the long haul and therefore we were also the ones with the biggest motivation to see change in Tim. Love is a massively strong motivating factor and no teacher or expert could have that level of love or motivation for him.

Acceptance of Tim

There had been no one around me to this point telling me that Tim was fine as he was. Everyone – consultants, educational psychologists, Portage, ABA, the School – had been trying to make me change him, constantly insisting he wasn't good enough. All the experts around me were sending me messages that there's something wrong and my child just doesn't live up to the mark – that he is deficient – divided up into a series of deficits and excesses, which only they are equipped to fix.

But the Son-Rise Program was challenging this truth between me and my child. They were also helping me to see I had a choice. From my point of view I loved him with all my heart and he was perfect. Inside myself I was caught between what had been drilled into me and my natural, loving instinct. The Son-Rise Program helped me to start to trust my own natural state towards Tim. I loved him. I accepted him. This whole process brought me a sense of inner relief – permission, as bizarre as this may seem, to love my child exactly as he is despite all the contrary messages I was receiving. It was as though I could start to breathe again, knowing that I am not alone on this unusual parenting journey. It was a wonderful feeling to know the Son-Rise Program would be behind me.

'Isms'

They talked about Tim's repetitive behaviour as being 'isms'. So far I had heard of repetitious behaviours as being called 'stims' but as I understand it, stims mean self-stimulating behaviours. The Son-Rise Program explained that the behaviours our children engage in are not only for self-stimulatory reasons but also to counteract sensory overload or to bring a sense of order to unpredictability – hence the choice of a new word, isms.

The Son-Rise Program used the word 'ism' instead of stim– so that people would be clear how to treat their child when in this state, and also to remove the negative connotations connected to the word 'stim'. Isms were things Tim did exclusively – wanting to shut us and the world out and just do these behaviours completely by himself. This was the first time Tim's stimming behaviours had been explained to me as something he *needed* to do. I could recognise that he spent many hours a day engaged in these behaviours, I had just never understood it in this way before. They explained that he may go into these exclusive behaviours because he felt so overwhelmed by sensory overload and was trying to shut everything out and gain some control.

Because sensory overload had not been considered part of the triad of impairments and because my ABA case leader had told me he just had to 'get used to it' and because no one had ever sat me down and explained all this to me, it really opened my eyes. They explained how in many ways, the world is too much for him and that it's not surprising he needs to shut off, close himself in, turn away. They explained something which I really needed to know in my heart. That he was turning away from us not because he didn't love us, but because we were part of the *too much*. I could see that with my lively personality and way of talking, it could be too much and that even my desire to connect to him might be overwhelming. It was all very helpful for me to start to understand.

They explained the extent to which he may hear sounds differently to me, not be able to tune sounds out or that he may see things differently, that he may taste, smell or feel things in unusual ways and that it may be unbearable for him – hence the need to ism or stim.

Knowing this started to help me with my fear of what I had seen as abnormal. In fact, his behaviour was *normal* considering what he was going through. I found this a massive relief and my view of Tim and his behaviours started to change.

In fact, Tim's behaviours *made sense* if he was trying to cope with so much unpredictability and over-stimulation coming at him from all angles all the time. I would need to switch off too if that was happening to me. I thought of Tim and his refusal to walk into loud rooms and how he would hold his ears and cry – suddenly – for no reason and how he would scream and tense at the sensation of water on his skin. Beginning to understand what Tim might be feeling and facing gave me a new and much clearer understanding towards the reasoning for his behaviour. How could we ever have perceived this as naughty? If someone is overstimulated and can't cope they need kindness and help, not punishments and reprimands.

Thinking About Tim's Isms

What were Tim's isms? Tim's exclusive behaviours involved looking at books and talking to himself, talking to his hand, putting his hands to his chest and clenching every muscle, lining things up, making high pitched noises, flapping his hands and sudden spontaneous leaps around the room… All these things seemed unusual to me – but could I now understand these differently?

These were things the Son-Rise Program were saying he *needed* to do. Could I jump into his world with him and was there a risk we'd both get lost if I did that? Being completely honest, I was afraid of this world of his – it felt like a great unknown that I found hard to relate to.

I walked out of that room and cried many times during the Start-Up Program, trying to come to terms with my feelings. This was not because of the Program itself, but because my heart was hurting so much and my emotions were so raw. I loved what I was hearing but I think the relief that there might be hope for Tim allowed a part of me to let go – a bit like when you've been working so incredibly hard and suddenly have a holiday.

Joining

They then talked again about the first vital principle of the Son-Rise Program. About how if Tim couldn't come into our world yet (not being able to respond to or learn from us) then we could instead go into his world and join him in the place that made sense to him.

When Tim needed to shut off from the world around him, it didn't necessarily mean he wanted to shut off from us, he just couldn't deal with us. Therefore if we could be empathetic enough to place ourselves where he was and hone our presence into something he could cope with, we may be able to start spending quality time with him in this way.

They suggested that if Tim started isming, we would ism with him. I was immediately concerned that if we did this, he would just ism more and more and never stop. Interestingly they told me that this was nearly everyone's first reaction, but that they'd only ever seen the opposite happen. They called this concept 'joining'. Joining someone in what they are doing is a fundamentally human trait. People are always joining each other in what they are doing. It was just that I had never flapped my hands or jumped up and down in excitement or spoken into my jaggedly moving hand. But could I do this if it helped Tim to feel less alone? Could I do this if it helped to create a camaraderie between me and Tim? Could I do this to help me to understand what he was getting from it? I think I could.

I recalled Jackie's strict instruction in the ABA – to never go near Tim when he was stimming as otherwise it might reinforce to him that this 'behaviour' was OK. If we were going to accept him, we needed to allow him to fully process in the way he needed to and be his cheerleaders along the way. This was the opposite approach and took me a little time to catch up with.

No one would be forcing Tim to stop isming. Son-Rise Program explained that if there was a reduction in his isming, it would be because of a reduced *need* to ism due to the decrease in his sensory overload and anxiety. They then explained that the joining between Tim and me could create more bonding and connection between us, which may lead to Tim to wanting to start to engage in other things with me. This was the platform to start to connect.

This, I think, was the first concept I fully grasped and it made me excited.

They had one simile which made complete sense to me. If your child has an itch and wants to scratch it, you don't keep stopping him as the means to make the itch go away. Instead you find out what causes the itch and treat *that* – then the child will not even need to scratch! If the itch is sensory overload (among other things) and the scratching is the isming, this is so obvious. I just needed to start to learn how to reduce his sensory overload and anxieties in order to help calm his world.

I could see that joining wasn't just enjoying being with him but was the essence of reaching him as a person and making the initial vital natural connections that he seemed to be so afraid of making. I couldn't have loved him more or tried to bond with him more. Yet he was still in this state. I definitely needed to try something new.

One of the biggest things was that Tim didn't want us near him, when he was isming – he wanted to be alone. He was just shutting everything out. In fact, he could be a bit like a trapped animal in his desperation. It felt like we were intruding or interfering if we were near him.

I know some people might say if he wants to do what he's doing we should have left him there, but having a bigger understanding of his reasons helped me to see that he probably didn't want to be there, but it was currently the only way he knew how to survive. Therefore, I knew I couldn't just leave him there. Joining him was the ideal solution as it put no pressure on him but gave him the company he needed.

By shutting everything out he was also shutting us out, who could love him and help him and be his friend. He didn't know yet that we could love and help him, because up to this point we had also been part of the process that was forcing him to change. Unsurprisingly, in his mind he perceived an element of us as a threat. I dearly wanted to turn this around.

That would be why we would have to learn to be with him in a way he could manage and relate to and start to build bridges from there in *his* time and on his terms.

I liked the fact that Son-Rise Program told me I wouldn't be doing this as a technique in order to immediately get Tim to cooperate, but because I loved him and wanted to reach him. Any willing engagement would come in time, naturally and when he was ready and wanted to. That would be the spark that his foundation for learning would be built on.

The difference between the forceful approach with a priority on conformity and the natural 'going with your child' approach was like chalk and cheese. Jackie had said, 'I'm sorry but *we're* the adults'.

Here they were saying '*You* have the autism and I don't, so I'm going to learn and take my cues from you and be your friend in the midst of it'. I know which one I find most respectful.

They explained that if we started really observing Tim's world, where he was coming from and how he was feeling and putting ourselves in a place to be part of that with him, he would start to feel that he was not alone in his complex state and the aim was that he would begin to want to connect to us, rather than push us away. The idea then is that when we invested enough time with him in this unpressured way, he may start to feel invested towards us and may become willingly engaged with us and able to go our way. In little steps. Not by force or bribery, but by his own desire and initiative.

Again, this is what I had wanted since Tim had started withdrawing from me. I knew his learning wasn't happening organically and rewards, systems, drills and repetitive tasks had felt very alienating. This felt natural, personal and very human.

Here, I could be myself, but I could see I had a lot to learn. Here, I would be choosing to find the most sensitive parts of myself, choosing to share with Tim only the parts of myself that he could manage and relate to in order not to overwhelm him, choosing to jump into his space and find an interest in all the things he loved.

I could see this wasn't a deferring or sacrificial feeling, where I would need to resign myself to do something I didn't want to or be someone I wasn't. I couldn't sustain that. With the ABA, I had tried to be someone I wasn't and that didn't help Tim at all. I'd promised myself then that I'd never be in that situation again. He needed me to be who I was – but at a level he could manage.

The Son-Rise Program explained that to focus on Tim's natural social connections and ability to relate was more important than to try and get him to learn reading and writing at this point. His interpersonal skills were his biggest issue and therefore would need the most attention. There would otherwise be a possibility he could end up being an adult who might be brilliant academically but unable to relate to people in any meaningful way. I hadn't read in any of the explanations about autism that it was an academic disability – only a social disability – so this made sense. I had also read that learning difficulties can accompany autism. I had been told that Tim didn't have specific learning difficulties. The thing was, though, that nobody could teach him and he wasn't learning anything new, as his state was never in a place that left him able to learn. His autism was one massive learning difficulty. Mum explained it the other day, when she said, 'If you were put in front of a firing squad and never knew when you were going to be shot at, you wouldn't be able to put your mind to anything else.' Tim's overloads and the unpredictability of his life must have made him feel like that. No wonder he wasn't in a state to learn.

Motivations

The Son-Rise Program explained that whereas *joining* is the right hand of the Son-Rise Program, *motivation* is the left. Joining brings your child to a place where he is ready to connect to you and motivation is the way you naturally develop your child's attention, so you can both focus on the learning and growing. And that is done by having heaps of fun! So far, we had only tried to persuade Tim to do things by offering him rewards, which really meant that he was being coerced. With any reward system there is always an element of doing something you don't want to do for something totally unrelated that you do want. If you are doing something you don't want to do, there is always that negative struggle, however great the reward might be. But I was being told there was another way. If I were to discover Tim's intrinsic motivations, I could discover what he *wanted* to do – without a fight. I could do what he wanted to do with him and use the activity to work on specific goals with him. This uses a different kind of energy. For once you are not fighting your child's natural state but going with it.

The idea was to go along with what *he* wanted to play – discover *his* intrinsic motivations. This way, he would want to stay involved. In the Son-Rise Program motivations are seen as the 'engine of your child's growth'. I knew only too well what happened when trying to get Tim to do some random task when he was unwilling. This is what ABA and the school had pushed for. But going with his motivations would enable us to stay interactive for longer… and staying interactive for longer meant more connection and possibility for learning. If he *wanted* to do something it would actually be coming from *him,* therefore less – if any – battle.

I could see that receiving a 'prize' for good behaviour is not the same as being *interested* in something. Being fascinated and motivated by something is a natural way to hold your attention whereas with rewards you are being forced and coerced into specific behaviours and actions. I also remember saying earlier that Tim's rewards were never enough. The Son-Rise Program explained that the motivation principle is actually the *opposite* of the system of reward-giving. If you do a boring task for a reward, you may get to hate the task and you will not have any intrinsic motivation to do it. Children with autism particularly need to try and try with certain tasks in order to master them and if they are intrinsically motivated, they will be more willing to keep going with the same activity.

Motivations would definitely help to trigger Tim's desire to try. How many times do we have to try something before we are able to actually do it? Many. If a child refuses to try – as Tim constantly did – this would seriously hinder his ability to learn new things. This could help spark his desire to persist as a major element of his ability to learn. You surely couldn't force someone into developing a genuine desire to try, so it would have to be done without force. If Tim was highly motivated by something and wanted to do it he would continue to try until he'd succeeded.

I understand motivations. I know that when I am excited and highly motivated by something I can go along with it for hours. I do it because I want to – not because anyone tells me to.

Linking Goals with Motivations

The idea was to link goals you have for your child with their intrinsic motivations – a genius idea. We spent a long time on the course thinking about our child's motivations and goals and how to link them. At the time I knew Tim's motivations to be parties, pass the parcel, Bob the Builder, chasing games, silly dancing…

In groups we discussed ours and other people's children and how best to make these links. I loved the creative thinking that came from this exercise. I also loved that I could think of one of Tim's motivations and one of his goals and link the two – and see myself actually making it happen. The empowerment of proactivity was starting to wipe away some of the intense frustration I felt with the fact that no one was currently doing anything purposeful to help him. It was such a relief to know that I would be proactively putting these ideas into place and making them happen.

Sometimes I felt stuck for ideas and sometimes ideas flowed. I could see why it was great to have a group in which to discuss all these things and share ideas. We did lots of brainstorming. These were teaching strategies that could genuinely help us and I was filling up notebooks with ideas on how we could start to help Tim.

Empowerment

Joining him and following his motivations were things I could do myself when I was on my own with him. I didn't need to rely on other people, therapists, 'experts', or school systems. I felt a spark of empowerment growing inside me. In my own time with my own son, with no one else around, I could start to connect with him. I didn't have to be a bystander anymore, waiting for the school systems to step up. Son-Rise Program were telling me that my relationship with Tim was key and I was the one who could jump into his world, be his friend there and gradually encourage him to learn and grow. They were showing me how. What purpose! My daily reactions and responses and the way I was with Tim were where progress lay. The ABA had insisted I step back from Tim's development to make it clear that I was his mother and not his therapist but the Son-Rise Program advocated that as I was the closest person to him, with the most love and the highest motivation, I could have the best influence. But in order to fulfil this role, I definitely needed their training.

Tim's attachment to me had been viewed as a major problem for a long time, with people trying to prise him off me, making me feel my emotional attachment to him was somehow wrong. Here, they encouraged me and helped me to see my emotional connection with Tim was the foundation of his development. Every time I had spoken to the school, I'd felt like I was getting in the way. But Tim wasn't someone's job – he was *my child*. I was beginning to walk a path to claim him back.

This thinking turned my world the right way up again. I had been disempowered for too long – having other people work with my child and being told that his bond with me wasn't helpful – waiting for Educational Psychology reports and speech therapy advice as to what to do next with him when all the different therapists never even spoke to each other and all the information I had on Tim was in jumbled pieces. This therapist was doing this, this teacher was doing that... It all had to be a trust issue for me because I was never allowed to watch. No, that system was too muddled. Someone needed to be at the centre of it all, bringing all the information together and really stopping the world to take notice of his development. I wanted to be in this position so much. I wanted Erik and I to be back in the driving seat, to be empowered – to have Tim's future back in our hands, like we did before the autism diagnosis struck and seemed to lever him out of our hands and into the so-called 'care' of the system. This sat right in my heart.

What State am I In?

So, if I was going to find a way into Tim's world and love him from the inside out and help him over time to learn, I needed to be the right person for him. They explained that this wasn't just about hard techniques but also very much about my attitude. I needed to examine my own state.

When they first talked about attitude, I related it to my own experience of course. It had been insinuated many times that I had a negative attitude as a teenager and I tended to think of attitude as being about whether you had a good or a bad one. In fact, people talking about my attitude had got my back up in the past and initially it did here too – that was *my* space, *my* decision, *my* right. It was about Billy Joel songs and getting rid of adult ownership over your life and breaking out on your own. My only experience of attitude really had been about being rebellious and my go-to place was to think of it in that context. However, they explained that my attitude was all about what I believed, how I felt and therefore how I reacted. They took me back to the fact that my attitude could determine how effective I would be at helping Tim to reach new heights.

I had been told many times in the last few years that Tim picked up on my emotions and that I should be careful with my attitude and responses towards him – which I tried to be – but the Son-Rise Program took this thinking to a whole new level. They explained that because Tim was so resistant to relationship and as we were the adults he spent most of his days with, his relationship with us was vital because we were his main connection to the outside world. We were the first people he would use to see what life outside his world looked like.

But even though I could see I would need to work on my attitude, I didn't really know how. I had been thrown into an 'autism world' I knew nothing about, where everyone and everything was telling me that something was wrong. They explained that if I believed there was a lack of hope for Tim's life, then it would be logical that I would continue feeling run down, low, exhausted and unsure. Consequently, all this would reflect on my feelings and attitude when I was with Tim. In contrast, if I could first turn around this belief about Tim and his autism into something that had all the hope in the world and love both Tim and his autism, believing to my core that there was every possibility for his development, I would feel more hopeful, excited and positive. Then I would have my feelers out for everything I could do to help him, knowing that so much more is possible. This, in turn, would affect how I would treat him, how I would talk to him etc, which would have an automatic impact on his development. It made sense but it was a lot to get my head around.

They explained that I had an element of choice here – that this thinking about autism and Tim's development was within my own control. I could love him, trust in him and believe he could grow in every level he needed and wanted to. The Son-Rise Program would be with me on this one. Having seen Raun's journey and those of all the other children the Son-Rise Program told me about, I genuinely believed this was possible.

In *Son-Rise: the Miracle Continues*, the book written about Raun's life, his father, Bears Kaufman, on learning about his son's diagnosis, asked, 'Could we kiss the ground the others had cursed?'

This is what they were encouraging me to also do right now.

They spoke to us about our role, representing the world of human interaction for Tim…

In *Autism Breakthrough*, (2014, p144) Raun says the following:

> 'Every single second you are with your child you are, for better or worse, our world's ambassador. You represent the world of human interaction. Everything that you do tells your child what it's like to be a part of our world.
>
> If you force or push, that tells your child that our world is one where she will be coerced. If you disapprove, that tells her that our world is a disapproving world. If you give control, that tells her that the interactive world is one in which she can feel secure and have autonomy. If you are approving, that tells your child that our world is an approving one.
>
> You are asking your child to permanently join you in your world. For this reason it is critical that you remain

extremely aware of the messages you are sending about what that world is like.'

I was often crying, often feeling grief and desperation, feeling uncertain and often distracted and preoccupied in trying to solve the daily challenges.

So from his point of view, he would see crying – he would feel sadness, grief, desperation, uncertainly, preoccupation. Why would he want to come out of his solitary place? It was probably more fun there. I could see very clearly that though I loved him, I was (unwittingly) a minefield of complex emotions that he would find it easier to stay away from.

This had to change. Of course, I wanted him to become closer to us and all the people who loved him, but if I was his first gateway to these human relationships that he'd have to walk through to be part of them, I could see why he would avoid them. I needed to be a positive and welcoming view of our world – and not at all falsely. But his developmental delays and the autism prognosis made me sad. How could I possibly be happy without pretending? In my mind I was only like that *because* I loved him and didn't want him to be in the state he was in. But as a way to help him and to start to draw him closer to me, I needed to be the total opposite – calm, relaxed, fun, full of attention, welcoming, happy even.

Happy? Are you kidding?

No wonder they spent so much time at the training helping me work through my own feelings. The thing is, up until this point, although I had known my feelings were important, I had not been aware of the level and the extent of their importance.

I reasoned that if I knew Tim would be OK, I could be happy, but I knew it didn't work like that. I felt so screwed up at this point that I really didn't know what to do with myself – the conflict inside me was reaching a height – I could see the point but I was sad– how could I possibly become this person I needed to be for him?

Surely if I did right now, I would only be pretending or 'putting on a show' for him. I certainly didn't feel like that. We all know people who make out that all's right with the world, even though they are hurting inside. That couldn't be what they meant, surely?

But could I *feel* like that? Could I *access* these feelings in me *because* I loved him? I thought of the ten-storey house and moving it brick by brick – *'just tell me what to DO'*

No one said it was going to be easy but I could totally see the *point*. Maybe I could let go all the anger and frustration I had been building up over the years and start to focus on more welcoming emotions?

My Mum (who has been one of the biggest keys in Tim's progress and is amazing) was, for fifteen years while I was growing up, suffering from serious depression. She couldn't access many good feelings throughout those years and when I allowed myself to think how I could have felt if she'd been *happy*, I know it would have opened up major parts of my world and I could have accessed those things more easily in myself – my outlook, way of communicating, feelings, it would have all been different – I would have been more *able* to get on in the world and would have *wanted* to be with her. As it was, my world closed down, I became angry and rebellious, left home young and refused to go back for a long time. How different *could* it have been? How different *could* I have felt and how different *could* my relationships have been? I know I am neurotypical, but if a child on the autistic spectrum is even more highly sensitive to the emotions and attitudes of other people, it makes even more sense to change.

Seeing the point was the first step – wanting to do it was the next – working through the 'how' would come. I wouldn't waste my time feeling bad. I would forgive myself but I could definitely see the reason to change.

The Four Fundamentals of the Son-Rise Program Social Curriculum

INTERACTIVE ATTENTION SPAN

When it came to the Son-Rise Program fundamentals, I had heard of the need to help someone with speech and with non-verbal communication. What I hadn't heard of though, was the importance of interactive attention span. In fact, I had never heard of 'interactive' attention span. I knew about normal attention span and felt Tim had a lot of it with regards to concentrating on one thing for a long period of time – electronic games, looking at books etc. But what they meant by this was how long someone could stay *interactive* with another person. Tim could not stay interactive. He looked briefly at someone or said a few words and then walked away. I hadn't even known that someone could build up their interactive attention span, a bit like a muscle. I was fascinated though as I could see this was a really important building block that could open up lots more pathways in Tim's development. The Son-Rise Program sees lengthening Interaction Attention Span as the prerequisite to all other learning and growth. I was glad they were going to give us lots of examples on how to do this.

VERBAL COMMUNICATION

Interestingly the Son-Rise Program discussed the fact that we had learned to read Tim's signals so easily was not always helpful. I was so used to Tim taking my hand and pulling me to things he wanted that I would immediately know what he needed and would get it for him without asking him to say anything. Unwittingly I was not helping him in this way. PECs, also, could have the same effect. If Tim only had to hand over a picture, instead of using words for what he needed, it would be taking away much needed opportunities for talking.

They explained that each time Tim wanted something, it was an opportunity to encourage him to talk and up to now, I had been missing these windows. They taught me that it was not particularly helpful to encourage Tim to say abstract words but was more helpful to encourage him to use words when he was motivated by something he wanted – this made sense. At the moment he was highly motivated by chasing games. If he could say 'go' or 'chase' we could immediately chase him. That would inspire him to say it more. He would have more and more reason to say specific words. This would really help.

My heart broke for the times that we had ignored what he said to us if it was not said in the right tone of voice or was not the exact word the drill required him to say. Forget all that – what do we want? For Tim to practice speaking. Therefore, I decided that if he speaks we will react – simple as that. The idea was that if he said 'Jump' we'd say a metaphorical 'how high?' We would react straight away and make him realise that using words got him instant reactions.

But would reacting immediately to everything Tim says make him spoilt? Bring it on – I'd give my eye teeth for a spoilt child who talks to me. That would be so much easier to work with than a non-communicative child who continuously zones out and turns away from me. I envisaged a loud, demanding, talkative child who wouldn't leave me alone – that sounded like heaven!

So much of this made sense and I couldn't understand why I hadn't thought this way in the past. Another great proactive tool I could take home with me and use straight away.

EYE CONTACT AND NON-VERBAL COMMUNICATION

For the Son-Rise Program, eye contact was all about sharing delight and camaraderie. From Tim's point of view it was about him receiving the deep message that he was loved and celebrated and to realise that connection with us could be fun and something he might want more of. Through eye contact we could communicate assurance, comfort, understanding and interest. We could share conspiracies, fun moments, feelings and celebrations. In fact, eyes communicate so much! As I understand it, most of a child's learning comes from people. Therefore if a child struggles to look into someone's eyes, they will miss so many opportunities to be loved and celebrated, to share connections and feelings which may ultimately make them feel better. So having fun and encouraging eye contact can create great leaps in all areas of development as well as building communication that is much deeper than words. For the children who can never speak, this surely would be a very helpful source of human connection.

I am aware that autistic people really struggle with eye contact, partly because they are already taking so much in, that looking at a person, with all their changing words and mannerisms can be overwhelming. This means they should never be forced to do this as the effects could be detrimental. However, eye contact through fun and shared moments of silliness can really build relational bridges.

FLEXIBILITY

Flexibility was something else I had also not considered but when I thought about it, Tim had almost none. Things had to go his way, he couldn't cope with changes to plans and he would get set on 'tracks' that he had to follow. However, they took my understanding a stage further. They explained that for a child to interact with a person, they also needed flexibility. People change their thoughts, ideas, directions all the time and if a child is ever going to go with this and not fight it out of a need for security, they would need to develop inner flexibility. It was an important tool in speech for this reason. I didn't even know that flexibility was something you *could* develop.

Analysing Where Tim is Socially

We had a session looking at the Son-Rise Program Developmental Model and it was interesting to see if I could plot where Tim was in each of these elements. Each of these social aspects had 5 stages:

1) Interactive attention span: Tim was definitely working at Stage 1 with his interactive attention span. He was not yet able to maintain interactive attention for 2 minutes or more.

2) Verbal communication: Tim was definitely at Stage 2 in this. He could speak between 50 and 150 words and he could speak in 2 and 3 word sentences or more. He had conversations that were consisting of one loop or more (each loop is one conversational exchange) and his words were generally clear and understandable. He could also spontaneously initiate

communication when he did or didn't want something. When I looked at Stage 3 though, he definitely wasn't there yet. It involved both answering and asking simple what, who and where questions and involved requesting permission before taking an action. No, we weren't there yet, but we could see where we were heading.

3) Eye contact and non-verbal communication: I would have put Tim between stages 1 and 2 for eye contact – he would make eye contact 2/3 times a minute and could just about sustain it for 2 seconds or more. He never made eye contact by choice at this stage – only with massive fun and encouragement.

4) Flexibility: He was also definitely working at Stage 1 with his flexibility. Stage 1 involved easily allowing our presence with him in his playroom and allowing us to help him in his activities.

Although this might seem a very low place to be, it was also very encouraging. As I mentioned earlier, before I learnt about the Son-Rise Program approach, I knew about eye contact, verbal and non-verbal communication but I didn't even know there was the possibility to build 'Interactive attention span' or 'flexibility'. Now I was aware of these things, I could work on them with him.

No wonder Tim hadn't been progressing. We had not been working on his real issues. These were the social goals at the core of his ability to connect and learn. These were the first real steps that would see him make genuine progress. I was sure of it.

Behaviour/Meltdowns/Tantrums

The Son-Rise Program *never* called behaviour 'difficult'. In fact they didn't see anything as bad. They were totally non-judgemental and trusted that the child was doing the best he could in the circumstances he was in. I loved this thinking.

They explained that the state Tim would get into with tantrums or meltdowns could all be helped by our attitude. There was much we could do to help him out of these states. I had always found it difficult to distinguish between a tantrum and a meltdown. For instance, when he wanted the card that day when we were feeding the ducks, it looked like a tantrum as he didn't get what he wanted but in actual fact, it could well have been a meltdown. He'd been in school that morning and may have built up a lot of internal stress. Whatever the situation, tantrum or meltdown, they explained that my attitude towards him would be key.

One thing I liked was that they were all for keeping the relationship intact with your child when he was having a meltdown or tantrum, as the relationship with you was vital. They were very much against removing your relationship from your child if they were tantruming as they knew how much your child *needed* that relationship and connection with you. Wow – this actually resonated with my inner feelings that I'd never put into words before. It had *never* felt right putting Tim in the Thinking Room and ignoring him or walking away from him when he didn't behave 'appropriately'. I now shuddered at the thought. Also, other than briefly quietening him down, it had never made for better connection, only more hurt and upset, which then just built up, causing more separation.

They also explained that in his tantruming, he was not trying to separate from us. In fact, he was actually trying to communicate with us – and that's what we want – for him to communicate. They explained the importance of our reactions to all of Tim's behaviour. They explained that if we were to light up like a Christmas tree every time he did something that we didn't want, he may actually enjoy this exciting reaction so therefore, find that these behaviours served a purpose for him and feel the need to do them more.

I had been used to ignoring difficult behaviour and praising good behaviour within my teacher training. The Son-Rise Program idea though was never to ignore, because you want to encourage *all* communication. Instead, the most useful ways are to react in a calm, slow, boring way to difficult behaviour and in a fast, urgent, excited way to behaviour that we want… One example Raun gives in his book Autism Breakthrough is this:

If you are cooking dinner and your child tugs gently at your shirt or speaks to you gently, you will probably say, 'Not now, gorgeous, I am cooking dinner', but if your child has a screaming tantrum, you will leave the dinner and dramatically run straight to your child to see what's wrong. Your reactions give out subtle signals to your children about the best ways to communicate all the time.

If I were to be sparkly and exciting every time Tim tried to communicate with me with words, and slow and boring every time he tried to communicate with me via tantrums, screaming and pulling, he would start to see which type of communication got him what he wanted more quickly. There were so many ideas here that I could try with Tim.

Control

They also talked about control. I honestly felt that I had been so worn down by control battles and the need to win them that if I heard any more about strategies to break him down I would lose it myself – but… their take was the total opposite of anything I had yet come across. They said Tim was controlling because he felt so out of control. That would make sense. Which elements of his life did he have control of? Nothing. He couldn't tell us what he wanted. He couldn't make what he wanted happen. No wonder he felt so out of control – and he was being moved from pillar to post often against his will and without understanding – (thinking of all the times getting him to leave playparks and getting him to go into the car to get to school, shops etc). They said…wait for it…that the answer was to *give him control.*

What? Give control to my child of five? Surely we are the adults and we should be in control and he should do what *we* ask of him. Yes, that would seem logical but that hadn't worked, had it? They explained, in order to let go of his need to control, he needed to experience that he had some control and some say in what happened to him. He needed autonomy. He hadn't yet been through the development stage to realise that sometimes he had to do what an adult wanted and sometimes he could do what he wanted. Also, due to his lack of understanding and ability to express himself he had lost so much of his autonomy. He needed it back.

So us trying to have control hadn't helped him. But giving him control? Eek! What would that look like? I could see that if he *did* have some control and some say in his life he wouldn't need to control *us* so much. OK, something to think about.

Trust his Processes

They also talked about *trusting* him. Again, what? Trust a child who can't communicate with you that he knows what he's doing? Surely, he needs lots more guidance than most because of his lack of understanding?

They didn't mean trusting him at the side of the road – thank goodness! But they did mean to trust his processes– that he will be doing what he does for good reasons and that he is doing what he does somehow to help himself and balance out his sensory difficulties. He was not being naughty, but was doing his best to look after himself. In fact they believed that he was doing his best to cope at all times. This rang totally true for me – how many times had I taken the side of helping him to cope, rather than reprimanding him for being 'naughty'? I honestly felt he was trying his best and that so many things overwhelmed him that he just couldn't manage his feelings, or what was being asked of him. That was when his overloads turned into what everyone saw as 'difficult behaviour'. I only had to think back to that dreaded meltdown on the last ABA training day, when I had been controlled into controlling him – I hated all this talk of control!

So therefore, I breathed out. I finally felt that someone was coming down on my side of the conflict that I had battled with ABA and even with Erik at times. Erik didn't feel in conflict with any of this new thinking though. It made total sense to him too. Phew!

Special Playroom

They talked about having a special playroom for Tim, explaining that the room needed to be free from distraction. Tim's sensory overload caused him such discomfort that in order for him to be comfortable there, he needed to be as free from these things as possible. The purpose of the room was to be a relief from all the overloads so we could focus on joining and interaction. Also, at the time, Tim could run about the house at will. They asked me to think about how many times I had to say *no* to him. Well, lots – nearly all the time in fact. I had to be constantly alert for the door, too, making sure doors were locked and he couldn't escape. They explained that from his point of view he would be playing with things around the house and would suddenly be shouted at, or removed from the room, or the object he was playing with, because of it being dangerous for instance, without any understanding of why. Because he currently lacked the skills to understand our explanations, he would find his world very muddled. He would also not be able to put his attention to anything if he was constantly told no to things he could not understand. If anything could suddenly happen that would upset or alarm him, he wouldn't be able to relax enough to access people or learning.

The idea of the playroom was that it would be a YES room. Everything would be allowed. He would be able to relax and start regaining a sense of autonomy. He could follow his motivations in there. He could do what he naturally felt he wanted and needed to do and we would do it with him. When was there ever a time in his life that he could actually totally do what he wanted or needed? And not only that but have a buddy alongside.

To try to help him stop for a moment and not run constantly, we could put a little lock on the inside of the door so we would both be able to stay there together instead of spending the whole of each session running all over the house! He could still run about – the space he could run in would just be a little bit smaller. Our other three exterior doors to the house always had to be kept locked anyway, so it would just mean being in a slightly smaller place, rather than having the run of the whole house. It would prevent us from having to constantly tell him to be careful and stop him doing things. Being together in one place would start to bring some freedom, despite the fact that this idea seemed like a paradox at first. Again, I could see that his difficulty with this could be a temporary thing, until he genuinely realised he could enjoy spending time with us in this way. It all made sense.

Television

The Son-Rise Program, with a focus on connecting and interaction, had a very strong message about television – well, all screens, electronic toys and computer games in fact. Basically they explained that they fed into children's exclusivity, fed their desire to zone out of relationship and removed the opportunities for human responsiveness and interaction.

By this point I could see the point of the focus on human interaction and connection more clearly and could easily see how television and DVDs would detract from that. But so far, Tim had seemed to need the television, or at least thought he had needed it. He had so far not been able to eat without it on or cope with having people round without having it as a comfort blanket and he couldn't seem to relax without it – it was his 'time out' place – as it was ours. Sometimes it was our only way of calming him down and often it was the only way we could get jobs done in the house or breathe out ourselves. Had we conditioned him into this need, I wondered? His DVDs were also his obsession – he would watch them until they were worn out – again and again. How would he survive if he had to live without them?

Someone in the room suggested that it could be a cosy thing to sit with your child and share a TV programme together and that for him it was a time of connection. The Son-Rise Program Trainer asked him to come up to the stage, where she made a point of standing side by side with him gazing out into the audience as if we were the television. She asked us to consider how much connection there really was – no interaction, no eye contact, no response to each other. Basically being exclusive together.

I had a lightbulb moment about how we would start making serious inroads into Tim's ability to connect and communicate. I wrote a note and passed it to Erik. 'I think we need to get rid of the telly'. He looked at me and nodded. Neither of us had any idea how we would cope with the enormity of this, but we just knew it was a done deal. We would get rid of his electronic toys too. We would focus totally on human, not electronic, interaction.

A Way to Understand Tim that No one had Explained Before

The Son-Rise Program explained that sometimes Tim would be exclusive (needing to zone out) and sometimes he would be in a state to interact. They could see that children could move in and out of these states throughout the day. Tim totally did exactly that. It was great to talk to people who could understand the reality of how he was.

His exclusive state was most of the time, but there were fleeting moments when I felt he was present with me. The Son-Rise Program advocated that being with him, we would really notice where he was – whether he was in his own world, in which case we would join him – or whether he was showing signs of being open and ready to learn. The first they called a red light, which meant not to try and teach him anything but just to join him. The second they called a green light. The green light was exciting because it meant that there was an opportunity, even if fleeting, when Tim looked at us or initiated something with us, where we could connect. Yay – connection! My goal! (and no clickers in sight) I felt I would be willing to join him for hours in order to have one or two moments of connection – I yearned for it that much.

So *when* to teach a child is as important as how to teach and what to teach. This was so new to me. Here, it was fine if he didn't comply – but was amazing if he did want to. The pressure was off – we just wanted to capture any moment that he was willing to try and communicate. It was such a different approach. No tasks to tick off, instead our undivided attention and an acceptance of him as a person, letting him know it was OK to be him in the place where he was and that we were there ready and waiting as soon as he wanted to look out of his window into our world.

I can see why other teaching systems might seem faster. Parents and teachers alike want results as soon as possible, however they are reached. Boxes need to be ticked as we need to prove that our children are progressing. But if the child isn't progressing in terms of their social and emotional well-being, and in their connections and relationships, they can't easily learn academically anyway. I could see this very clearly. I had also made the decision that I would far rather my child could cope socially than ever be an academic genius.

Tim's State

Ignoring Tim's state when teaching him, which so far we had all done in pushing him towards our own agenda meant that we had missed opportunities when he was ready to learn and wasted energy trying to force him into compliance when he simply couldn't.

When I look back at the ABA videos, I can see Tim is saying 'no' to us when we request certain things, but we are pushing through his red lights and trying to make him do them. He is also telling us what he wants but we were all taught to ignore his green lights because it wasn't coming from an arbitrary agenda. What incredible opportunities we had been missing!

A neuro-typical child is mostly able to adjust to learning something in a given timetable even if he doesn't want to, therefore it is hard to understand why a child with autism can't do the same. Learning that Tim needed to shut down and that he was doing the best he could helped me to understand that he couldn't 'learn on demand'. The Son-Rise Program process made complete sense. A lot of quality time would need to be spent before he could access learning in this way.

How Can We Practically Put an Approach Like This into Practice?

It makes sense that the Son-Rise Program approach cannot be followed in a regular classroom. Schools were never created to put child development first. They are all about timetables and agendas, which is why ticking boxes has to take such a priority that, sadly, teachers don't always have time to see where each child really is. Even if they could, following a child and being responsive to him in this way would not provide sufficient concrete outcomes, and therefore progress wouldn't be so easy to document. Horror of horrors – school league tables might go down… Saying that, if a child isn't making progress anyway, what's the difference?

Schools are built to teach academic subjects, not to teach the social interactional skills required to get a child to the place where he can begin to meaningfully learn. Before a child can benefit from school surely, they would need to be able to be comfortable with other people in their space, to understand and be able to follow basic instructions and be able to communicate some basic needs and intentions. Tim was not there yet – and his school was not equipped to teach the skills that get him to that place. They were geared to teach children already at that place.

As a teacher, I'd had it drilled into me to always have a clear objective and outcome for each lesson. I would have a method of how to do something and would know what I wanted the children to achieve. I had also spent many hours writing out plans for Tim's ABA programmes and checking tick lists of what had been achieved. Tim hadn't been ready for this approach to learning. Much as any teacher might like to teach in this way, if it doesn't work, you can't. I needed another way – a way I'd never taught before.

The Son-Rise Program approach was a totally child-centred way of learning and because of this could not be slotted into curriculum boxes.

But How Can We Do This All the Time?

We couldn't. If we were to embark on the Son-Rise Program at home, we would need to find volunteers. I felt challenged by the idea of asking yet more from my friends. We had already done a sponsored walk to raise money and the Caudwell charity was paying for us to do this training. We had also recruited ABA tutors a year ago then had to let them go. Did we really have to ask other people again to help us? It was embarrassing – couldn't we just sort our lives out ourselves? Which of our friends would want to come and volunteer time to play and work with Tim? Surely they all had enough troubles in their own lives and nearly all our friends were pushed for time. This felt a bit too much out of my comfort zone.

But back to the goal. Did I want Tim to grow and develop? *Yes.* Did it not make sense that I would need to teach this to other people so they could do it for me when I couldn't? Yes. Did it therefore not make sense to ask? Yes…but…so why did I think that everyone would be too busy and wouldn't want to help? The Son-Rise Program had plenty of stories about people who had loved playing with their children in the playroom – and how the volunteers themselves had grown from the experience. And the final question…. if I was going to be asking Tim to explore a world outside of his comfort zone, shouldn't I be willing to do the same? Eek…. Again, I get the message – I could see the reason…so this wasn't just going to take Tim out of his comfort zone, it was going to take us there as well. OK, here we go!

How Do I Deal with my Own Feelings?

The world, society and even friends and family could say hurtful things, even without realising sometimes. I had been told at one point that I'd be a 'lovely Mum to a normal child'. However, I knew I had found an unwavering place within myself where I loved Tim, naturally, exactly as he was and that I would always be his safe place of acceptance.

The Son-Rise Program was fantastic in helping me deal with all the angst and torment I felt when people judged my parenting and the pain of Tim never being invited to playdates. Since Tim's diagnosis, such things had never been mentioned, and so were left for me to deal with personally – reliant on my ability to reason and forgive, whereas The Son-Rise Program acknowledged these emotions as a key part of my life. As I was dealing with my gorgeous, unique child I would also have to cope with ill-informed, negative input from other people and process whatever feelings rose up in me. It makes total sense that so many parents who have children with special needs, end up at mental breakdown point themselves. It's as much about taking care of yourself and processing your own emotions as it is dealing with your child.

I came to a place where I could understand why Tim was behaving the way he was and I was OK with that – it made sense. I had a plan to lead him as far into relationship and learning as I could. I then needed a plan for how to cope with the judgements of other people and the way that made me feel. I was in a place where hurt quickly led to anger. That screwed me up on the inside if I didn't manage to forgive quickly. I took on board all they were teaching me. It would start with me letting go of my judgements of other people. I wouldn't judge them if they held negative or hurtful thoughts about my child, however unfair it all felt. This fitted in with my faith. I had become a Christian at the age of 17 after a serious car crash and had experienced the feeling of being fully forgiven and I was learning to unreservedly forgive others when they hurt me.

Just as Tim's autism was a learning process for him, forgiving people was a learning process for me. I would choose not to judge people if their reactions to my child appeared really insensitive. How could I reason that I wouldn't react the same if I had a well-behaved neuro-typical child and was watching someone else's child have a meltdown? I decided to choose to believe that if people criticized my parenting and Tim's behaviour, they purely didn't understand and that if they really did understand, they would care – if they fully knew how his life felt for him. This was a mantra that helped me through many a socially painful moment.

Is It a Sacrifice or is It Something I Want?

When Raun was little his Mum spent three years of her life giving her almost undivided attention to him in this totally loving, relationship-filled way. My initial feeling was one of incredible sacrifice. Could I possibly sacrifice like that too? Three whole years of life? The Son-Rise Program had an answer to that too – it's not a sacrifice if it's something you want– and if it's something you want for yourself, you are working on a goal but not sacrificing anything. If I wanted to sculpt an amazing model, I would work on it bit by bit and day by day, not thinking of it as a sacrifice but working step by step towards something I wanted – my end product. I could see Tim in this way. I wanted to work with him bit by bit – I couldn't think of anything in life I wanted more than to spend time with him.

Back to beliefs again; if I didn't believe that Tim could seriously improve, why would I go to such lengths? I started to see increasingly how beliefs were at the core of this journey. I pictured him looking at me, talking, laughing, asking to see friends. I pictured him chatting to other children and being part of a larger world. I could see it in my mind's eye and I could feel how it would feel when we were there. I was totally open to learning all the strategies I could – and I also knew my goal was so clear and exciting that I would want to stick to it.

Extreme

This all seemed incredibly extreme to us – a playroom, possibly taking Tim out of school, getting rid of the telly, a whole new approach and lifestyle change – and yet it also made sense for where we were.

Something Raun Kaufman says in Autism Breakthrough is '*Autism is extreme and requires extreme measures*' – it was clear if we were going to break into the extremity of Tim's exclusiveness, we would need to try some of these extreme measures.

I didn't mind how extreme this was as we were in desperate need of serious change. Odd bits of therapy hadn't seemed to help – like lots of little drops in the ocean but never enough. Force and coercion for hours hadn't done it either – it pushed Tim further back into himself and seemed to cause him emotional pain. Would sustained love, attention, chosen reactions and responses start to do the trick? Would the Son-Rise Program techniques actually work?

Hopeless to Hopeful

Towards the end of The Son-Rise Program Start-Up, I started to feel completely differently about Tim and his autism. Looking back, it was not a conscious thing but I gradually began to see things differently. Before my training in The Son-Rise Program, I had been viewing Tim's autism as a tragedy, a dead end, as a hopeless thing that I could not change or do anything about. I had seen it as something that could just get worse and that however hard I fought, I wouldn't be able to make a big enough difference or change the path of his life.

But, as the week had progressed, I began to see that Tim's processing and connecting issues were all things that could change and grow – that he was in no way written off. And that there were many ways I could help him with every aspect of what he was experiencing. There was something I could *do*.

This led to a sense of empowerment and excitement at all the possibilities for my relationship with him. My head started to fill up with all the ways I could connect to him, help his speech development, reduce his overloads and start to see progress. I became genuinely excited – and this excitement left a lot less room for grief, sadness and hopelessness. You can't really feel hopelessness to the same level when you have a spark of hope.

Chapter Seven – Let's get started

When we came back from our five days of training, Erik and I couldn't wait to get started. We spent the first whole day on the floor with Tim, at his level, being with him, responding to him, positioning ourselves for eye contact and celebrating when he cast glances in our direction. We were seeing him in a completely different light.

It all moved at quite a pace – I was beginning to recognise when he was being exclusive and when he was available, but seeing it and responding were two different things. I could see it would take practice. As we watched him in his heightened states of repetitive and exclusive behaviours, we could now understand why he needed to do it. But on that first day we equally had huge moments of contact and connection and lots of fun and silliness. We joined with him, played with him and celebrated his every attempt to communicate with us.

Many of these techniques were firsts for us – focusing on eye contact, encouraging him to continue doing what he loved instead of stopping him, using these things to draw out his interactive attention and creating high levels of motivation for him to speak. It was as if we now had a manual to work from. When watching him walk around and talk to his hand, for the first time I didn't get wound up while he did it. I didn't need to expend any energy in worrying about what I should be doing or how I could stop him, or how long he'd scream when I did. I had a new mindset.

The first time I joined Tim was in the lounge, lining up DVD cases on the table. He looked at me as if I was a bit odd, and clearly didn't really want me to join him – taking all my DVD cases and putting them in his own pile. However, I calmly found a few more (not the ones he was playing with) and carried on lining them up. I remember when he looked at me out of the corner of his eye, I gave him a huge smile and said something like, 'Hey! It's so nice to see you!' which he found funny. From there, he wanted to draw around the DVD cases and allowed me to share for a while in his activity, so we started drawing around the cases and connecting together. It was actually working – straight away. Wow!

Erik and I followed Tim all over the house that first day, celebrating every bit of eye contact and response and delighting in everything he did. It was the first time I had ever let go of tasks and expectations in order to prioritise connection. My new understanding was starting to make all the difference.

I Now See Why We Need a Playroom

A few days later, when I was joining him and we had started engaging and laughing, the telephone rang. I decided not to answer it, but hadn't reckoned on Tim trotting off to pick up the receiver. And while I was talking, Tim turned the telly on. When I had finished the call, I tried to reason with him to turn the telly off – and it turned into a major battle. And we had been engaging so well...

I could *totally* see the point of a playroom!

Tim's Playroom

When we mentioned in our church what we were doing, a carpenter friend of ours, Kevin, offered to turn our bedroom into Tim's playroom – even more amazing, he wanted no money for it. In fact he did a job for someone else and instead of asking them to pay him, he asked them to contribute to Tim's playroom. That paid for all the materials and he gave all his time for free. Is this what the Son-Rise Program® Trainers meant when they said we would be surprised at people's willingness to help us and be part of this project?

Erik and I had decided to turn our bedroom over to Tim, as it was the biggest room in the house, in order for it to become his bedroom/playroom. We would move into Tim's current bedroom, which had just enough room for our bed. We didn't have enough rooms for Tim to have a separate playroom, so his bedroom would also need to be his playroom. Kevin took off the door to Tim's room and replaced it with a new one featuring a two-way mirror so we could watch the volunteers working with Tim and see his responses. Kevin then put up four big shelves, two on either side of the room, up high, so that Tim would have to ask for what he wanted. Excellent!

The whole playroom-building experience totally threw Tim though. He was very unsettled having to sleep in a different room and having someone else walking in and out of the house. His behaviour became more erratic and his responses more limited. With our new understanding, we expected this level of insecurity and were confident that he would settle back to normal once it was all finished. And we were right.

First Son-Rise Program Sessions

When we had our playroom set up and Tim in a flexi-school situation where we collected him from school every lunchtime, we started our proper first afternoon sessions. Initially, Tim cried for almost half an hour and his stress and tantrums started kicking in straight away. This was to be expected as he never liked any kind of structure around him and always wanted to be free to run around the house from room to room.

Tim's Initial Resistance and His Reasons

Despite the fact that we actually wanted to give him autonomy, comfort and freedom of expression, the irony was that to start with, we needed Tim to find a way to *realise* that he would be given the fun and freedom he needed. We couldn't explain it at this point and until he experienced it, he couldn't know. But if he ran all over the house there was never a point of stillness where we could start to be with him and relate, allowing him to start seeing that being with us could be a good thing.

I knew that when he could have fun with us, he wouldn't have any desire to fight. In some ways he was fighting the unknown, as he always did. At this point, as I mentioned before, we couldn't explain concepts or happenings to him. We couldn't say, 'Come with me into this room and I will do what you want to do and I will be your friend and we will have fun together'. It would have been so helpful if we could have done. Equally we couldn't say, 'We can't have chips now but we can have them tonight' or, 'I am going now but I will be back soon'. Tim seemed to believe that when I left the house that I would be gone forever.

Tim would only start to accept something new if he could see for himself what was involved. As he struggled with the concept of time, we knew that he couldn't grasp that his play time would only be for a short while. Sometimes I thought that he believed everything he did would last forever. Therefore, initial resistance on his part while playing in the playroom was fully expected.

Because of these thoughts and beliefs, during his first session with Erik, he kept trying to persuade Erik to open the door, taking his hand and pulling him there. Erik stayed calm and loving with him as he attempted to engage Tim in activities but let go affectionately when Tim was having none of it. The biggest difference here was that he stayed present and supportive with Tim all through his emotional desperation and when Tim finally decided that he would see what Erik had to offer, after half an hour, Erik was ready to love and play with him. It was incredible to see Tim's body visibly relax as he rested against Erik. Erik cuddled him and spoke softly to him. By being so close to Erik, Tim was already showing signs of being available. Tim was not initiating, so Erik suggested a ball game and Tim agreed.

To engage Tim a little, Erik put a ping pong ball in his mouth and spat it out across the room – this made Tim laugh and he then wanted more so he started requesting that Erik 'eat the ball' again. This was an opportunity for Erik to ask Tim to look at him and the game continued with requesting, eye contact and response for a good ten minutes. Finding a way to engage Tim was half the work at this stage. We hadn't yet found his highest motivations in the playroom so were trying different things. At one point, Tim was repeatedly flopping himself on to a beanbag and Erik joined him in the best way he could. Tim himself then initiated a game of pretending to be asleep. He demanded that Erik also pretend to be asleep. It all went quiet, then Tim sounded the alarm and Erik woke up all surprised. Tim adored this reaction and wanted to play again and again, so this was yet more opportunities for eye contact, talking and responding. I could see how when your child wants to do something again and again, instead of getting frustrated at the repetitious nature of it, you can *use* it for all the things you want to teach.

This was such a gorgeous way to play with Tim. It felt so loving and so natural, so human and personal and responsive. I could now see that Tim's difficulties were massively based around human interaction and that this was the way to reach him. Oh my goodness. I remembered how I had visualised his autism as being like a block of ice. *This* was a way to melt it! I could almost tangibly see the 'melting' take place. We were empowered!

I knew we were at the beginning of a long journey and had some big things to shift but having seen the response and delight in Tim and the loving, spontaneous nature of the approach I felt ready for the long haul. I could see how this could bring him to a place where he could be with us happily, even if it would take a while. This was the beginning of the 'extreme measures' but it felt OK and I thought back to Samahria Kaufman's journey with Raun and how she saw it as working towards what she wanted and not in any way a sacrifice.

This was totally what we wanted and now we had been given tools. We were on our way.

We explained the Son-Rise Program approach to Siobhan and she tried a session with Tim. He adored wrapping parcels and playing pass the parcel at this stage and she entered the room with him armed with heaps of wrapping paper, scissors, sellotape, and a CD player. He was so excited! When he realised that Siobhan would play again and again what he wanted to do and didn't say it was time to stop but kept saying 'yes, we can do some more', the look on his face was a picture. His talking was very sporadic and he would clench his fists to his chest and would make occasional leaps around in excitement – but it was excitement, not misery. He was highly *motivated* and Siobhan was using every opportunity to encourage him to look at her and to tell her what he wanted in order for her to make it happen.

Moving Between Exclusivity and Interaction

Over the next few months, Tim moved constantly between interacting and being exclusive with the interaction gradually outweighing the exclusivity. One of his isms, as I previously mentioned, involved putting books out in front of him, making repetitive noises and saying occasional words. We had hoped that the words he said were relevant to the books he was looking at – until one day we found him on his own, poring over the telephone book and talking in the same way. Clearly his talking wasn't related to the pictures he was seeing. We realised this was an ism as he was doing it both repetitively and exclusively. We were learning all the time to analyse where he was in terms of being exclusive and interactive.

During our play sessions with Tim, we were also starting to recognise red and green lights. Initially, we often mis-read him, especially as we were changing from a very directed approach to a totally responsive one. Once Erik was joining him in wrapping and unwrapping DVDs and he asked, 'How many DVDs are there?'

Tim didn't respond at all. Erik couldn't make him hear him and he couldn't make him respond. Erik could see he wasn't in a place to respond so he let it go. By asking Tim a question, he had been testing the water to see if Tim was open and responsive, as he seemed to be letting Erik in, but he wasn't. So Erik went back to joining him by wrapping and opening parcels. On analysis, Tim was open to a connection through joining but wasn't yet ready to fit into any other agenda than his.

Emotionally Attuned Intervention

It was interesting, though, because Tim did start to look at Erik more when Erik was unwrapping parcels, with an element of camaraderie – being on the same side. There wasn't any feeling of 'you versus me'. It was very much 'in it together'. I liked this. We played for hours like this.

Emotional Bond Developing

Another game they played was that Tim would touch Erik on various parts of his face and he would make silly noises. So, if Tim touched Erik on the chin he would make one kind of noise and if he touched him on the nose he would make another. Tim found this highly amusing and kept reaching for Erik. So Erik used this to help him with his speech by saying, 'Do you want to touch Papa's chin? Look at Papa then…what do you say?'

'Pa..pa… can… I… touch… on…the…chin?' Tim would say most of this without looking at Erik while Erik moved himself about constantly positioning himself to make it easy for Tim to look at him. He finally gave Erik a brief flash of eye contact as he finished speaking and Erik cried out, *'Yes, you can!'* and they immediately immersed themselves in a silly chin-touching/ridiculous noise game.

After a while of continuous noise-making, Erik needed to breathe, so he pulled Tim off and said 'I can't do this anymore!' but then added, 'Do you want to do it again?'

'Yes!'

'Can you *ask* again?'

Then Tim suddenly changed tack and said, 'Play with ball?'

Coming Back for More Play

This was the great thing. We were going with him. We were not dictating. It was a very fluid, constantly moving process but the emotional bond was momentarily sky high and Tim came back to us for more of this because he liked it. Erik was using every opportunity to encourage Tim to look at him and acknowledge him. He sometimes asked Tim to look at him and told him how great it was when he did. He held a ball close to his eyes so Tim naturally looked towards him when he wanted it.

In my opinion you can't go wrong with this process. You can't do harm and you can only create better and stronger bonds with children.

When Tim said, 'Play with ball?', Erik knew he wanted to play a particular game where Erik opened his arms wide and would throw the ball from one hand to the other while Tim tried to get it off him. Erik looked at Tim.

Tim was looking meaningfully at him and opening his own arms to show Erik what he wanted him to do.

Erik asked him, 'Do you want me to open my arms wide?'

And Tim said, 'Yes.'

'Can you say Papa, can you hold?'

Tim echoed, 'Can you hold?'

'Arms,' prompted Erik.

'Arms,' said Tim.

'Wide?'

'Wide?' repeated Tim.

'Do you want me to do that? Yes?

'OK!' said Tim.

And the game started. Every time it came to a standstill, Erik asked Tim to ask him again.

This looks like Tim is saying something and being rewarded by a game. What's the difference here from ABA or the school system? The biggest difference is that we as the adults are willing to let go of our agenda. There is no coercion. Tim is asking because he *wants* to and not because he has to. We were also waiting for the desire to initiate to come from him and celebrating his every attempt at communicating by engaging with him. Importantly, we were prepared to immediately go back to joining him if he returned to his exclusive behaviours. Finally, we were not only praising him when he got his communication accurate, we were celebrating every effort he made.

Tim's interactive attention span was so short at this point that the game only lasted about a minute.

Let's Get the Television Out of the House

After we had been doing the Son-Rise Program for a while, Erik and I decided to take the step of removing the telly. Our beliefs as to why we were doing it were exceptionally strong, which is why, bizarrely it didn't feel like we were doing an awful thing. If I had honestly believed we were being unfair on Tim, I would have found it hard to do but I actually felt we were only being helpful to him. We weren't just looking at his present-day requirements, we were looking long term and how different his life would be if he could interact and communicate with us more easily. I had no qualms. I was, however, concerned as to how he would react.

When Tim was at school one morning, Erik and I took the telly from our bedroom and the one from the lounge and put them out in the garage – then I went round the house removing all the DVDs that I could find, Tim's and ours – and put them in a box. I took the box to the garage so that I wouldn't be lying when I said to Tim that they weren't in the house. Then I went to collect him from school.

He came into the house and immediately looked for the telly. His reaction, however, was totally not what I was expecting. He looked for the telly and for his DVDs, but he genuinely didn't seem bothered that he couldn't find them. He never asked for them and I chose not to say anything about it. Instead, I took him to his new happy place – the playroom – where he immediately started playing one of his favourite games, without bothering to look further for the missing telly. While he couldn't tell me his feelings, he was perfectly able to make us understand when he was unhappy about something – and no telly certainly didn't seem like a tragedy to him. He didn't get upset or run around looking to any major degree – he just let go of it and started playing with me. I couldn't believe it, but I was delighted. Perhaps by now he understood that playing with me was more fun than watching telly.

We kept him off the telly and electronics for two whole years. In fact, we all went cold turkey with the telly for the first six months as Erik and I didn't want to ask Tim to do something we weren't prepared to do ourselves. Our house was quieter with no background noise – but it had a warm and friendly atmosphere where we were always open for interaction. Books and toys were continuously around and over a period of time, Tim seemed to get bored and started picking up books and comics to look at them. It was at this stage that he started to learn to read.

After six months, personally, I really missed comedy and Erik and I put a little telly back in our bedroom so we could have some switch off time for half an hour or so in an evening. We put a blanket over it and interestingly even when Tim saw it, he seemed indifferent, maybe because other elements of his life had become more fulfilling and stimulating.

Interestingly, when aged ten Tim confided in me that he remembered when I took all his DVDs away. It was obviously a big thing for him as it had stuck in his memory, even though he hadn't been able to talk about it at the time. I still believe that it was the best decision ever. When aged fourteen, he even told me he was pleased I had done it. He had suffered no ill effects at all – only positive gains.

Dictation Sessions

When Tim realised we were willing do things he wanted us to do with him for long periods of time, he started wanting to dictate stories to us. Brilliant. If he was initiating this, we would go along with it. This was what it was all about. He was using words to ask us to do things and we were responding. He then took one of his story books and asked me to write in it. He wanted to dictate the words and wanted to tell me exactly where to write them.

I had to confront one of my own inner rules that you don't write in books that you have bought, as how can you then pass them on to other people? It felt wrong… but then I turned my thinking around. This was one of the areas where Tim *wanted* communication – it was something *he* was initiating – it was going to *help* in his communication. I reasoned that it didn't matter if we wrote in an entire library's worth of books. His development was far more important than any amount of material possessions. This was obviously part of the processing he needed to go through and I chose to trust him that he had good reasons to want to do this.

As it happened, this process of dictating stories went on for over two years – and it did move on to blank exercise books. It became the default activity he nearly always wanted to do. It was hard work and required a serious attitude decision each time, as he was so specific and pedantic but the fact that he was communicating at all was so brilliant and that's what I was now aware of.

We became as user-friendly around him as we could and he could be as controlling and dictatorial as he needed to be. He would tell us exactly what to write, where to write it and exactly where to put full stops, which he called 'dots'. Soon we began to see fantastic ways to use this activity. He was not flexible enough to let us question him on what he wanted to say yet, even though what he dictated made very little sense to us and sometimes he wanted just one nonsensical word on a page. However, as he wanted us to write these things so much we could ask him to look at us as he asked us and could check with him sometimes if we had 'got it right' – another opportunity to engage with us. We always tried to be as fun and silly as we could with him.

He then progressed to wanting us to draw pictures with his dictated stories. Even now, it's a surprise when recalling just how many pictures we drew, and the hours and hours we spent writing nonsensical stories. There isn't one volunteer that doesn't have vivid memories of the dictation sessions and the sometimes sinking feeling about our artistic abilities when Tim said things like, 'Can you draw Nana at the table playing a trombone?'

It was a very intense process and hard to just go along with it. There was no imagination that we could relate to within his thinking, but we now knew to accept his processes instead of saying things like, 'but that makes no sense' and 'why don't you put this instead?' and 'what do you really mean with that?'.

It took a continuous outworking of our chosen attitude, especially as he never seemed to tire of it. The pictures went through phases, with drawings of characters sitting round tables with presents in front of them; pictures of family members all on stage playing various instruments etc… We were of course, following his thought patterns but we obviously couldn't stop ourselves trying to work out where he was going with certain thoughts and ideas. It was people he knew, cartoon characters, musical instruments, presents – lots of things he was motivated by. His thoughts were all being outworked through our (often very bad) drawings. Interestingly, he never minded that most of us couldn't draw. We never tried to correct him or make him tell us his thought patterns but we were using this process to start to encourage a desire in him for social interaction.

We were using these interests of his to engage with him at every level we could, seeing if there were little windows where we could join him in his thinking and if there might be a little flexibility in his thought patterns. When he asked us to draw something we could ask him where on the page he would like it, what colour he would like it and so on. This started to expand our communication and introduce elements of flexibility in his thinking. Knowing the point wasn't to correct him, teach him or suggest things went against my grain as a teacher. We just kept reminding ourselves to connect, connect, connect – and always that connection was more important than any achievement. Because connection *was* achievement. Connection *was* the goal.

We could see where he was in his flexibility at this stage, because when we suggested adding something of our own to the picture or maybe drawing something in a different colour, he would ignore us – as if we hadn't spoken – or he would get cross, making his 'no' very clear. He had his agenda and nothing was going to get in the way of this, so we would back off and continue to let him lead the activity.

I could see that with this new approach he would have every reason to want to be with us and start to enjoy our company. We would put no pressure on him but would only love to be with him and go with whatever he wanted or needed to do.

In fact, the more we adapted to the approach, the easier it became and the more it made sense. We all had the belief that he could progress this way. Now it was all about adapting, changing, growing, learning and giving Tim the biggest gift of our time and attention for days, weeks, months, years, however long he needed.

What an unusual thing to do. We were trusting our child that he knew what his processes were and we were giving him control. Large chunks of the day were in his control but we were making connections. It's like a drug. You can become addicted to the high you feel when your child makes a connection with you. This wasn't theory anymore. We were outworking the Son-Rise Program in practice. It was hard work and challenged us on all levels – our feelings, our work/life balance, hardly going out and feeling quite reclusive. Yet I felt a tremendous excitement about the inroads we were starting to make.

Volunteers

We had tried to find people to help us before, but this felt a little different as we were more convinced of what we were doing and asking of our friends. Thank God we belonged to a church filled with people who loved us, as it gave us an immediate platform to ask for the help we needed. It still didn't feel natural and took us both out of our comfort zones but we had a goal and a plan. We booked a hall and a time and we invited anyone who wanted to find out about what we were doing to come along and join us there. About twenty people came. I had a talk prepared about where we had come from and about Tim's autism and how we were already helping him. We showed some of the Son-Rise Program DVDs of children who had progressed and talked about what we would need them to do if they wanted to be part of this journey with us.

At the end of the afternoon, six people said they were serious about helping us and one said she would have to wait until she had left her full-time job but would help us then. Another didn't think she could work with Tim, but would be willing to come to our house to help me clean. Wow!

We trained our lovely volunteers in all the aspects of the Son-Rise Program we had learnt and they would come as much as possible to play with Tim. He was still currently full-time in school so we could only do short moments in the week and longer times in the weekends. We would continuously discuss how Tim was and how he was doing, how we felt and what had happened in the playroom. It was important that we all felt OK when we were in the playroom with Tim, as he picked up on every bit of stress or angst. Any negativity or feeling of boredom would push him away and yet any good feeling of fun, love and connection warmed him into wanting to communicate – which was the whole aim. It was hard to expect someone to be happy if they came in the house distressed about something in their own lives, so we would often talk things through and put ourselves right before we went in there. We all supported each other as best we could so we could be in the best states to play with Tim.

I am so unbelievably grateful to my friends – Gel, Janina, Rosie, Dani, Steve, Cathy, Rachel, Karen, Joy – for the fact that they gave of their time so willingly – and that they also found places in themselves to be just what Tim needed them to be.

Who wouldn't want to be loved in this non-judgemental way? Everyone wants someone to care about what they care about and do what they want to do with them. Everyone wants to be loved unconditionally and everyone wants to be celebrated –albeit in ways that they are comfortable with. Even for a child who doesn't have an ounce of developmental difficulty and is totally teachable, it is a brilliant approach…

I remember thinking that I would like to be loved in the way that the Son-Rise Program approach loves people. It would definitely bring out the best in me. We are all complex and need love – not just children with autism.

Volunteer's Views

STEVE: It was quite a few years ago, now, but some things still stick in my head. Tim adored the trampoline; we were on it together for hours… and hours… and hours... and hours! He never seemed to grow tired of it. It was repetitive stuff, but did it mean that Tim let me into his world? Absolutely it did! On that trampoline we were certainly connecting, soul to soul. And it was probably good fitness for me, anyway! Indoors, I have clear memories of reading Thomas the Tank Engine stories to him; he loved hearing about 'The Fat Controller'! He also liked dictating things for me to write down. This included numbers. Everything had to be exactly as he prescribed; "i's" had to be dotted, "t's" had to be crossed. I remember once writing numbers down, starting from 1. When we got to 7 he completely freaked out. It took me a while to realise that it was my 7 that he didn't like – I tend to use the continental form of the number which has a horizontal line in the middle. With Tim, though, you couldn't do that sort of thing. It was important not to allow his tantrums to upset us and to stay calm throughout, while trying to find out what was causing the upset and putting it right if it was within our power (sometimes it wasn't!). We did lots of English and counting which was great, but the main thing was the eye-contact, communication, praise, excitement and connection. Tim had a little chant that went "Gootagootagoot, gootagootagoot". Sally had no idea where it came from. I figured I would join in – anything which might build empathy, really. Oh – and I remember the pass-the-parcel games, too!

My question to Steve – what made you help us? 'You were my mates, Sally, and no one likes to see their mates unhappy! Simple as that!'

JANINA: 'Once we latched on to something that *he* was allowing us to do with him, we ran with it. He used to reel off all these things that were on the back of the DVDs he'd had and we used to have to draw them. So we used to have to use our memories of what the DVD logos looked like – BBC logos etc – but if we got it wrong he would say it was wrong and we'd have to do it again – but we had nothing to copy! I've got to say, when I see DVDs now it makes me chuckle – he had minute attention to detail in everything and if you didn't do it his way, you definitely knew about it.

'But he was including us – and the whole thing was, it wasn't for us to change him, it was for him to change *us* into a way that we could relate to him. You can't walk into somebody's house and tell them what to do. We went into that room, not wanting for him to join us – it was for him to invite us into what he was doing – to include us.

'The biggest thing was, you desperately wanted for him to be OK with you doing things so it didn't matter how many hundreds of times we did the same thing, because he had accepted us and we were allowed in his world – almost like a privilege. There were only a few of us who could actually 'read' Tim – you just knew the way of doing things and once you knew that, you could then slowly bring other things in. We slowly built his ability to take instruction

– we went from him dictating every single thing we did, to him being willing to do what we were asking and that's when we were able to slowly bring in new things…

'With what we were doing, we knew there was going to be an end result – we didn't know when but we all knew, eventually, this little boy who's stuck in his own little world was going to come out the other end with a lot of skills but for him to have that he needed to go through this.

'We had to allow Tim to 'run his course' – for days, weeks, months! But it was his way of expressing things. I never had a doubt because when you gave the presentation about the Son-Rise Program you gave us stories and testimonies of it working. We knew what we were taking on. We were prepared to try and help. There wasn't a doubt of this never working. We had an idea that Tim needed x, y and z and we had to keep going with it. Yes, it was hard work – you walked away thinking 'bloody hell!' But it was never draining as in 'I don't want to do this again.

'Some three years later, that very first time when he stood up in church and sang, Rosie, Dani and I were at the back of the church in tears because we could actually say we were part of that – and it's that whole thing of feeling like we just knew – and you guys knew who was part of that – to get that little boy up on the stage singing.'

My question to Janina – 'What made you help us?' I've always wanted to do something for somebody – if it makes your life that little bit easier. When I started coming to church, I got to notice you and your little boy. He didn't like being in one position and he was very distraught and I could see that you guys struggled just to have him sitting with you and that he was so distressed. I know it takes a lot to stand up and ask for help, so if I've got time, why wouldn't I volunteer?

What to Do About School?

Tim was still in school at this point. We felt it was a massive decision to take him out – in fact, we didn't know if the three of us could stand up under the strain. We both had to work and we were also worried about our lives imploding if we did full-time schooling at home.

We so wanted to do as much of The Son-Rise Program as possible with Tim but we panicked. We felt that to take Tim out of school full-time would create too much pressure for us as a family. For a start Erik needed to work and I was teaching part-time – how could we do this? But how could we not do this? The answer we came up with was for Tim to attend school in the morning and have sessions in The Son-Rise Program in the afternoon. This wasn't ideal but it was the best we could do at the time, if we were to keep ourselves sane. Then, we reasoned, he would be at least getting some social/community input in the mornings and we could start to connect to him on a one-to-one in the afternoons.

When we researched this arrangement to see if it was allowed within the education system, we found that typical children were allowed to be flexi-schooled but children with statements or particular needs weren't. What? That's discrimination! We looked into it a lot more, asked, were told no and obviously, decided to ask again. We knew this was what we wanted. We knew that to be in school full-time was too much for Tim, but to be home full-time was too much for us! There *had* to be a way forward for this. This seemed to lack reason.

Erik did a 'sit in'. Being a social worker, he knew the system and he went to the office of the lady who was head of Special Needs in West Sussex and sat down outside her office… and waited… and waited… until… he had to go home because she actually wasn't coming in. Not a very dramatic sit-in! But because he had been there, she called him the next day and arranged to talk about it further, when she explained that it would have to be a Panel decision.

Panel were a group of people who didn't know us or Tim but who had the right to make decisions about his life. We weren't allowed to talk to them, but we were allowed to write – very gracious of them! We wrote and waited and waited. I wondered what we would do if they said no. This *had* to be the answer. But how can people who don't even know him make decisions like this about his life? Deferring your child's life to people who don't know him or care is one of the greatest feelings of disempowerment I have experienced.

I remember I was training a group of schoolteachers locally when Erik dropped in to tell me the good news that they had said yes. A way forward. Phew! Just sometimes policies can change and people can come down on the side of a child. What didn't feel nice was that Tim's life was at the mercy of people who didn't even know him. That was something we would still experience a lot more and it was a feeling I never got used to.

Following this news, we spent the next three years taking Tim to school in the mornings and doing sessions in The Son-Rise Program in the afternoon.

Systems, Panels and Experts

We were about to embark on a world of systems, panels and experts – people who didn't know Tim making decisions for his life. We were also at the beginning of a journey full of autism 'specialists' who would visit Tim for an hour or two in school, sum him up and work out what they thought would help – as in what most 'autistic children need' and write a report which seemingly nobody adhered to. My friend calls it 'parachuting in'. Do I sound sarcastic? There's just something so frustrating when your child's development is so important but is so out of your hands. I just think parents need to be much more involved. We are the ones who have our child most of the time and have their best interests forever. In the last ten years we have had heaps of fun experience with systems, panels and experts. I use the word 'fun' to stop myself from swearing.

I can see why parents take their children out of the school system, to regain empowerment and focus on what their children really need, rather than what some random stranger dictates they need.

Tim's First Sports Day at School

As I mentioned, Tim was still at school in the mornings and it was coming to the end of the school year – at this point he was nearly six years old. I was looking forward to Tim's Year 1 Sports Day. I looked forward to the prospect of seeing him take part in this school activity, especially as he loved running. Erik and I pulled up outside the school and heard shouts of excitement coming from the field. There were loads of parents and children and the field was buzzing with anticipation and the feeling of summer. I scanned the field looking for Tim's class to see if I could single him out. I saw his class but I couldn't see him anywhere. So I looked over towards his classroom.

A child was lying face down on the grass, sobbing and refusing to move. Two classroom assistants were trying to get him to stand up but he was having none of it. Erik and I walked over. We got down to his level and spoke to him. It was OK. It didn't matter *at all* if he couldn't be part of Sports Day. We wanted him to know that. We would happily take him home now and it would all be OK. We walked with him past the field of shouting, excited children and comforted him and each other. It was OK. He wasn't ready. It was totally understandable on a sensory overload level that he couldn't cope with this right now. We wanted him to know it was OK, we loved him totally, it didn't matter at all and we would help him.

This might not seem like a big thing – but the big thing that had changed was in me – my understanding and my attitude. Despite my disappointment, I didn't need to despair – we were working on it. He was not ready to cope with such an event, yet. We would look after him and nurture him and give him the input he needed to make him stronger in this area, until he was ready. And if he never was, we would love him just the same.

No Doubts

Looking back, I find it interesting that we never questioned whether we *should* do The Son-Rise Program with Tim. We knew we were allowing him control as part of a process to give him his autonomy and we chose to trust him in that process. It was obvious he had a need to do this and it was a way to reach him. Though we didn't know how long it would take, we never felt the need to waver from the path. The path made sense, even though we knew it could take a long time.

Chapter Eight – Throwing ourselves into his world

For the next year, during which Tim turned seven, we threw ourselves totally into the world of connection, development and friendships. Our volunteers came every afternoon and would be immersed in play – connecting with Tim wherever he was – trampolining, dictating stories, reading books, silliness, or rough and tumble.

Out of the playroom, we tried everything and anything to see what would motivate Tim to stay connected to a task and found that there was something in painting that he quite liked. My friend, Dee, had recently taught me silk painting and I found that Tim really enjoyed it too. I would create the shapes and pictures with the special pen and he would spend ages putting the paints onto the silk and watching them spread out and to the edges of the material. We made loads cakes from packets, over and over – even though he never wanted to eat them, he liked the process. We would take out chime bars and drums and make music and we would look at books together.

I would invite his friends round and we would make cakes, do paintings and *anything* that he could do with a friend alongside. He was not yet ready for real interactive play, but he could play and do things alongside other children and that was something we constantly encouraged .

Deciding to have no telly for a while can really open up your life to more creative outlets. There is so much time to be filled and we started to find that outside the sessions Tim had in the playroom, he was choosing to engage in activities where we interacted together.

Whenever we were at family gatherings, Tim still was driven to engage in his dictation activity with whoever he could find to be willing. At my Nana's 92nd birthday, he sat next to my brother and his wife, pedantically dictating to them what to write and where to write it. He got cross when they didn't cooperate totally with what he wanted – and we had to explain in advance that he could be like this. We were constantly having to explain him to other people, but he also had an endearing quality which drew people to want to work with him. He was such a mixture – charming yet complex.

Tim was pulled like a magnetic force to his need to ism and his powerful interests. Wherever we were, we had choices – to go with him, try and stop him or ignore him. Well, ethically we knew stopping him was wrong and ignoring him was unkind. As we could now see the reasons for his needing to do these things, we didn't consider these an option. Going with him and being with him in the process was the best option. However, it was a rollercoaster ride – we never knew where he was taking us. It was also constant.

When we got tired, people who didn't understand our situation would suggest that we just tell Tim we wanted to do something else for a while, but this wouldn't have worked. Tim was a constant powerhouse of energy always headed in his specific direction and if we were not drawing that energy into interactive tasks and connections, it would be poured into exclusive thoughts and isms.

Whereas the telly had previously been his down time, dictating to us became his new downtime, which meant that loads more time was being spent on interaction. We tried to have interests outside of all this, but it was hard to maintain things other than work due to this constant pull on our time.

Erik and I ended up putting all of our 'un-Tim' time into developing businesses with the goal of becoming self-employed and more independent to eventually allow more time for the things we needed to do. I was highly motivated in the creative element of work and he had a great entrepreneurial spirit which kept driving him forward. He was always looking for ways to help us to be freer in terms of our time and finance so that we could put more undivided time into Tim and his development. At one point we had a bit of a laugh when discussing all the businesses he had thought up and some which he had started which hadn't worked. He was a great believer in trying and trying until something succeeds. This was our mindset for both Tim's developmental path and business.

I had a very clear vision for a musical scheme of work for primary schools and worked on this at every spare opportunity I had. I was convinced I could create a product that would sell. It also made my regular work more fun if I had a higher purpose of creating a product. I wrote a series of structured, easy-to-follow of lesson plans and made over 600 videos of children playing the games, to help the teachers for children from Reception through to Year 6. The growing scale of this project hadn't been my intention at the beginning, but my creative ideas just kept coming turning this into a far more ambitious venture. I think, in the midst of all the uncertainty about Tim's life, this was something I could control – and besides, it was a worthwhile undertaking that I knew there was a real demand for such a product. Because of what we were going through, it took ten years instead of the few I had originally intended, but Active Music now sells worldwide and brings in a decent portion of our income, allowing Erik and I to spend more time with our children.

Mindset

I remember coming home from work on some days – a whole day teaching in a local school – and sitting outside in the car, gathering myself, and knowing that the degree to which I had given my attention in the day to nearly 200 children was nothing compared to the level to which I would be needed when I walked in the door. That's when the real work would start.

I once commented to my Headteacher that it was easier to stay on at school and work than to work at home and she said, 'Can't you just tell Tim you have work to do?' This made me realise how hard it was for other people to understand. Tim wouldn't have understood these words and not only that, if I wanted him to learn to communicate I would have to be available and communicate all the time too. Ten minutes a day wasn't going to do it and if I did leave him alone at any point without trying to draw him in, he would immediately retreat into his exclusive world. I think that's one of the hardest things for people on the outside to understand. Unless we connected with him, Tim would be exclusive all the time. We couldn't afford to leave him alone. We needed to be open and flexible around him *all the time* if we were going to make a difference.

What helped me here was my mindset. Although I was tired, I was genuinely excited about Tim's development. My motivation never waned and my love for him only increased. I had also learnt the Son-Rise Program® principle of noticing and celebrating all the good things Tim could do, which provided constant fuel for my motivation. In fact, I was also starting to use aspects of The Son-Rise Program techniques in my every-day teaching. The more I learnt about it, the more I could see that what a fantastic approach it is for every child. Which child wouldn't want an adult to see where they are really coming from, join them where they are, love them unconditionally, never criticize when they are wrong and celebrate every step of their achievement? I would! When you do this, children develop more trust with you, becoming kinder and more trusting themselves.

Church

Because of our decision not to force Tim into unnecessary stress, we decided that as he could not access the children's groups in church, that we wouldn't even attempt to make him join. He could just about handle generally being 'around' during the music, so we decided we'd go together for that part of the Service and then one of us would bring him home and do a session in The Son-Rise Program with him. This was definitely the right thing to do. We were going to work with him and help him to develop more strength before attempting to include him in groups he wasn't ready for.

However, I personally found it gutting to leave a room full of friends to come home and be on my own with Tim during this time. While my excitement and motivation with what we were doing towards Tim's development never wavered, I have always needed the company of my friends to renew and replenish my sense of self. This was one of the hardest aspects of our new life and therefore, I had to be really creative in finding ways and moments to see friends.

Environment

It was becoming increasingly clear to me that his environment had a massive effect on Tim. The environment at home was altered to be accessible for him. It was nurturing and flexible, so he could be assured of immediate interest if he wanted to communicate and therefore he started opening up. By contrast, the environment at school in the mornings was loud, unpredictable, full of the needs and demands of the other children around him (which I increasingly realised he found hard to deal with), sudden bells, the scraping of chairs and adults constantly having specific expectations of him. It was as though sensing other people's expectations caused an inner stress so great that he couldn't function and he shut down.

While obviously we wanted him to eventually be able to learn in such an environment, at that time, he wasn't even progressing in his language skills, due to his stress levels. I also realised that the environment wasn't just about the space, noise and unpredictability, it was about the attitude and flexibility of the people around him, too.

Sounds and Music

Tim's reactions to sounds and music were complex and, at times, contradictory. At the age of four he had sung elements of James Blunt songs in the car, pouring out renditions of 'You're Beautiful' and he would sing nursery rhymes such as 'Ten Green Bottles', in his own way repeatedly, seeming to enjoy it. He would sometimes go up to the piano and play random notes when he wanted to and occasionally he strummed on Erik's guitar when he felt like it. He'd been able to take part on his fifth birthday, when Bungle the clown, had children at the front singing a very silly song, replacing words with sound effects which had the children rolling around with laughter. The only lessons he didn't always resist at school were music activities and he had even been able to stand at the back of the hall and sing some of the songs for the school Christmas plays.

However, by contrast – if I so much as touched a key on my piano, never mind play it – Tim would scream, 'No no no!' and either try desperately to stop me or run away in distress. His reaction was mostly the same if Erik tried to play his guitar. He just couldn't let us do these things. So we were left wondering whether it was the actual sounds causing him distress, or the fact that we were the ones producing them, as it was taking us away from being available to – a form of separation anxiety, perhaps.

Sometimes Erik would decide to be strict and tell Tim that he was now going to play the guitar in the kitchen and that if he really didn't like it he could go to his room for a little while. But it never worked. On other occasions, Erik would leave Tim with me and go off to the furthest room in the house to play, but Tim immediately run after him, demanding that he stop.

Nobody had any definitive answers. Jackie from ABA had said that it was all about his need to control. When he was making sounds that he wanted to hear, he could tolerate it but when we made sounds he couldn't cope, proving that it was all to do with his wanting and wishes rather than any physical pain. She had also suggested that we introduce him to our instrumental playing by playing Tim some of Erik's recorded music and singing rather confronting him with the live version. But we already knew that Tim could happily listen to CDs of Erik singing, so this wasn't the issue.

However there were occasions when he was distracted in a room full of people and someone would play a few notes on the piano and he didn't actually notice or jump up to stop us. But this could have been because he was already shut down due to being stressed and overloaded, anyway… It all seemed so random.

While I was busy creating Active Music DVDs, Tim sometimes saw them over my shoulder and seemed interested watching the children play the singing games. I encouraged this so that he would repeatedly watch them, and occasionally would hum or join in some clapping, evidently enjoying it.

Because of this, Erik and I decided to let him come along to some of the all-day music workshops I regularly ran for forty children in my school on a Saturday. He was often very excited to come. Erik would bring him along for a while, depending on how much he could cope with. Often it would take Tim a while to get from the car to the staffroom. Occasionally a few of the other children would come in to see him, which sometimes created a bit of connection which he liked but it could just as easily overwhelm him. His stress levels and sense of fear at these times could engulf him to the point where he could hardly think, process or function. If ever it became too much, Erik always took him straight home.

At break time, he would venture out to the playground and I would play a game I knew he could handle and encourage a few of the other children to join in. This was often a simple game of catch, chosen because I knew it was something Tim could manage. Then he would be willing to come into the hall with me with his new-found connections and momentary confidence. When he was with me, I ensured the group played games or sang songs he knew and it gave me such a sense of belonging and happiness that he could be there taking part. After about forty-five minutes he often would have had enough. Erik would take him out of the room and while I was sad, I was also really encouraged that he had managed this short time. Any good connection with others was positive.

However, he appeared to be in actual pain when reacting to Erik and me making music, which of course I wanted to protect him from. I really didn't know what was going on, but I felt we needed a definitive answer as to the underlying cause so we could work out a strategy on how to treat these various reactions, as these issues arose every day. You would surely treat behavioural choices in one way, but pain in a different way.

Tim would also cry at some music, as it appeared to evoke a deep and painful sadness for him – particularly at beautiful hymns and Christmas carols. And he would listen for hours in a trance to Katie Melua and James Blunt. The whole sound issue was puzzle that we just couldn't understand.

The Effect of Expectations

Another thing I learnt about Tim during the beginning of our journey with The Son-Rise Program was the effect that expectations had on him. When I took away the weight of all my expectations from him, he tentatively opened up the door to connection but when I had a specific expectation of him and he knew it, the door immediately slammed shut. Add to that a time pressure and the door pretty much bolted. Now, I know you can't go through life ignoring other people's expectations and there are certain things you have to do, but we were experiencing an extreme situation here. We chose to do as little as possible that caused him pressure. We decided not to take him to the shops too much or to other people's houses, just for the moment. Instead we spent more and more time engaging with him at the level he could cope with and playing again and again, purposefully taking expectations off him.

Joining was brilliant for him, as it created a way for us to shift from where we were to where he was and when we were close we could actually reach him enough to take pressure *off* him. Pressure came off him when he was laughing, playing and being silly, so that he also didn't need to ism during these times.

Gradually he was becoming easier to be with and more willing to allow us in his space. These moments with him at home were gold-dust. They were infinitely precious and gave us a very real insight into what was realistically possible for him, so long as he was approached in a way he could access.

We knew it would take a while for these changes to be embedded sufficiently for him to function more easily in the outside world. Meantime, we were keeping a close eye on his developmental changes within the specific environment we were creating for him at home and were enjoying the small but positive changes we were seeing in Tim's connectedness.

When Tim was distressed, his cries and screams would penetrate my heart. And he would cry until he was too physically exhausted to continue. Since starting the Son-Rise™ Program Tim's episodes of extreme distress were becoming less frequent, replaced by more laughter and connectedness. That had to be a good direction.

Pathway to Learning

In *Autism Breakthrough,* Raun Kaufman talks about the hippocampus – the part of the brain that takes in and registers new information. Apparently, this part of the brain plays a part in forming, processing and storing new memories as well as connecting certain sensations and emotions to these memories. The memories aren't stored there, but once processed they are sent to the cerebral cortex which is where they are retrieved from when needed. In hindsight, I now realise that Tim had a problem with forming and retaining new memories, as when I told him something it didn't seem to register. Therefore, it couldn't be processed then stored, and wouldn't be available as a memory to be used later on.

But Raun explained that new neurons *can* be generated in the hippocampus every day if stress is reduced. In Chapter 16, he explains that Dr Scott Faber discussed with him why he felt the Son-Rise Program was so effective. 'He found that when the children with autism were joined, given control, handled with a non-judgemental and welcoming attitude (all of which he termed an 'emotionally attuned intervention') and placed in an environment which was not overstimulating, their stress hormone levels (adrenalin, cortisol) dropped to normal ranges.' Raun explains that when your child shifts out of fight or flight survival mode (which Tim had been in all his life) and his stress hormones return to normal levels, the door is open to breakthroughs on several fronts. 'When cortisol levels are reduced, the process of hippocampal atrophy ceases and reverses itself, with cells growing and reproducing in the hippocampus again'.

So, could taking the environmental stress off Tim help him to relax, think, learn, take things in, and store them? Given that this part of his brain was so obviously not working, I was keen to see if it could start to open up this vital and pivotal part of his processing.

Raun Kaufman also talks in *Autism Breakthrough* about mirror neurons, (p36). He explains:

> 'These are a special class of neurons present in every person's brain. Among other things, mirror neurons enable us to identify with, learn from and connect with other people. Mirror neurons fire in our brains when we see – or sometimes even hear about – someone else taking an action or having an experience. For instance, when we are watching a basketball game and someone shoots a basket, the same pattern of neurons fires in our own brain that would fire if we were actually shooting the basket. What you might think of as empathy is a mirror neuron phenomenon. Mirror neurons allow us to walk in someone else's shoes.' (2014, p.36)

I can relate to mirror neurons of course – wincing if someone eats a lemon, crying if I watch a sad film, watching a dance move and copying it. However, I could see Tim's mirror neurons weren't firing. He wasn't able to copy, imitate, watch then do. He also wasn't able yet to identify with others' feelings.

G. Rizzolattie, an Italian neurophysiologist and Senior Scientist of the Research Team at the University of Parma, explains mirror neurons in this way:

> 'We are social beings. Our survival depends on our understanding the actions, intentions and emotions of others. Mirror neurons allow us to understand other people's minds, not only through conceptual reasoning but through imitation. Feeling, not thinking.' He goes on to explain, 'Mirror neurons are essential for imitation which is key in the learning process. From birth, this group of neurons are active and they allow us to learn to eat, dress, speak…they enable us to reflect body language, facial expressions and emotions. They are key for child development as well as relationships and education.'

The potential good news for the shutdown of Tim's mirror neurons was the fact that Raun Kaufman in *Autism Breakthrough* went on to explain that mirror neurons begin to fire in the developing brain when children are joined.

'It turns out that the simple act of stepping across the bridge from our world to that of our children may help to stimulate the exact part of their brains that seems to be having such difficulty.' (2014, p37)

I found these two elements of neuroplasticity really interesting. So, with actively taking pressure off Tim and sparking his mirror neurons by joining him, we were giving him a very good chance to learn, grow and develop.

We were embarking on an experiment to see if his brain *could* start taking in new information in a Son-Rise Program environment. I could see that when he was relaxed, happy and connecting with us, he could begin to take in new things – like letters and words for instance. When we had been doing The Son-Rise Program for about four months, Tim had started to put together more simple CVC words such as cat, dog and pig. I was beyond excited that not only could he make this connection with sounds and words, but that he *wanted* to. He gradually started relating simple words to pictures and for me, this proved that the pathway to learning was beginning to open naturally. No one was forcing him to do this. He was starting to do it because he wanted to.

Starting to Sound Out Words and Sentences

As we continued to play with Tim every day in The Son-Rise Program playroom, we began seeing some changes in his ability to learn. As Tim started putting letters together, I realised that he could read more and more words. I started making word cards and finding puzzles with corresponding words and pictures. None of this was imperative but I found that he actually wanted to play word games with me. I had to catch him at a willing moment but I could show him words like 'pig' and 'dog' and he would sound out 'p-i-g – pig!' and 'd-o-g – dog!'. He was delighted that he could do it. He was beginning to form memories and retrieve them from information he had learnt.

Eventually I created word cards and he could put words together to make sentences. At this stage words and sentences were disjointed and he couldn't create meaning from them easily, but the very fact that he could put letters together to make words must mean some part of his brain was now working. His school teacher told me that he just read like an automaton and that he had no understanding of what he was reading – but I thought that was unnecessarily negative and I chose not to look at it like that. I was celebrating all the things he *could* do. The rest would come. We were able to start playing around at an introductory level with words and numbers in a fun way.

Tantrums and Difficult Behaviour Diminishing at Home

After five months of playing in The Son-Rise Program playroom, I note in my diary that in the whole of that period we had only had to give Tim 'time out' once. That was incredible! The changes had gradually been happening but I had only just come to this realisation. We put this down to spending hours in his one-to-one The Son-Rise Program playroom allowing him the control he needed, joining him and playing with him with all his motivations, without sensory overload.

We also knew that another reason for this success was having no computers or TVs. Now, instead, we played in the playroom with him and our relationship with him was so much closer and easier, which meant he probably didn't feel he needed to push against us so much. We also understood him better and realised that, more often than not, he was struggling to cope, rather than being naughty – and we respected him for that. We were also consciously adapting ourselves into people he could and wanted to relate to. He found it easier if we were calm but he also loved our silly celebrations, like when we did ridiculous dances or pulled exaggerated facial expressions. Instead of needing to shut us out, he was starting to enjoy having us in his space in tiny increments. All these things had come together and were really making a major difference with regard to his inner feelings and behaviour, especially at home.

What Tim Now Chose to Do in His Own Time

When Tim wasn't in the playroom, we noticed that instead of isming and talking to himself, he was beginning to read the stories in the books he was poring over. He was still muttering to himself but his mutterings were actually the words on the pages. This was clear proof that he was starting to connect to the stories in front of him. He also started to engage in elements of imaginative play by making little playmobile figures talk to each other as he obviously had very clear stories in his head of what he wanted to happen. He would make farms and have people interact with each other. It wasn't always easy to see the purpose of his play or understand his stories from the outside, but he would be engrossed in this activity for long periods of time.

Choosing to Read Me a Story

One day, when he was aged six, I sat with him in the lounge and he actually read a book to me. He even let me help him with words he could not read. This was a massive moment for me and the cosy togetherness of it felt beyond exciting. Learning was happening, skills were developing, flexibility was emerging and Tim and I were sitting like any mother and child, reading a story!

When his friend, Kylie, came to play, he would sometimes read his stories to her too. At one point she looked up at me in surprise and said, 'Can Tim read?' She seemed shocked, perhaps because Tim was unable to demonstrate his abilities at school.

The fact that he could sit with us and read meant that he was developing in interactive attention span and verbal communication. And the fact that he was allowing me to correct and help him was proof of development in his flexibility. These were clear and very exciting ways to chart progress. It was subtle inner progress that would undoubtedly lead to more obvious progress down the line.

Typing on a Keyboard

At this time, Tim started to show an interest in typing words on our computer. We were keeping him away from watching screens and playing computer games, but I felt if he was showing an interest in creating words and sentences in this way, this could be a useful purpose for a screen. Sometimes we would let him type onto our computer and he would write out stories, copying from his books or from re-iterated stories in his head. This helped us to see his thought processes more clearly. This is an example of his writing from that time: 'Mr Wolf was his friends is come to look at the invitation plees come to my birthday party tomoro at 12 ocloc don't be lat Mr Wolf looked puzzled she was glad they added but sleepily......NO NONO! said Mr Mumy and Mr Daddy your birthday is yours Mr Wolf's shopping list'

While it was muddled, he was typing out his thought processes. It was clearly a mixture of the stories he had been reading and helped me see how he processed them. He was able to find the letters, put them in order to make words and he *wanted* to. That was the part I found most exciting – and he was giving us insight into his world by writing it down.

Musical Playdates: Linking a Motivation with a Goal

With my training in The Son-Rise Program, I could see that one of Tim's motivations was music and that one of our goals for him was to spend longer periods of time feeling comfortable with other children.

For my dissertation when doing my music and teaching degree, I had studied the Hungarian composer, Kodály and his method of teaching music to children. This involved, among other things, singing games. Over the last few years of my teaching I had run a variety of music clubs where I had played hundreds of singing games with numerous groups of children of all ages. I had also run music workshops, often with 40 children for up to six hours a day. Tim hadn't attended, even though many children were his age, because he was unable to even enter the hall due to the noise. However, he could start to learn these games and play them at home when under no pressure. I had seen that Tim could engage with his classmates to a level when he was playing some musical games.

So how would it be if I invited friends round to play singing games? They were things he could do and the other children could come and enjoy it too. There would be opportunities for him to engage in elements of fun and social interaction in his own, safe environment and perhaps it would help him to start to build some relationships. We started having little parties at our house with small groups of children and only doing the things Tim could engage in. At one point we hired a hall and had a singing games party which involved playground games, parachute games and singing games in circles. With familiar games and familiar children, he could access this. This was working – the combination of what Tim could do, with other children being around him, and enjoying it too. He loved the chasing games, he enjoyed throwing and catching and he joined in the singing games.

He would be in close proximity with children for two hours. Although he still couldn't talk or connect easily other than in a one-to-one situation with an adult going his way, he *could* engage in this practical way and as I mentioned before, we had learnt to focus on what he *could* do rather than the things he couldn't yet do. It made such a difference to how we felt and Tim genuinely enjoyed it. It was also good for the other children to see him having fun and sharing the things they liked. We always kept these parties short and held them in the morning when energy levels were high and tempers were at their most mellow!

These musical 'play-dates' became a regular feature of our lives because they worked so well. We started having 'parties' at any time of day with any child who wanted to join us – and what child doesn't like parties? This was a great way for Tim to mix with others with no pressure or expectations – and he was willing to engage because his motivation was so high.

So, Tim was engaging with groups of children in a way that he could access and enjoy and he was being joined and connected with every day in the Son-Rise Program playroom. In this way, throughout the next year we made steady progress.

Tim was now heading towards the end of Year 2 and approaching the age of seven.

An Attempt at a Holiday

It had been seven years since we'd been on a sunny holiday and we were desperate for a break away from everyday life. I so badly needed some freedom and a break that we threw caution to the wind and booked a holiday in Spain.

Because Tim needed to follow his agenda and had high expectations for dictation and all the things he needed, we knew it would be complex, but I figured that we might get at least some willing engagement from him out there and see at least a little of the beach and sun. We thought it was worth a shot. Even if it was hard, we would take any good moments we could.

The thing is, going abroad was something that I had such a yearning for that I found it hard to reign in my expectations. I am a traveller at heart. I had been to Australia for nine months when I was twenty-one, backpacking alone for four months and was at my happiest with all the freedom I found, meeting new people and visiting different places. I had worked for seven months in South Africa teaching street children, and skydived and ridden ponies into the Lesotho mountains. I am in my element exploring new places, creating memories and meeting new people. Basically I craved adventure. It had been a long time.

Spain to me meant exploring the little cobbled streets, wandering through the markets, sitting under palm trees and feeling the warm sun on my face and the soft sand beneath my feet. I do know that holidays with children are different to holidays without children but I wasn't fully prepared for just how restricted this one would be.

Tim had felt comfortable on the plane and the journey to Spain had gone fairly well. We then arrived in our dream resort – not the expensive kind, but with deep blue skies above, beautiful white houses and a sparkling swimming pool. We were so excited. It was beautiful. A full fourteen days of sunshine – such peace and expectation. It all seemed to be going so well... Before the screaming started at the shop because he wanted a magazine – and of course there wasn't an English one to be had. He showed an even stronger desire than usual to talk to himself and became immersed in his isms. He then refused to go to the beach which I was dying to do.

I had allowed myself to dream about plans, feelings and visions for this holiday and my expectations were high. My need for a holiday was through the roof.

However, I soon realised that we were more restricted than we were at home – because Tim was really struggling. The whole new environment was just too overwhelming for him.

Tim didn't get words like *if, maybe* or *we'll see*. He had to have certainty. This is OK when you can give certainty, but on holiday you don't know anything about where you are or what you can do. For Tim it must have felt like the certainty had been ripped out from under him. He said he wanted to go out if we could get a magazine, which is something we regularly did in England but we didn't know if we could find a place to buy an English magazine in Spain. He couldn't relinquish his refusal without that promise.

We couldn't go exploring, because he had to know exactly what was going to happen before we did it – but of course, *we* didn't know. For us, the unknown and adventure was the fun of a holiday but it didn't work that way for him.

On the first morning I woke up at 6 am, got up, showered, put on my shorts and pretty white top, organised packed lunches and found myself ready for a whole day out before the others had even woken up. That's how excited I was. In my head, freedom had begun and we were going out for the whole day in this beautiful, new environment. Tim wanted to go swimming first, which was fine. We would go out after that. After swimming Tim demanded to do some dictation. I reckoned we could do a little as he was seriously insecure and his need was high but then we would be able to go out. However Tim became exceptionally controlling, which I took to mean that he was finding this new environment stressful, so

I relented and took all the instruction that he wanted to give me, trying to be as attuned to his needs as I could as I knew this would help him feel better. The thing is, for some reason by the time we had finished, he was not in a great mood. We decided we should eat before going out. That took another hour. *Come on!* Then Tim refused to go out. He wanted to stay in the dark flat, where we had been all morning. He didn't have any concept of the beauty out there that awaited us. He had no imagination or desire for it. He just wanted anything that would make him feel secure.

I was doing my best to be patient. I knew if Tim could feel my expectations on him it would be like red rag to a bull – but come on! We were on *holiday*! It made no difference. We didn't leave the house until 3 o'clock in the afternoon. By then it felt like most of the day was over. I'd been so excited and ready to leave the house for nine hours now but had, as always, not wanted to push Tim against his will.

We could have forced him. We could have carried him kicking and screaming to the car to take him out on a picnic. But that would have hardly been a great experience for him. It would destroy the trust we had been building up with him and would show no respect for the genuine difficulty he was having in coping with his new environment. We went the way of willing engagement. It always took time. We respected him for his difficulties and gave him the time to do what he needed to do, while constantly encouraging him to try and come out of his internal mode of safety and repetition to see and experience something new. If he could see a purpose he could relate to, he would be more willing to engage.

The thing is, I still wanted to cut loose and just go off in the car, exploring. I wanted to walk along beach fronts, paddle in the sea, sit in cafes, sift through clothes in the market stalls, basically run away from all our restrictions. I could see all these things but not access them! Sometimes I felt in the midst of all this coping that there was no time to be the person I actually knew myself to be.

A couple of days into the holiday, we stumbled upon an English bookshop which sold Tim's favourite audio books and there were lots there he didn't have. On the first day we bought him one and from his reaction realised that buying an audio book was as exciting for him as going on a trip out. So we decided to use a chunk of our holiday budget on buying Tim an audio book at the start of each day. That made him excited and willing to get ready and come out with us. He would then come to a café if he could have a biscuit and apple juice. This café was on a terrace in the sun, so gave Erik and I a momentary holiday feeling. After that if we went to McDonalds to buy chips, he was then willing to come with us to the beach. Or he was willing to *try*. Sometimes as we approached the beach he would pull back and resist and though I respected him and realised there were so many things he was genuinely struggling to cope with, I was also battling my own huge desire to break free and run down to the beach and soak up the Spanish seaside atmosphere...

Tim still needed to do his ism of walking around and talking to his hand. He found some low rocks in shallow water which he loved pacing around on in his own world, oblivious to everything else, speaking his own stories into his jaggedly moving hand. Loads of people were playing in the water and walking on rocks and it wasn't at all obvious that Tim was doing anything unusual, other than to us. We could then take a minute to sit on the beach, dream, drink in the sun on our faces and feel as if we were on holiday. I got used to making half an hour feel like a whole day.

We let go rules on this holiday. My Dad, when hearing my despair, suggested we let go our no telly rule and let him watch some. I was concerned that it would start up Tim's whole need and demand for the telly even when we were home, but with the level of despair being as it was, we decided to risk it. We let him watch half an hour every evening and that gave him something to look forward to. We even let him play for twenty minutes on Erik's phone each day when at the café.

We also a couple of times gave up our no dairy rule and let Tim have bits of ice creams. Often we shared them – Tim had a little and Erik had the rest. I had to be careful of the effect all the dairy and the sugar could have on him out there, while out of his comfort zone and when he was already highly sensitive and controlling. But we set the boundaries here.

In fact, it was all about knowing the plan in advance and having things to look forward to for Tim. Our days started to slip into the same routine. We would go to the bookshop, buy a new audio book, go to the beautiful terraced café, buy McDonalds chips and then have a moment on a beach – however long Tim could last there.

Mostly at the beach we played full on chasing games. No resting, making sandcastles or splashing in the shallow water for us! Tim couldn't stand the sea. He was actually afraid of it. He would walk near the edge but would hardly ever put a foot in. We would sometimes carry him out into the water and he would put his arms round our necks and cling on for dear life. The easiest way Tim could enjoy the beach was with chasing games. With these, he was fully animated and happy.

We created an element of home from home for Tim at the flat, so often we bought balloons and wrapping paper and made it feel like a party, just for the three of us. This was still a major motivation of his at the time.

We didn't get cross with Tim at all on this holiday. We knew he had all his sensory overloads and was not in a place to understand reasoning or ifs and maybes. That wasn't his fault. It was our job to help him, but we did both find the restrictions really hard, especially as there was nowhere to express our frustration.

I took to walking off and writing about my feelings in my diaries but that wasn't enough. I knew if I could talk and cry with Erik then we would find a perspective, a way of looking at it, a way to be closer through it all, however we were hardly ever on our own. We knew that even if we showed a tiny element of our own feelings it could lead to a highly charged meltdown on Tim's part. He was not yet able to process these emotions from us without deeply panicking. It was as though his security depended upon our happiness and any spark of difficulty on our part threw his equilibrium too far.

We knew that Tim was highly sensitive to any negative emotion. We had chosen to share our negative, frustrated, angry, sad emotions with each other or with friends but not to bring them out in front of Tim. We still had them, of course, but they would need their time and place and we would keep our happy, easy going, fun and positive emotions to share with and in front of Tim. These emotions were genuine too. We weren't putting on shows for him – we could just see he wasn't ready and couldn't deal with negativity from us. At home it was a little easier to find a way to balance this out, but in Spain there were no outlets.

Tim was never at a place if one of us was unhappy to ask if we were okay. He would run off and cry and it would become all about him. Then we would have to deal with the difficulties he had because of our frustration, so it became easier for all concerned if we just kept our negative emotions in check.

I knew that with a chance to talk all this out, I would be able to regain my Son-Rise attitude and see the world and our journey again from a place of genuine hope, but it was hard to get the time to properly talk things out.

Tim was still finding the dynamics of Erik and I talking to each other difficult to process. Sometimes in the car, Erik and I would start a conversation and Tim would start screaming because he didn't want us to talk. Becoming angry would not help. Reasoning was not something Tim could understand or was ready for. It was a continuous battle and left us both feeling frustrated. These feelings when in such a beautiful place were so contrary. The holiday environment was all around us but we could hardly access it.

Once, after the audio book, the café and the chips, we had driven down to a beach. We drove along the seafront then had to turn inland to find a place to park. Oh my goodness, the noise! Tim started arching his back, screaming and kicking. I so wanted to comfort him and explain to him that we were still going to the sea but just had to park. Life was hard when such simple things could not be explained.

Another time we decided to be rash and after our morning routine we drove to Torrevieja, about an hour away. This was a very special place for Erik and I as we had spent two weeks there when we were first together. However, walking along the beautiful promenade, Tim suddenly saw some rocks in the sea and really wanted to go and walk about on them as he did at our local beach. However, these rocks were dangerous – they jutted high above the sea, with great crevices between them. They were nothing like the low rocks Tim was used to walking about on. There was no way we could let him on them. Explaining this to him however, was not easy. We could only say 'no' and help him through his processes. This suddenly turned the day from hopeful and 'out there' into 'OK, so we need to calm him and head towards home now' mode. Erik and I had both learnt to cope with putting our own needs second – (or often tenth) but we were both so genuinely disappointed.

The thing is, if you were to look at our holiday album you would think we had the best holiday ever. It sounds ironic, but I became so adept at taking happy photos – brief moments of connection and fun, smiling faces and holiday feelings. Every day I would take loads of photos then come back in the evening and sift through them all – weeding out the unhappy ones and keeping only the great moments. If a stranger were to look at these photos they would literally see a happy family of three having a great holiday. I don't know if this was helpful. I had always loved photography and loved capturing moments between people. For me, these tiny captured moments were still the truth – just a very small part of it. The things I took pictures of had really happened. But photos are silent. You can't see distress in photos or feel despair. You can only see what you see. Deep down I think I might have been trying to create a carefree frontage to our lives when it felt the complete opposite.

Erik says sometimes, when we look back at photos, that it gives a very unrealistic impression. However, years later, Tim talks about this holiday with good feelings and memories – so we had obviously done the best we could for him. All I know is that there is a part of me that yearns for freedom and I didn't find very much of it on this holiday! To choose which memories to create and keep gave me an element of control as to where I put my focus.

This autism journey was challenging me to the very core of my being every day. There was no escape or certainty of relief in sight and that was another layer of stress that I was also dealing with daily. Saying that, my relationship with God and my Son-Rise Program mind-set helped me get my perspective back and served as my ultimate, my path, my way through, my hope for the future. There was a clear path in helping Tim and the more we could help him the more we could all experience eventual freedom.

Our needs and Tim's were clashing almost continuously, but we were still choosing to see life from his point of view as much as possible and ease his path as much as we could. The comfort we had, was that the Son-Rise Program approach had given us a foundation of certainty that we were doing the best we could by him – we just had to continue walking the path.

Chapter Nine – Conflicting messages – which way to go?

After the summer holidays, when Tim turned seven, he moved up to St Andrew's Primary School. We had chosen to continue the journey of mornings in school and sessions in The Son-Rise Program® in the afternoons as it had been working to a level and also because we still had to work. Tim didn't move up with all the children he knew as we didn't think the school they were moving to would best suit him. So we found a new one.

Interestingly, I had also just got a job in the same school that Tim was about to go to, as a music teacher two days a week. The Headteacher insisted that I must never talk about Tim in the staff room and that I had to be very clear when I had my 'teacher' hat on and when I had my 'parent' hat on. I found this a bit harsh but I knew that it was not fair in the staffroom to start talking about your child to a teacher who is on a break. That was obvious. I also knew that I would be expected to focus totally on the children in my classes without my attention being compromised by any states that Tim was in.

I had chosen this school for Tim as it had been highly recommended to me by a close friend who had worked there, as a school that had been particularly good with certain children with issues. It was a Catholic school and there was a strong, caring ethos running through it. They were in agreement that we could continue to bring Tim to school in the mornings and do sessions in The Son-Rise Program every afternoon. In essence, we would both be responsible for his learning and development.

On the third day of being there, I wasn't working and I picked him up at lunchtime. The car was parked on a very fast main road and as I walked round with him to help him in, he suddenly went rigid. He started crying and refused to move. He was having a major overload meltdown right on a busy main road. Traffic screeched past while Tim screamed and cried. I stood behind him with the door held as far in as I could hold it. I panicked as more lorries rumbled by. I knew I couldn't force him out of this state or easily manoeuvre him into the car. In the middle of this a stranger called to me from the other side of the road – was I okay? She crossed over with her children and when the road was clear, started talking to me. It could have been this distraction that changed Tim's state, but eventually he softened and was willing to get safely in. It turned out the stranger was a parent in the school – I got to know her well and we are still friends to this day.

This behaviour was quite usual for Tim. He would manage and hold things in until he just couldn't take it anymore. Getting into the car had been that moment. There was a lot to take in and he was basically telling me in the best way he knew how that it was all too much.

We were tentatively quite pleased with some elements of his time in this primary school. We were initially quite overwhelmed by the amount of care, thought and provision that was put into Tim by the school and we felt there were little elements of progress being made. He was beginning to be able to follow small instructions even when being directed to doing something he didn't choose to do and he had moments of being a little more flexible, cooperative and willing. Meanwhile, we were playing with him in his Son-Rise Program playroom every afternoon and focusing on his flexibility, eye contact, communication skills, and desire to be with and connect with people. These were our goals and it seemed at this point that school were willing to be part of this journey with us.

Tim's awareness of concepts outside of his own world were very limited and he would still talk in his own way as a release from over stimulation but we knew we were heading in a slow but steady direction that could gradually release him from these needs and help him to open up his world.

He was still on a very different path to the other children who were already developing their writing, understanding, talking, mathematical thinking and socially were in the midst of friendships, arguments, playground squabbles, making up whilst learning all the time. Tim was outside this world. He could be alongside the other children and there were fleeting moments of interaction and fun, but Tim couldn't be treated like the other children because he was so rigid in his willingness to cooperate. This was aggravated by his understanding and language skills being still so under-developed in comparison to his peer group. He was in a year below where he was supposed to be and still significantly trailing behind his classmates both socially and academically. I didn't allow this to affect me though. It was *his* development I was interested in. If I compared him to other children, I risked losing perspective and the strength I needed to continue along our path.

Sometimes Tim stood in the doorway to the classroom saying loudly that he didn't want to go in. The teacher told me later that that was probably what all the children were thinking, but wouldn't say. Tim was trying to tell us even then that this environment was not right for him. We were stuck at this point, because we couldn't live off just one salary and I couldn't see how we could do things differently. He still couldn't yet learn in the ways the other children could – listening and responding to a teacher's instructions, going to tables in groups then talking and working together. He was in a world of his own but occupying the space alongside the others. The 'parallel universe' thought was in my mind often. He spent most of his time in a separate room with a classroom assistant who would be trying to get him a) to sit still b) be willing to *try* to listen and c) be engaged enough to start to do what was being asked of him. He was already naturally able to achieve these elements in his playroom at home, but just couldn't seem to muster the ability to do them here.

Often the noise and unpredictability of the classroom would set him off into meltdown modes where he would refuse to do anything he was asked to do and would just wander off and find something he could cope with to do, regardless of the teacher's wishes.

Christmas with Tim aged seven and a half

At the age of seven and a half, Tim was still moving constantly between exclusivity and interactivity. He knew about Christmas and was very excited. By this stage he could read well and he was still really into audio books. He was even starting to understand the stories he was listening to. He wasn't able to discuss them much yet but we were working on that. He was also very much into Playmobil and elements of imaginative play. My sister and her family joined us at my parents' house and when it came to giving out presents Tim was almost beside himself with excitement. He ran round the table, spun himself around and leapt about with excitement but interspersed with all this were interactive conversations that made complete sense. For example:

Erik: What is it?

Tim: I got a Charlie and Lola book and DVD box set! Happy Christmas everyone! Thank you for my lovely present!

Me: Tim, what are the five stories? What are they?

Tim: Charlie and Lola

Me: But what are the five stories?

Tim: (reading) We honestly can look after your dog, my wobbly tooth, woops, it wasn't me, I've won and snow is my favourite and my best!

Nana: Tim, have you read those before?

Tim: No, I haven't listened to this before…

We had been working on Tim's ability to respond to us, have conversations and answer questions and amidst his need to be exclusive and talking to himself, his ability to converse was gradually developing. Hope, hope, hope – it was all possible!

His presents were all based around reading and imaginative play this particular Christmas – a Playmobil circus, a magic set, as he was starting to like the idea of magic and lots of audio books which he loved to read along with while listening. His cousins received a Nintendo DS games console, and while they were very excited and this could have been hard for him, Erik and I played with him lots with all his new toys and never wavered in our resolve to protect his vulnerable brain from being overstimulated by these devices.

A conversation a few days later while playing with his circus:

Erik: What are you doing Tim?

Tim: I'm making a circus

Erik: Wow, is there a band in the circus?

Tim: Yes and a fairy waving her wand – is that a fairy?

Erik: Yes that IS a fairy

Tim: And is that a magic wand?

Erik: Yes, that IS a magic wand

Tim: Is it a fairy for girls?

Erik: You mean is it a girly fairy?

Tim: Is it for girls?

Erik: Yes, but boys can play too

Tim: Is for girls and boys?

Erik: Yes…

And then he resumed his playing.

Later in the holidays he was making cakes with a friend, Bella:

Bella: Do you like mine Tim?

Tim: Pardon?

Bella: Do you like mine?

Tim: Yeah and I like mine too.

While he then fell silent again, he was able to respond appropriately when spoken to. In the silent moments when friends were there, I often felt I needed to fill in the gaps but I had to be careful to also give the children the opportunity to connect on their own level. Despite the long silences, I held on to the fact that Tim was gradually able to engage in short conversations and we knew what to do to help him develop this skill further.

Re-Framing Tim's Development

At this point, someone looking at Tim from the outside might say that he hardly ever talked; he rarely made sense; he jumped about sometimes and showed odd behaviour; he only very occasionally followed an adult agenda for him and he has interests in very unusual things. Problems, problems, problems…

But I didn't see it this way. Instead, I saw that Tim's ability to speak and converse was there and developing; his desire to be with people was definitely there and growing every day; he was able to read, allowing his interest in different topics to grow; he was responsive and friendly; his need to be exclusive was diminishing. Hope, hope, hope! Even though the journey seemed long and we were often tired or overwhelmed at not having a 'normal' life ourselves, we never ever lost our reasons for treating Tim as we did.

'He Will Not Follow our Agenda'

The school's biggest problem was trying to persuade Tim to follow an adult's agenda, as he was still finding this really difficult. Did the teacher force him and risk a meltdown, or did she go with him and try to entice him away with encouragement and rewards? This often wouldn't work anyway as the enticements were never rewarding enough for Tim. This was the main difficulty. It would be easy to conclude that he was spoilt and just wanting his own way, but he wasn't doing any of this with a conscious purpose and I knew it was far more complex than that.

The processing issues within his brain could not make sense of the environment, so he was overwhelmed, constantly in flight/fight mode, trying to ward off anything that would tip him over the edge – and most of the time he was on the brink of being tipped over. I knew that this was not naughty behaviour. We were still helping him bio-medically with oils and supplements to help his nervous system and he was still on his special diet. But every time he walked into school, his anxiety deepened, his communication skills eluded him and he seemed totally unable to listen or understand – even though he could manage a lot of these things in the playroom at home.

To actively redress these stress levels, we were purposefully having so much fun with him at home, going with his needs and motivations, playing games on his terms in a way he could enjoy and were connecting on a very deep and loving level.

Once, in school during a fire drill, the Headteacher spoke to all the children lined up in their classes on the playground. The whole school fell silent. 'Does anyone have any questions?' she asked.

Tim put his hand up.

'Oh no,' I silently begged. 'Please don't ask him – he doesn't understand the question'.

But she did ask him and because he hadn't grasped the context, he started talking about what he had done the night before. The Head suggested he share that with her later, but I felt that had exposed him. Why couldn't she be subtle? Why couldn't someone check with him what he wanted to say before he spoke in front of the school? I felt that the more the other children were exposed to Tim's difficulties, the less chance he would have of being treated equally by them.

Another time, when the children in Tim's class were lined up in their classroom, some of the children called me over. 'George is being really mean to Tim – he keeps trying to get him to say something rude to the teacher to get him into trouble.'

Because Tim struggled with meanings of words and didn't realise what rude or swear words were at this point, one of the boys thought it would be funny to ask him to say something rude to a teacher.

I felt a burst of indignation at the boy standing in front of me, who thought he could make a joke out of Tim's difficulties and desire to please. However I knew it would take more than a short reprimand to change this boy's thinking. I knew he would stop temporarily at this point now he knew that I knew, so I walked away. But would this happen again when my back was turned?

It was a stark reminder of Tim's vulnerability to teasing and bullying. It just fuelled my desire to want to help him – to communicate his *own* feelings and his *own* free will. However, school is not a helpful place to teach a child to find their voice. Most of the time they are not allowed to talk and if they are, it has to be about the subject in hand or answering a specific question. Tim needed to talk continually, about anything and everything and to be encouraged to do this more and more for its own sake, so that he could learn that communication was fun, useful and always well-received. Then he would see the point of trying with his emerging ability in the world of social communication.

Tim's Track

Tim's internal track was silent but very powerful. He was hell-bent on following it and if nobody tuned into it at any level, he found it very hard to cooperate. He needed to acquire more flexibility. I knew we needed to prioritise the work we were doing on his inner flexibility, as this was still keeping many doors closed for him. Friendships were hard as he couldn't go along with what someone else wanted to do yet and he was still not showing real interest in how other children were feeling or what they might want to do. School was difficult as it is all about following someone else's agenda. It was frustrating. His speech was developing in his own way to suit his particular needs, but until he really began to be inwardly flexible and become more responsive, I could see that the interactional element of his speech would remain stuck.

From a Son-Rise Program point of view, he wasn't 'cooked' enough yet and needed more time in a one-to-one environment, working on these things. But Erik and I still couldn't work out how we could increase his time in the playroom.

'He Needs to Conform Before We Can Teach Him'

The Headteacher made it clear that when Tim learnt to conform, then they would be able to start to teach him. I could see the logic to this. However, he couldn't properly conform. I genuinely believed he was doing his best and that all the sensory overload issues and anxiety coupled with his lack of understanding of what was expected of him were blocking his ability to conform. Again, it comes down to force versus connection. Do you *force* the child to conform against every ounce of his will, or do you seek to build a relationship with him and gradually reach him to the extent that he *wants* to start to take adult direction and willingly starts to conform? All my instincts chose the second option. We were working on the latter every moment he was outside school and we were honestly seeing elements of progress, even though it wasn't yet sufficient for a school setting. Willing engagement was my goal and the school had no strategies to achieve this.

We were focusing on these aspects of Tim's development all the time, but soon we began to see a divide with our agenda and that of the school. The school had their task-oriented agenda and it was every bit as inflexible as Tim's processing currently was. They wanted to conquer Tim's inability to conform as far as they could, by way of outward structure and set expectations. They disregarded our knowledge of Tim almost completely and the fact that we allowed Tim to follow his processes at home seemed to them as though we just 'let him do whatever he liked'. Conformity was their goal as was ticking boxes to prove progress, but Tim could hardly put pen to paper yet, in the way they wanted him to, so I think they were losing heart.

I actually don't blame them. Autism isn't an easy condition and even if schools try their best, they are only able to follow the advice sold to them by professionals who they believe know best. I don't know any teacher or headteacher who has *ever* been advised to take advice from parents as to how a child should be treated. We knew we were working on all the issues that would help him achieve goals of autonomous learning and willing conformity in the long term, but we had a way to go. We could have got there a lot faster with a full time Son-Rise Program away from the restrictions of the system, but our financial situation wouldn't allow us that freedom.

We Needed to be Stricter

The school suggested to us that Tim wasn't conforming with them because we weren't being strict enough with him at home and in fact it would help *them* if we started to use a structured timetable with him at home. The idea was that this would help him adhere to timetables in school. We thought we would respect their request for a while and try this. We wrote up a really clear timetable for Tim – time in the playroom and with whom, time to eat, time to get undressed, time to brush his teeth, time to go to bed… However, it only stressed Tim. Instead of going with him and giving him time and space to come to his own understanding about what he needed to do, it rushed him and worried him, so consequently didn't work.

I acknowledge that for the school this was a really difficult situation. From their point of view, here was a child who couldn't conform to the extent that he couldn't even sit still and learn properly, which meant they then couldn't do their job as a school and teach him. Therefore, they felt they needed us to work with them on 'getting him' to conform. I do understand that thinking. I had just learnt a new and better way, which I was sure would have a better long-term outcome.

I knew that he needed more joining and connection before he would be *able* to conform to the expectations of others. We needed more time with him.

So How Do You Comfort Him?

I was sitting in the school hall with thirty infant children all around me, surrounded by puppets and instruments one morning, when Tim's familiar and heart-breaking scream resounded through the building. I had become accustomed to keeping Tim in a corner of my heart while I kept my professional teaching hat on, so I continued giving the five-year-olds my full attention. Of course, my natural mothering instincts were on full alert, but I knew I wasn't allowed to intervene. His screaming and distress, however, went on.

Eventually, the Headteacher asked for my help, explaining this was a last resort as the school were supposed to be able to deal with 'these issues'. She asked me to come into her brightly lit office where Tim was still inconsolable. She stood there, arms folded and said she wanted to watch how I comforted him.

What?

I needed her to leave me on my own with him then, so I could turn the bright lights off and give us some privacy. Her very presence was creating tension at a time when Tim was unable to tell me what had happened.

I knew only too well what the Headteacher wanted me to do – to calm Tim, talk to him and persuade him to go back to the classroom and carry on for the rest of the morning. That would have been seen as success. That would have actually *been* success!

However, I could see he was beyond that. Strategies wouldn't work. Calming him by taking him away from the stressful environment and all the expectations would work, but I knew that was working against what the Headteacher wanted. The only comfort I could realistically offer Tim was to take him away from there. As it was near the end of the morning, I managed to calm him down enough to sit quietly and wait for Erik to come. But what I wanted was to be able to comfort him in privacy, work through his emotions with him and come to a place where I could reach him again.

The Headteacher told me that his meltdowns disturbed the whole of the Key Stage One area with the three infant classes and that she had to look out for the needs of the other children. Where did this leave Tim? I still stuck to the fact that there must be a *reason* for his meltdowns and that we were on the way to helping him reduce them.

Still in an Infant Environment aged seven

At St Andrew's, because Tim was still in an infant environment and could still play, they somehow found ways around his lack of ability to conform. The infants had breaktimes different from the older children, so had lots of space to run about and do their own thing. Sometimes when break finished, Tim would refuse to line up and would run off to far-flung corners of the playground or into a playhouse to hide, needing to be enticed with offers of things he wanted to do, such as cutting pictures out of Argos catalogues, to come back in again. But being an infant classroom there was still scope for children to do their own thing…

Interestingly, now Tim can talk clearly, he tells me he remembers this and explains how it all felt for him. He wrote about it all in a diary about his school experiences and can't believe he used to do it.

At one point we requested that Tim stay for lunch – a simple request you might think. The Headteacher wrote to us, stating that she would have to write to County to approve funding to employ someone for that time. It would obviously take weeks to get funding and yet more weeks to interview and employ someone – just for my child to join others for lunch – which we weren't even sure was the best idea. At times I wanted to scream out for a semblance of simplicity in our lives. We let it go. We weren't totally sure we wanted it and when we saw the ridiculous lengths that the school would have to go, it seemed disheartening.

Some Positive Elements

Towards the end of this academic year, just before his eighth birthday, Tim attended another Sports Day. He was really cooperative and seemed to enjoy it. I stood around with the other mothers, some of whom I had become friends with by this stage, just watching all the children and cheering them on. Secretly I was watching out for Tim every second and inwardly celebrating that he could take all the instruction from them and was able to manage this situation. He didn't win any races – in fact I don't even think he had an interest in winning – but he had some fun moments with the other children – laughing and looking as though he was sharing silly jokes and at the end, I managed to take a lovely photo of him with a group of friends. There were elements here where I felt he had really begun to feel part of a group and could enjoy the other children as well as the activities.

One major point where the Son-Rise™ had made a real difference to Tim was that he began to adore the praise and cheers of others. He had moments where he loved achieving things and loved his achievements to be acknowledged. This was a spark that we knew was developing and needed constant nurturing as this was a major step towards him relaxing and enjoying other people and could be a key to him wanting to take instruction more.

School Expectations

As I mentioned previously, the expectation of children at school is conformity. If they can't conform, they need help with their behaviour so that they will conform. This seems to lack reason. What if it is not for reasons of behaviour that they are not conforming? What if it is for deeper underlying issues? Surely you work on those underlying issues until the child does not need to display the 'difficult' behaviours any more. We knew what those underlying issues were because we had a clear understanding of how Tim's autism affected him and so we were sticking to our goal – working from the inside out rather than the outside in.

It was difficult for School to understand the extent to which we were working with Tim in the afternoons. It may have appeared that we were merely playing with him, but all the time whether in the playroom or not, we were working on the most important elements of his development through play by first entering his world. It was our constant focus.

I think that many headteachers think they already have the answers for autism, especially if they've had a visit from an 'expert' and that lack of progress is the fault of the child's autism, not their teaching approach. They seem to believe there are no strategies that can help a child with autism and therefore aren't open to change and growth. This was our experience, anyway.

I think a lot of children with autism are just seen as an inconvenience in a school as they struggle with the things schools want most. It's such a shame that many people in schools aren't aware of the positive impact they could have. If children could be played with at the level where they really are, if social interaction was emphasised over ticking academic boxes, if children could use and follow elements of their motivations, if talking could be concrete and other children could be brought in to play turn-taking games, our children couldn't help but improve in all the areas they need to. Instead, adult-led programmes are put into place, rigid routines are set up, which cements a child's need for routine rather than challenging their flexibility, motivations are ignored in preference of dictating what the child 'should' be doing and the child's red and green lights are totally ignored in preference to timetables and conformity.

It's even more of a waste, because the children with autism who are in mainstream schools with one-to-one support, often have their assisted time taken up being persuaded to conform with what the rest of the class are doing, instead of having their own development analysed and their processing issues addressed in order to genuinely benefit their own development.

I also question the point of asking a child on the autistic spectrum, who cannot grasp basic concepts yet, questions like, 'So what do you think the skeleton of the dog is saying?' as Tim was asked in infant school. And what could he possibly gain by joining in an activity where he had to depict Arctic weather patterns through playing percussion instruments, aged eight? At that stage he knew about rain and sunshine, but the Arctic? These were way too conceptual and didn't reach the way Tim thought or processed at all.

But no one seemed interested in exploring the way he thought, learnt, processed, absorbed information, or where he was in his social understanding or had any interest in working with him towards the next level. As a teacher, I have had to work a lot on providing proof of children's progress. Well, you can only do that if you know where the child is in the first place, then you can see if progress is being made. Given that no one spent any time analysing what Tim could do, as opposed to what he couldn't, there was no starting point and no focused direction for his development and learning, so how could teaching happen?

The concept of, 'If a child doesn't learn in the way that we teach, we need to teach in the way that the child learns' is a very familiar one. But no one was willing to look at this with me.

I had not encountered any school willing to adapt their teaching programme to the needs of a child who still had to learn and practice the art of processing their world and communicating their feelings.

The Issue Again – Force or Connection? Year 4

So, I was back to that familiar issue again – force or connection. The school wouldn't let it go. Had force *ever* worked? No. Had focusing on connection and interaction worked? It was starting to. It helped Tim access a state of relaxation, fun and silliness, which in turn led to willing engagement which in turn led to learning. We had seen elements of improvement and we were excited about what we had achieved. This was the option we were going to stick with, as it was the approach that had brought the most effective results – so this was an intelligent conclusion, as far as I was concerned. It sometimes seemed incredibly hard for people on the outside to understand this. However, I didn't need anyone's understanding, which in itself was interesting as I am someone who is often seeking advice and approval from others! This time though, I was totally convinced. It was as though this whole concept had been planted firmly in my heart and understanding and I just knew it was right for Tim, however long it would take.

Regular Son-Rise Program Sessions

At home Tim had been having his regular Son-Rise Program sessions all year. Rosie, Dani and Gel continued working with Tim and a friend, Karen, did sessions with him for a while.

Then along came Rachel to join Tim's Son-Rise Program team in the afternoons. She was an out-of-the-box thinker, with a larger-than-life personality and a reassuring presence. She was highly creative and open-minded and she had a very natural and humorous manner with Tim. I could see where Tim was at with his reading and writing and would make lots of worksheets for him to complete with Rachel, and for short moments Tim could focus on learning with her. They had a great relationship and Tim always enjoyed his sessions with Rachel. In fact, Tim loved Rachel so much that she became one of his powerful interests. He started writing a series of books all about her. I mentioned before that Tim could hardly write – what I really meant was that Tim could hardly write what other people directed him to. When his ideas and motivations were sufficiently powerful, he could write sentences and put his thought processes down on paper. The school did not know this, though, as anything he was motivated by was not allowed in school.

Out of seventeen titles, this is a short selection – Rachel Morris Sings that Song, Rachel Morris the album, Rachel Morris give me the type of food activity book, Rachel Morris's Christmas Eve, Rachel Morris makes the Gingerbread Boy

This is one page from 'Rachel Morris – police is coming'

> A policeman wears a blue T-shirt and a policeman wears a red T-shirt as well. They were very cross – very cross about the DVD player screen. The screen flyed away and on a plop! Back on to Rachel Morris's house. 'Hey guys, I'm grumpy about something'. 'What's up?' But Gel took the DVD player away from Ellie. But it's to Ellie and Mrs Lapely Loop couldn't have it now. 'It's for prizing up only for grabs' said Rachel Morris grumpley. 'That screen is for Ellie Mustchin, this is now, prize up for grabs only, just only, NOOOW!'

Tim could write. While he was muddled, he would still take bits and pieces of information from all sorts of books, characters, people he knew and things he was interested in. We needed to get inside it more and see where he was coming from and use these stories he loved to take him further in all his creative processes. Again, school wouldn't do that.

Transition From Year 2 to Year 4: Are You Serious?

Have you ever felt that you have not been listened to by The System? Sorry, joke. Of course you have. If you have a child with autism or any element of extra needs, of course you have.

Tim had spent a whole year learning to manage in the environment of his new class and most importantly the children in it, many of whom he had forged tentative relationships with outside school, which was a great achievement. Would it be logical then to remove him from the environment where he had achieved all this, skip a whole academic year and put him into a totally new group of thirty children with whom he had built no relationship at all?

We had been refused our original request when Tim first came to St Andrew's for him to be back-classed and so that he could stay at a place which didn't push him too far out of his learning capacity, despite the fact that he is a summer-born child and needed more holding time to practice his gradually developing social skills.

School, however, had understood Tim's need for this and had told us that even though County wouldn't allow it and Tim was registered as a Year 3 child (seven-eight year olds), he could start his time at St Andrew's in Year 2 (six–seven year olds) as it was more infant and play-based. They said he could transition throughout the year into Year 3. This was not ideal but it was better than throwing him in at the deep end into a Year 3 class with much stricter timetables and no playing within the classroom. The school were really trying to meet us halfway here.

However, throughout the year Tim started to develop relationships and connections in Year 2 and began to develop tiny elements of cooperation. As I said earlier, he was totally involved in Sports Day. There were definite signs of progress.

However, School had either forgotten, or they could see how hard it would be to move him and it was suddenly just a couple of weeks till the end of the year. He hadn't been gradually transitioned and, because of the legal stance from County, would have to make the leap to a totally new year group and totally new class. The class he was in were six and seven year olds. He was seven. The class he would be going to was for eight and nine year olds. He would be eight over the holidays, but that wasn't the point here. He now suddenly had to be forced into a whole new class, missing out on an entire year's worth of social and academic learning.

From a summer where he was progressing and actually starting to relax and belong a little, he had to return to school to face a whole new class of thirty children along with a massive leap in academic and social expectations.

What shocked me most, was that the SENCO herself said she thought moving up a class was the best thing for him. She told me that if she thought Tim would progress or develop at all in the lower year she would have kept him there. What? So instead you put him *up* a group? I could see that the school staff really didn't believe Tim could make any progress. The SENCO then told me that it would be 'really hard for the Year 4 class to have him.' Charming! They didn't seem to want him *anywhere.*

What logic would take a child out of a situation that was working? Surely if something is working you should do more of it? Despite our protests and appeals for understanding, no one listened or was willing to be flexible.

The System Rules

The system ruled. There was even a document out at the time entitled 'Every Child Matters'. What a ridiculous title. No, my child didn't matter. The *system* mattered. Doing what was right for Tim at this time would have had no detrimental effect on County at all. One of their arguments was this: (It made me laugh) 'If he stays down a class there may be an element of him not being able to reach his full potential as the expectation for achievement would be for that of a younger child'.

The best bit was to follow… 'Naturally you would like the best for Tim and would not want him to be disadvantaged by this'. Excellent! They know him and us so well. Honestly, the lack of communication would have been like a hilarious sit-com if it wasn't so important. They talked about joined-up thinking, they talked about every child mattering, but they didn't think about *talking to parents!*

As I mentioned earlier, I sometimes used to think that just by the fact that I was a parent, I may as well have the word NULLIFY written across my forehead in indelible black ink whenever I talked to a school or a system about my child. It made no difference that I was a teacher, too, or that I had learnt so much about autism or that I knew my child the best. No. There was a faceless panel of people who could play God. Who sat around a table and talked about our lives and our child and made decisions about his future which could either make or break him. And they didn't even know what he looked like.

Year 4: Tim aged eight

So, despite all the good that was going on inside Tim, he was forced after the summer – bless his heart – to return to a whole new group of children and totally different social and academic expectations.

It was a shock to him. At eight, when he started Year 4 he was still only in school for the mornings but he had four different one-to-one teaching assistants. The Headteacher said he was so difficult to work with that she couldn't possibly ask one person to have him for more than two mornings. But where was the consistency for Tim? What about his need to spend time every day with the same adult to build a relationship? To talk to, develop trust with, to have fun with and create a rapport that might start to bring down the barriers and get him to a stage where he could learn?

He was given a desk at the back of the class, set apart from the others. This was intended to give him space if it became too loud and he needed somewhere to retreat to.

The class was full of lively children and was continuously buzzing with chatter and work. The children were very able to apply themselves and there were lots of long-standing friendship groups that would obviously be hard for any new child to break into.

'Volunteers', Not Friends

At this point, as Tim could not manage to engage with the others enough to persuade them to play with him or join in their games, he had 'volunteers' at every break time to play with him – either chasing games, skipping games, playing with hoops etc. If anything broke my heart, it was that my child needed volunteers as he still couldn't properly connect to make any friends. However, I adored walking from the school building to the staff room, seeing him surrounded by a group of children, all totally engrossed in a game on the playground. My Son-Rise thinking comforted me and told me that it was all part of a process and that he would have friends eventually. It was my biggest lifeline throughout all these bleak school times when it was hard to see how anything could come right. I knew that he was still a 'work in progress'. No one was shutting any doors and all progress was still possible.

I did find I had to be continually aware of Tim's internal state and very occasionally I would choose to keep him off school when he was totally overloaded and needed processing time. Of course I had to keep that quiet. Once the Headteacher caught wind of the fact that I occasionally kept him home for such reasons and she told me point blank that I was only ever *allowed* to keep him off if he had a *real illness*. For goodness sake! Anxiety and overload is part of autism. Our children need looking after and their state needs looking after. Since when are parents not allowed to look after their children? Schools don't take into account a child's state. Internal overload can be debilitating. The child can't take in new things, concentrate or cope with ever-increasing demands until they have had enough down time to process and unwind to the extent that they are ready. All I was doing was proactively helping him to ease a real problem, but the system seemed to be working against me here. Their thinking was he would learn that he only needs to kick up a fuss and he would be allowed to stay off school. The thinking that a child is merely kicking off out of naughtiness shows no respect or consideration that the child might be dealing with a heck of a lot and may need help.

When we were in the Son-Rise Program playroom, we could respect when he needed to switch off and when he was available to learn, which, as mentioned earlier is the red light/ green light concept. When Tim was overloaded, he would shut off from us and ism as part of his processing and as a way to wind down, which we respected. We stayed with him but never forced him to react, respond or do a particular task at these moments. When he was ready, he could interact and learn again. In school he was expected to have his green light on all the time, which was exhausting for him. This, I think, is why many children end up having to mask their difficulties in schools. They are forced into boxes where they don't naturally fit but they have no choice. I was glad I knew a different way to show respect to Tim throughout all his time at home. I have never known anyone in a school show respect for a child's need to process or re-group.

'No Point Him Being Here'

One day, I went to pick Tim up at the school entrance at 12.30 and was met by the teaching assistant who had Tim with her. 'There's no point him being here,' she said, right in front of him, as if he wasn't there. She showed me a piece of work – a Maths sheet where some sums were written inside pictures of elephants. None were attempted.

'How did you approach him?' I wanted to ask. 'Did you attempt to make any connections, use any of his motivations, laugh with him maybe? Get him on side? Or did you just sit with him in a quiet room waiting for him to sit still and attempt these boring sums?'

Yet, it wasn't my place to say this to her as I had been expressly forbidden to talk about this. How ironic that I, as his parent, who knew so much about him and his processing wasn't even allowed to suggest ways that would help him with both his connection and his learning.

You couldn't use normal approaches with Tim. It always required more – more connecting and trust first, more rapport building, more fun and giggles. Then through games and using his motivations, he would find a place where he could access the focus to get something done. I knew all this and my knowledge of him could have really helped them work with him, but not at any point were they willing to acknowledge my ability to get the best out of him. The Headteacher once wrote us a letter stating Tim's timetable and also explaining that if they needed help with Tim they would go to an 'expert'.

John Holt in *How Children Learn* (p20) explains a train of thought which can be summed up in this way: 'You cannot learn anything about yourself from your own experience but must believe whatever we experts tell you.'

This is a tiny part of an incredibly interesting thought process, basically about a child's autonomy over what is dictated from above. This is exactly how I felt I, too, was being treated. I knew so much about how Tim processed, ticked, worked, and knew how to help him on all levels from exactly the place of trusting and learning from our own experience. All my experience and knowledge was being invalidated. I spent about 75 waking hours each week with him on an intimate level. The person they took their advice from saw him for about one hour of his entire life.

Home/School Links

I started to feel that Tim's teaching assistants were becoming less communicative and simply delivering Tim out to us, then immediately heading back into school when Erik or I picked him up at lunch times. I needed to know how he had been each morning. Even a short chat would give me a feel of how he had been – any major upsets or any great connection moments. I was always respectful of the TA's time, but I needed to know this, because I was going to continue the work at home and being able to talk through what had happened at school created continuity for him. It worried me that his TAs would hardly say a word to me.

I approached the Headteacher. 'It's almost as if they're being told not to talk to me,' I explained.

'They are' she said.

I sat dumbfounded. *What*?

'It's not in their job remit to have to talk to parents. And anyway, it's their lunchtime' she said.

Again, *what*? This was the school that still emphasised their amazing home-school links and had reassured us that there would be good communication between them and us. Autism requires a lot more than a few written words in a home school book. By this stage, my trust had been severely damaged when in a meeting they had told me that it had once taken four adults to remove a screaming Tim from a classroom. They said that as they had 'dealt with it' they didn't need to tell us. *Come on!*

Seriously? The adults he was spending all his time with were being advised not to talk to us? It could look that this might be a reaction to someone who would lock them into conversation for hours, but I only ever needed a few words just to get a quick overview for the sake of Tim's development and ongoing continuity. We were *both* educating him – the school in the morning and us in the afternoon – and good communication was the glue that supposedly kept the whole thing together.

I was told that if I wanted to talk, I could make an appointment to talk to his teacher – who, by the way, hardly ever saw him. Or, to the Special Needs Coordinator, who was hardly ever in school. Both of these people were colleagues who I liked very much and got on well with on a personal level. However, neither of these teachers ever spent quality time with him. The people I needed to communicate with were the ones who spent the whole morning with him. They knew his reactions, his responses, his emotional state, how he had coped, what he had refused to do and what he had cooperated with. This blatant, unapologetic lack of communication was fuelling my increasing frustration with the school system.

Tim's Initiative

Once, in the car on the way to school Tim suddenly blurted, 'Mum, I don't want to sit on my own. I want to sit with the other children.'

Oh my goodness! What a sentence and what a brilliant thing to *want!* From choosing to do his own thing, he was now showing interest in mixing with the others in the classroom setting. I could hardly contain my excitement. 'Why don't you go up to Mrs Hamilton when you get to school and say that to her?' I encouraged him.

'So I shall say I don't want to sit on my own, I want to sit with the other children?' he asked. He always needed reassurance when he had to say something to someone else – and he needed to practice his sentences so he wouldn't forget. He practiced this sentence all the way to school so that he would feel ready to say it to her properly.

I was really encouraging to him, helping him to practice his sentence in order to embed it into his memory. I was so full of hope and expectation. I kissed him goodbye and watched him run into school thinking, 'Please God, let his desire be heard and let them see how huge this is.'

I was teaching that day, but as it happened I didn't see Tim at all in the morning and as usual wasn't allowed to mention him in the staff room. When my teaching day was over, I passed Mrs Hamilton sitting alone at her desk in the classroom. I knew I was supposed to ask for an appointment to talk about Tim, but I was just bursting with anticipation as to how his desire and ability to communicate it had been received.

I took a chance. I went in and tentatively asked, 'Did Tim say anything to you this morning?'

She looked up at me and said, 'Yes, it was really odd. He came up to me and said something about wanting to sit with the other children.'

'And?' I could hardly breathe…

'Well of course I couldn't let him' she said. 'I can't change the rules – I'd need to ask Mrs Jackson if we are going to change anything and if he thinks he can just change things, he'll never learn to accept the rules.'

I stood there, dumfounded. My precious child had actually managed to retain the sentence in his head, drawn on massive reserves of courage to ask, *which I had encouraged him to do,* wanted to be with the others and it had all been thrown back in his face.

For the love of God couldn't someone acknowledge him, respect his efforts, hear what he was *communicating* and respond back to him? How else was he going to feel it was worth making all that effort?

We Know the Way to Go – We Need to Jump into It

At that moment I knew that we needed to break from the School and immerse him full-time in the Son-Rise Program attitude if Tim were to have any hope of growing, learning and developing. The Son-Rise Program is all for initiative, response, flexibility – on the part of the adult as much as the child. It is all about noticing the effort and encouraging every ounce of communication. I knew that was the way we needed to go – all the time. What was I doing bringing him here? I knew he was improving so much by the very fact that he had asked for such a thing, but it was just being ignored because rules had to be kept.

Communication is more important than rules! Communication *leads* to the understanding of rules! Where was the flexibility on the part the school? Where was the ability to respond and be with him where he was? Without that, he didn't have a chance.

I did question in my mind whether the decision to not back-class Tim had been made because they didn't think it mattered what class he was in, as he would need one-to-one support anyway and was so far behind that he would never be able to be on a par with the other children socially or academically. When I really thought about it, this came right down to beliefs. If the teachers didn't believe Tim could grow and develop, why would they bother to try? In contrast, we totally believed he could grow in every area of his development and because of this we were constantly working with him to achieve those goals.

Quick, Meltdown Ahead!

One early morning on the playground when all the children were chattering and lining up, I could see that Tim's emotions were starting to overload. His anxiety levels were rising and he was starting to resist any attempts at cooperating. I overheard the teacher say to his TA, 'Quick, get Tim on the computer'.

My teaching day carried on but my mind was racing. *Tim needs to express his emotions – work through them, come out the other side. Therefore he needs to unwind his anxiety with fun and good communication. He needs to cry, shout, express his fears and frustrations. He also needs to be loved through this process –so he feels safe and knows it's OK to feel all these things – then he will come out on the other side. This is how we're treating him at home. By putting him in front of a computer he is literally being shut up.*

All his feelings remained inside as no one was interested to know what they were or why he felt the way he did. And with all this bubbling away inside him he was expected to just carry on and conform. It wouldn't work – it didn't happen that way. He didn't function in that way. He could never work through his own emotions in school as the school's priority was to keep him quiet. But not all communication and learning is quiet!

The computer shut all his feelings and anxiety back inside himself. His attention was diverted and the school had quiet, but Tim was not learning how to safely feel or process any of these heightened emotions that led to his continuous meltdowns. School had their strategies to 'deal' with him from the outside but what was really happening to him on the inside?

I'd been told that he screamed sometimes for twenty minutes, that he kicked chairs, did no work for long periods of time, couldn't listen to instructions and disturbed others. I knew all that and I still adored him and I still believed that all these things were solvable. You can be very isolated in your parental beliefs sometimes. There were *reasons* for his behaviours. We were working on them. It was a process.

My diary at the time says this:

> 'We are losing him. It's like all he is, all he feels, all his excitement and all he can do and aspire to is being wiped out because he will not conform to sitting at a lonely desk in a large class of 30 and do everything exactly when he's asked to do it. And where he's getting left behind and lost and upset and there's no future way forward that we can see, it's us as parents, who know him, who know his capability and believe in his potential that need to stand up for him. But if I have that attitude at the School they treat me as if I can't see reality – that he basically can't conform and won't conform and that if he doesn't learn, he'll never get on in life.'

But there was more to him than the sum of his difficulties.

I spoke about his feelings and how he needed emotional connection in order to learn. I explained that I believed Tim could learn if accessed in the way he needed but they spoke to me as if I was not facing reality. I still believed so strongly that if Tim had the input that worked for him, he could learn.

My diary says this: 'I thought about it. Does he laugh at school? No. Does he relax at school? No. Can he input his thoughts and have conversations? No. He can't access any of these things. But this is not the end of the road. It's actually the beginning. This just isn't the right place.

'Look Ahead to Supported Working'

The differences in our thinking were incredible. The Headteacher told me that that Tim would just have to learn to manage his difficulties for all his life. I would have to look ahead to 'supported working' and think backwards to what kind of secondary school he would be able to cope with.

Supported working? He is only 8! I still want to give him every chance! Does nobody around here believe that a child on the autistic spectrum can grow and progress?

Time Out of School for Therapy?

Tim was still struggling with sensory overload issues especially with regard to his hearing. He would often cry in assembly and hold his hands tightly over his ears because the sound was so loud, but even though the teachers removed him they told me they believed he was just attention seeking.

Attention seeking? Surely any child wanting to grab an adult's attention would find more varied and interesting ways of doing so. Surely he wouldn't cry at the same things and under the same conditions each time just to get someone's *attention*? Also, sensitive hearing is known to be an issue for children with autism and I had been aware for a while that Tim's hearing was causing him more problems than just being too loud.

The concept of Auditory Integration Training had been recently brought to my attention and in the information booklet from the Sound Learning Centre in London I learned that AIT could benefit children with hypersensitive or painful hearing, poor sound recognition and poor language processing. They explained that 'When sounds are uncomfortable or painful due to over-sensitive hearing, a natural reaction is to block these sounds out by covering the ears or by learning to ignore the sounds mentally. If this does not work, then a standard defence mechanism is to mentally 'switch off' or 'tune out' altogether.'

That was exactly what Tim did. That was why people found it so hard to tune him back in as he was battling the constant need to tune out.

The Sound Learning Centre information booklet went on to explain that 'If hearing is distorted in one or both ears, difficulties in speech reception (the ability to hear and understand) and expression (the ability to speak understandably) can be expected.' They also explained, 'Sometimes the lack of speech comprehension is interpreted by others as unwillingness to comply.'

Totally! I knew that Tim's lack of willingness to comply was far more than a lack of discipline. Maybe this place had some answers for me. So if Tim were to be tested and we found out that his hearing, after all this time, *was* distorted, it would give a reason as to why he was having so much difficulty with his speech and understanding of language.

So what could be done if it turned out his hearing *was* hypersensitive and distorted? Can his hearing profile be improved? According to the Sound Learning Centre, that's what AIT was for. Tim would need to listen through headphones to a modified and filtered musical programme through an electronic device for twenty minutes twice a day for ten days which would retrain his ears to hear in a more balanced way, which would then hopefully improve his hearing and therefore his processing and access to language.

Imagine if by tweaking his hearing, his pain levels, speech and understanding could all be improved. How did any of us really know the level to which this was affecting him?

I could recognise Tim's processes so clearly within all their explanations. There was no guarantee of this helping, however. I understood that. It was all a case of 'it might/may/could'. Therefore it was a risk. But in September we received confirmation that the Caudwell Charity were offering to pay for Tim to try this, which took away a large chunk of the risk. If this might help Tim in the area of his hearing, it was too good an opportunity to miss.

The issue was when to go. Half terms were only one week so we would need to ask for a week off school to do that. If it was Christmas or Easter it would be possible but would be a lot for Tim to cope with a whole term of school, his entire holiday being taken up with therapy in London and then straight back to school. We asked if we might take one week out of school for this as it made the most sense.

The Headteacher said she would need to ask advice on this.

Ask advice? This is therapy that could really help. We were only asking for five mornings away from school – and his hearing issue was affecting everything. When she came back to us she told us that she had taken advice and was disallowing the time off for therapy. She wouldn't say who she'd spoken to or give a reason.

Later on, a child came bouncing up to me in school all excited. 'You'll never guess what Mrs Wagter? We've been told we can go to Disneyworld for 2 weeks – in school time!!'

This was the straw that broke the camel's back for me. We could rebel and take him anyway, but I had to work with these people on a professional level and many had become friends. It was a confusing place to be. I just felt I couldn't fight other people any more as to what was right for my child.

Where is Our Energy Going?

Our energy was going on all the wrong things. Trying to convince other people of what our child needed, trying to explain approaches that would help him and being dismissed, asking for what we needed and being told it wasn't possible. I knew all the things we needed *were* possible. We just needed to be in an environment that could work with what we needed.

Erik and I sat down at one point and realised just how much energy we were putting into all this. 'Just imagine' I said, 'if we stopped putting all our energy there and put it directly into Tim and what he actually needs.'

Conflicting Messages

We realised that Tim was receiving conflicting messages. At home we did not force him to do work he couldn't grasp or stress him with overload or unrealistic expectations. We were constantly trying to provide a relaxed environment where he had a large amount of control. We were allowing him to be himself. We worked with him gently. Only when we had his willing engagement would we use that to start to build all the skills he was lacking.

At school he was receiving the messages that he was being irritating for having sensory overload issues, that he would only be praised if he did what he was told – even if that wasn't possible for him, that he had to fit into the agenda of others in order to be accepted and that his own feelings and interests were unimportant. These conflicting message couldn't continue with poor Tim trying to cope in the middle.

I knew Tim was so full of emotions, feelings, thoughts, ideas, but somehow he couldn't access them and they couldn't be expressed here at the school. The school had no place for this world of his. The Headteacher told me that using his motivations was pandering, but we already knew his motivations were the starting point.

John Holt, in *How Children Learn* (p124) says this, 'It can't be said too often. We get better at using words whether hearing, speaking, reading or writing under one condition and only one – when we use these words to say something we want to say for purposes that are our own'.

This was written of course for neurotypical children but for children with autism, surely this should be doubled in emphasis. If a child has the ability to think of something and say it, their words should be fully received and responded to. Motivations fuel the desire to talk which can set this valuable process in motion. They are not pandering. What is more important here?

John Holt also talks about trust and explains how important it is to trust children – just as The Son-Rise Program had encouraged us to trust Tim's processes. John Holt even explains that we find it so hard because we, ourselves were not trusted as children. This also correlates with The Son-Rise Program thinking. What a thing to do. I was being tempted to trust my own instincts, knowledge and experience over what the world was dictating to me that I should do.

The School suggested we think about sending him to a special needs school (even though the special needs school itself had said he was too bright to be there) so we looked again at options. We visited one primary school that had an Autism Unit. When we went into the room, there were computers on every desk blaring out computer games because it supposedly 'calmed the children down'.

However, our goal was connection and communication and we knew that computers put Tim back into his own exclusive world again which was the *opposite* of where we were aiming for. No chance. We had a goal and these places were not going to take us there. In the special needs school we visited, we saw children sitting in separate corners not communicating with each other at all. Tim needed lots of communication and to do lots of talking, not spending valuable learning time where children didn't readily communicate and weren't actively encouraged to do so. That wouldn't cut it. The schools we saw all seemed to be full of ABA-type agendas which the child would have to slot into. Tim needed to break free of these shackles if he were ever to sort out his processing and find his real self.

Final Decisions

On the weekend before we made the final decision, we took him to the beach. I remember looking into his face and seeing that he couldn't access any of the carefree feeling of the wildness of nature, or the fresh air on his skin. He was tightly wound, showing only acute anxiety which to me looked like pain. I knew we needed to love and unwind him – just that to start with – and if that meant taking him out of school to do this, then that's what we would do, the sooner the better.

I could stay working part-time as I was and Erik, who was self-employed, would need to mix and match his timings around Tim and his programme. My parents, who were always supportive, were willing to help too. We would mix and match our work and make this happen.

Chapter Ten – Stop the world we want to get off!

We needed to get rid of all hindrances and go full throttle on all the things that worked – freedom! If we were to give Tim any chance to create more fluency within his processing, we had to do more of what had been working. It was so exciting to think that we could be free to work every day on what we knew Tim needed. I knew he could develop. We had seen how putting nurture and connection first had made such inroads, but every time he came to school, rules were prioritised and because of all the demands on him, no one could reach him at the emerging level where he functioned.

Let's take the pressure off

We would take away everything that caused anxiety, instead putting connection first. We would love the stress out of him. Tim's defensiveness, lack of cooperation, and responses were all signs of pushing people away. He didn't sync with the way the people around him communicated and behaved but it shouldn't mean we should force him to fit in or write him off. He had an unusual prosody to his voice and an unusual way of moving. He still did a lot of self-talking and was highly focused on younger or unusual interests. But this shouldn't mean we coerce him out of this by teaching him the 'right' things to be interested in. He was unaware of other people, having no interest in their thoughts, feelings, desires or needs. He also had no sense of how others perceived him. But this didn't mean we should control and organise him. We knew that under those issues was a boy who cared, who had feelings and was really sensitive, who was desperate for friendships. We had to create a better way.

We knew that Tim still couldn't allow people to get close enough to deeply love him, to play with him, to enjoy him. This is where we would focus – we would connect and respond one-to-one until he let us in for longer intervals, when we would start to re-build his way into our world, gradually expanding to include others. I could see it. It was in my vision. I believed it. We had to give him this chance.

I couldn't wait.

We had to cut ties completely with the school, knowing if we had made a mistake we couldn't get back in. It was a tough call because, despite the difficulties, Tim had a community around him. But as I still worked in the school, I planned to keep Tim in touch with as many of his friends as I could.

I did find this decision made me desperately sad. While I knew this was right, it didn't stop me feeling a sense of separation, of being different to others and ostracised to a further level. I would still be working with all these children on their musical learning, plays, choir rehearsals and all our sessions were so full of camaraderie and fun – but Tim would now never even have an option to be a part of it. I had treasured him being with me in the same building – and valued the occasional moments when I had seen him happy and engaging with others. I wouldn't see that anymore. However, I knew no growth could happen here for Tim and I was desperate for change – for real growth. I was certain we had the knowledge, the tools and the resources to make it happen.

The Beginning of Our Home-School/Son-Rise® Program

Rachel, who had been working with Tim for two afternoons a week for a few months now, had agreed to work every morning with Tim if we took him out of school. My parents had recently been left some money at the passing of an elderly relative and, being the selfless people they were, instead of travelling or buying possessions, they chose to invest it in Tim's life.

We had many talks leading up to our decision to take Tim out of school. It would be like an extension of what we were already doing at home. Erik, Rachel and I already knew we could work together and we all had a passion to help Tim succeed. We wanted to help Tim *overcome* his issues instead of learning to *compensate* for them. Rachel supported me emotionally through the whole process and was there alongside us during this decision. When it was made, she prepared to work with Tim regularly as his main tutor every morning.

No More Compromise

One home educating book recommended taking three months of unstructured time to 'de-school' your children. This made me realise that most children need to un-do themselves from the system in order to start to live within their own rhythms and frameworks. It also helped me realise that it can take a while for all children to de-stress, not just children on the autistic spectrum. We planned for Tim to have session in The Son-Rise Program every morning with Rachel, followed by a social activity every afternoon with Erik or myself and that we were going to have a full Son-Rise attitude integrated into our daily lifestyle.

I felt that at last we could work with Tim as raw material from where he really was – not where he 'should' be and because of this, the progress he'd make would be real. We didn't want to condition or maintain him – we just wanted the essence of who he was to be with us and to grow from there. There were no higher powers looking over our shoulders making us do certain things or tick particular boxes. We could take our cues from him as to what he needed to learn and go with it.

I was aware of the massive responsibility, but felt confident that the three of us – myself, Erik and Rachel – would be more than able to rise to this challenge.

Focus on What's Important and Don't Waste his Time

One thing I felt very passionate about was that I didn't want to waste Tim's time. He only had so much learning energy in a day, so he didn't need to spend hours cutting pictures out of catalogues or playing computer games as he had done at school, where they were used as holding activities with no specific developmental goal. As a primary school teacher, I had taught the thirteen subjects as laid down by the National Curriculum, but on analysis, there were only three that we needed to focus on with Tim at this point. English, Maths and social interaction.

The Son-Rise Program Social Curriculum

All our advice on helping Tim to relate to people came from The Son-Rise Program, particularly their social curriculum. The Son-Rise Program Social Curriculum gave me great security that we were following a clearly devised plan for Tim's specific social development. He had made huge progress but we were still part-way through this curriculum and we needed an opportunity to finish it.

Despite the fact that social skills can seem very vague, the Son-Rise Program, as I mentioned earlier, had analysed and broken down every intrinsic element of social development into clear, obtainable levels with lots of ideas and activities for taking your child from one level to the next. I didn't need to look further for advice in this department. We could work out Tim's current levels and work on each element to gradually move up the levels. This was the most clarity I had ever seen with regard to documenting progress in social skills. The teacher in me loved the fact that we had a clear guide.

I must say here that by social skills, I don't mean purely learning to be socially appropriate. The Son-Rise Program Social Curriculum is not about teaching children to say the right thing and to fit in. It is not about teaching them to be something they are not. It is about nurturing them into being more who they are and developing their intrinsic ability to relate to other people.

Outside the Son-Rise Program, other than repetitive rote-learning, I had only ever found social stories or social groups as being recommended to help children with social skills and these had never scratched the surface for Tim. He didn't understand the messages from the stories and he wasn't yet ready to speak as part of a group. He needed help on a more fundamental level.

English

With English, I knew that we needed to work on Tim's basic understanding of the language, both in speaking and writing. In fact, I wouldn't have minded spending three years focusing on this alone. I did not want to focus on learning about African rainforests when Tim couldn't yet formulate a sentence that made sense. I also knew that any learning would happen twice as fast if we could use Tim's motivations and we were now free to do so. I had really seen that these were the engine of his growth.

Now we wouldn't have to be held back by dictated timetables offering lessons on designing Viking shields or learning songs about Harvest, we could actually do what would really help him. Our vision was that once Tim's language skills developed sufficiently, he would be able to study any subject that interested him. People say the humanities open up your mind and make you more aware of the world around you, but Tim wasn't ready for this. He needed to be taught on a much more interactive level in developing his language before he would be able to understand these subjects.

Maths

In terms of survival and independence, we felt that, after English, Maths was the most important other subject to focus on. It would be vital for Tim to begin to understand numbers, their relation to each other and how they related to real life.

So we determined to use motivations in every one of these areas.

Pathological Demand Avoidance

In hindsight I've learnt about pathological demand avoidance and I'm interested to see the relevance of this to Tim's issues. The term pathological freaked me out initially, but I now understand it's basically a term for extreme. I had thought that all children on the autistic spectrum had profound demand avoidance, but I now realise that it is a bigger issue for some children than others, and this was true of Tim. On the Pathological Demand Avoidance (PDA) website it states: 'This demand avoidant behaviour is rooted in an anxiety-based need to be in control'. They say: 'while the demand avoidant behaviour is relatively uncommon, it's important to recognise and understand its distinct behaviour profile as it has implications for how a person is best supported'.

Interestingly, Tim didn't fully fit the profile but in these ways he did: 'A high anxiety which drives a need to be in control and avoid the ordinary demands of everyday life' They also say: 'Raised anxiety which fuels demand avoidance and diminishes their well-being can make it challenging to engage children in learning. Families and staff recognise that structured, predictable and direct strategies that work well for children with autism and Asperger's syndrome are less effective for children with PDA who respond better to flexible, collaborative approaches. Amongst the best ways to support a child, they suggest positive and trusting relationships between the children and adults, having learning based around their personal interests, to collaborate with the child, to use indirect approaches which are creative, individualised and flexible and which can be adapted to synchronise anxiety and demand.'

Reading this, years after we took the decision to take Tim out of school and teach him in this way was a lightbulb moment for me. They were suggesting we teach him in exactly the ways we had chosen to teach him, the ways The Son-Rise Program had taught us and what our own natural experience and instincts had guided us towards.

The brilliant thing about our new journey was that we could totally follow Tim's motivations on a daily basis. By following motivations, I don't mean just following his whims, as he had gone past the stage of needing us to join him in that way. Tim was now showing his green lights and an increasing ability to be present with us. Because of this, we now had a bespoke teaching timetable. The difference in our agenda from that of the school, was that it was based on knowledge of his development. We were firm, we had boundaries and while learning, we expected him to try do what we were asking of him as he was now capable of this. The very real difference was that we were asking him to do things he could already do and build up gradually from there, using every spark of interest that came from him. Most importantly of all, we could change our agenda at the drop of a hat whenever we felt it necessary. Erik described the difference as a school being a huge liner, unable to change course for any individual child, while we were a little motorboat, able to quickly alter course when necessary, for Tim's further development or over-learning.

Throughout every session Tim's responses, thoughts and feelings were very much part of the agenda and some of those early sessions were quite challenging. When we first started working at home, Tim was constantly negative. He would say to Rachel, 'You are a horrible teacher. You are making me do bad learning, I can't do this...'. He was in a highly emotionally resistant state and his moods would change from one minute to the next, however laughter was always on hand and Tim had kindness and personal attention on tap. He just needed some fun, some silliness, some space and to feel loved. We had no need to get into control battles, instead providing trust and enjoyment, where before there had only been misery and failure.

From our part-time Son-Rise Program we had already given Tim a foundation of willingness to participate, relationships, interaction, fun and a trust in us as people. We weren't starting at the beginning. We were already a long way down the road.

On one occasion, Rachel was showing Tim some Maths she wanted him to do, while he wanted to do something else. Rachel held firm and when Tim began to get actively cross and resistant, she firmly and lovingly told him that she was more than willing to talk to him, but she couldn't while he was in this state. Rachel continued to maintain a calm, loving attitude in the face of Tim's vocal objections, until after some twenty-five minutes, he came and sat next to her and completed all the work totally unaided. While he was cooperating, he still held on to his anger at this point. However, afterwards through shared games, fun and silliness he was able to let go of his anger and regain his loving relationship with Rachel.

This episode had shown that Tim could learn to process his own resistance and come out on the other side without force or coercion. I found this exciting.

What – Laughter?

Once I was working in the lounge while Tim was having a session with Rachel. I had become so accustomed to hearing crying, screaming, upsets and angry outbursts over the last few months, but I was not accustomed to the next thing I heard. Laughter. Intimate, conspiratorial, spontaneous and hilarious laughter. Forgive all my adjectives, but it was really like that. I jumped up and went to look. They were seated around a game and Rachel was making Tim laugh to the point of tears with her reactions to winning and losing and all her silly comments. They were both genuinely laughing! I watched and felt an incredible sense of relief. Laughter. What a beautiful sound. What a beautiful feeling. I realised Tim could learn this way – interactions, upsets, making up, laughter... I was watching his stress gradually leave him and his desire for fun and interaction take over. Wow. Thank you, thank you God. Thank you, Rachel. Thank you, Son-Rise.

Every day was an adventure of learning, resisting, working through things and coming out on the other side.

How We Taught Him

When Rachel was teaching Tim a new game, he would start out highly resistant. She would allow that and let him watch grumpily from the corner of the room, where he had retreated, while she played. It didn't stop her playing but if he didn't want to that was fine. The next time he might hand her a few pieces while he watched, still keeping his distance. The next day when the game came out again, he may tell her the name of the character he wanted to be and Rachel would play the parts of both people – herself and Tim's character. Rachel would have so much fun in her reactions to what was happening in the game until Tim felt genuinely ready to come over and be part of it. He then often showed he could learn the game incredibly fast and become really good at it. This was then a game he could play with lots of different people in different settings, enjoying the challenge and the relationship with whom he was playing.

So it wasn't that he couldn't learn – it's that he needed the right way in. He needed the adult with him to allow him his uncertainty, not judge him and be with him through the process, even though it was quite a long and complex one. The games Tim was starting to learn were conventional ones that everyone knew, such as Junior Monopoly, Uno, Boggle and Scrabble. The great thing about this was that all his friends also knew these games, so for the next few months whenever friends came round, out came the Monopoly. It was a great way to interact on a conventional level where the other child didn't have to compromise or do specifically what Tim wanted. On occasions, I could even sit back and do something else while Tim and a friend sat around the Monopoly board and chatted and played. I loved these games!

Through allowing Tim his pathway into learning, it was providing access points for language acquisition and understanding in a really relaxed, fun environment. From then on, games were constantly a staple for specific learning targets. Even when we went to other people's houses, I would take board games and would often find myself sitting on the floor with a group of children playing, despite my desire to catch up with the other adults. This was necessary for Tim to stay occupied and happy with others around as a way into different environments with new people.

Relevant Learning

Because of Tim's struggle with concepts, we needed to teach him in a way that incorporated this.

Maths lessons consisted of counting in twos, then in fives without using terms like multiply as this was too complex. Tim had to start at the beginning as nothing he had learnt in school had been retained. He would throw two dice and add up the numbers and he started gradually to understand and use number lines. In his English lessons, he was learning the difference between fact and fiction (the difference between what actually happened versus the ideas that were very real and important to him in his head). He would annotate photos and write diaries about what happened to him. Everything in his learning was relevant to his life.

At this stage, Rachel worked with Tim on his English and Maths, while Erik and I worked with him on his social and self-help skills, though we could often interweave this with the learning going on in the morning.

How Did Rachel Incorporate The Son-Rise Program Fundamentals into Tim's Daily Learning?

NON-VERBAL SKILLS: Rachel always encouraged eye contact in fun, friendly ways, communicating via her eyes and expressions etc. In fact, Rachel was partially deaf, so needed Tim to be looking at her when he spoke. She regularly reminded him of this and Tim in turn would take hold of her chin to turn her face to his when he spoke sometimes, perhaps to be assured of her full attention. This led to a wealth of communication, much deeper than words. Rachel was communicating her acceptance and love of him, as well as her willingness to listen to him. They hugged all the time, too. Often I would find Tim lolling comfortably over Rachel while they played a game. He needed this physical contact, for reassurance. I was so pleased that Rachel was totally happy to hug him when needed. If Tim cried, she wouldn't hesitate to cuddle him. This human contact was much needed by Tim, but hadn't been allowed at school.

VERBAL SKILLS: Rachel always listened when Tim spoke and took him seriously. She spoke back and encouraged him to keep the conversation going, to express himself and she would celebrate with him when he managed to make sense with his words. Her celebrations often made Tim laugh. Communication was her constant priority.

INTERACTIVE ATTENTION SPAN: Now he was starting to understand more, Rachel could spend longer engaging Tim in explanations and games etc. When she would explain tasks to him that he couldn't yet grasp, she found that he would switch off quickly or complain, but when she used humour and lots of fun, she could help him maintain attention and learning for longer periods.

FLEXIBILITY: Rachel would gently challenge Tim on his thoughts, what he wanted and whether he could do things differently while giving him as much certainty and security as she could. She would ask him to read what he'd written, think about it and start to think for himself about changes he may need to make. Rachel, while having a plan, also modelled flexibility in herself and her ways of dealing with Tim.

Erik and I used these fundamentals daily, too. With all Tim's reactions I could assess where he was within these elements on an ongoing basis. I could see when he was being particularly inflexible, maybe he was struggling to communicate verbally, maybe he had lost his ability to hold interactive attention for a while and needed to switch off, or maybe he wasn't picking up on the non-verbal signals of the people around him. By being aware of these issues and having a plan to take him forward in each one, I knew we were on a path that could only help him. When I looked forward to Stage 5 of the Son-Rise Program Social Curriculum, it gave me great inspiration to continue along this path as it led to a massive amount of social and emotional independence.

My Mind-Set about Autism

I never looked at Tim and thought, 'You are on the autistic spectrum so you can't do this and that'. Instead I thought, 'You are struggling, so I will help you through it and onto the next level. I hadn't heard of fixed and growth mindset at this time, but looking back, the growth mindset is what I had. I was also focused on helping him to overcome his difficulties, not compensate for them. I didn't want to say, 'As he finds communicating so difficult we will do something else.' Instead I wanted to focus on making communication as fun, interesting and worthwhile for him as possible, so that he would want to learn it more. I knew that this would be a slower path, but I also knew that the changes could give him a much stronger life foundation. This was very different to the thinking about autism I had come across in any school. I knew that with a growth mind-set around Tim's personal development, he could progress and I felt I never wanted him to be restricted again by negative, fixed thinking or closed doors.

Tim's Emotions

We found that by being present with Tim through his meltdowns, he was starting to learn to let go of all his frustrations and emotions. The brilliant thing was that he would then turn himself around, say sorry from his own desire to do so and carry on with his work. His meltdowns were starting to diffuse in a very loving way, maybe because he found less to resist against and then he started to learn a new way to deal with his emotions, totally naturally. No one was preventing him from expressing any of his emotions, even the loud, scary ones. There was also lots of fun to be had once he was out on the other side, which he now liked and the sooner he came out of his meltdowns, the sooner he could access this.

I think emotions are not taken seriously enough with children on the autistic spectrum. Academic achievement is often put before emotional processing, whereas I believe it should be the major priority. When emotions can be expressed and the child can experience and learn to process them, the world is their oyster in terms of relationships and learning. I still believe Tim was only ready for this emotional processing because we had laid the foundations from all the love and closeness of his Son-Rise Program journey to date.

Why was the Focus Room Working for Tim?

Tim had relief in the Focus Room from all the sensory pressure and the busy-ness vying for his attention in the outside world. He didn't have to try and understand every social rule or keep up with thousands of conversations all around him, scraping chairs, sudden bells, high expectations. All that fell away while he was in a place where he could just be himself, be fully accepted within the muddle he was in and grow from the place where he really was. He could have fun, play with adults who were 100% there for him and through this he could start to think and to learn. We could see the process happening so clearly. That's why I knew if we kept doing this and only this, he could make significant inroads in his development.

Tim was developing slowly but surely in the Focus Room. We told ourselves it didn't matter that he was behind his peers and when people liked to tell us repeatedly that the gap would ever grow wider, we made a conscious decision to not worry about it but continue to focus on Tim developing to *his* next level. After all, we had too much work to do with Tim's talking, listening, responding, writing and reading to waste time looking regretfully over our shoulder at what was happening with other children and making pointless comparisons.

Reading was his best skill at this point and it gave me hope that he was able to decode words and read them. He still found it hard to understand exactly what he was reading and couldn't talk to us about the story but he could *read the words.* That was a massive start which gave a foundation for other learning.

Screen Time

Between the ages of five and seven, we had found it useful to significantly limit Tim's access to screens, in that he didn't watch any TV or DVDs and he played no computer games. However, he did use a computer sometimes for typing stories, which he thoroughly enjoyed doing.

At about seven and a half, because of his love for story we started to allow him half an hour every evening, when he watched an episode from a favourite children's DVD. Interestingly, he never argued or campaigned for more time and this went on until about the age of nine. On very special occasions, we allowed him to watch a film on DVD, which he adored as something to look forward to.

The Sound Learning Centre

Now we had broken free of the system, we could choose when to take Tim for his Auditory Integration Therapy. We worked out that

Erik could go and stay with him for the whole ten days. I still had my teaching duties at school, but I had also been asked to deliver an Inset training session in London, so I could combine that with visiting them for a couple of days.

I had envisaged a massive building full of complex equipment, but from the outside it was just an ordinary house in an ordinary street in the middle of London. In the Therapy Room was the sound equipment and the chair to sit in with the headphones. During his initial assessment, for all the familiar reasons, Tim started out cooperating and then refused. Erik said he was asked to do all sorts of physical things like crawl from one side of the room to the other and walk on his heels and his tiptoes. Everything he was asked to do added to his anxiety and therefore lack of cooperation. He couldn't see the point, which was a big factor for him and when he had to sit in a chair next to Erik, opposite someone asking him questions, Erik said his anxiety started to go through the roof. They only managed to test one ear. It was a new environment and there were high expectations of him to perform these specific assessment tasks which was a red rag to a bull for him.

Through what they managed to test, they found that Tim had a distorted hearing profile and some hypersensitivities to certain frequencies in his right ear. They also stated that there were clear indications that he was hypersensitive at some frequencies and was affected by certain sounds which may well be uncomfortable to him. They acknowledged that Tim was very sensitive to certain sounds and became distressed by them, as they observed, 'He often makes various sounds and tends to speak loudly'.

They stated the following: 'Tim's hearing profile will have affected his ability to process or reproduce sounds correctly, in the right order and in time. He also has slow response times and finds it difficult to follow sequential instructions. Tim is suffering from Auditory Processing Delay.'

They organised a programme for Tim – twice a day he had to go for half an hour sound therapy with the headphones on. I was gobsmacked that he was willing to do all these things – but he did! He sat peacefully in a chair with headphones on listening to music with parts missing, trying to re-create new pathways between his brain and his ear. He looked so sweet and compliant sitting in that chair with great big headphones on, doing everything he was asked to do. It was as if somewhere in his subconscious, he believed it would help him.

Light Therapy

While Tim was there, he also had Lightwave Stimulation Therapy. This involved him leaning against a device that looked a little like an old-fashioned camera and popping his head inside some sort of box, staring at particular lights for 20 minutes twice a day. I knew very little about this, other than that it was recommended as helpful alongside his Auditory Integration Therapy. The idea was to address any light processing deficiencies which may affect mood, learning, behaviour, social difficulties etc. Bright lights had always made Tim uncomfortable. His mood changes and sleeping patterns had always posed a problem too. To be honest, it seemed to me that this came as an extra to the AIT although I'm sure it had way more significance than I had the current ability to register or understand.

Erik told me that once Tim knew what to expect on a daily basis, it really helped him. Then when they started to know the area of London where they were staying, they established a routine of going to a café then a second-hand shop to buy a DVD after each morning session – which was huge treat for him and helped him to handle the long waits and the inevitable stress of being in unfamiliar surroundings.

While I was there, I asked all the questions I could. I was trying to get an answer to a particular long-standing question that we had been debating for years. If Tim showed distress at specific sounds we made, was he really in pain or was this part of his control issues? On one of the days, a student called Ben talked to me in depth for almost an hour – he was really interested to listen and try to answer my questions. We made an appointment for me to come back and talk further the next day. I only had one more day before I had to go back to work and so this day was vital for me to find some answers. We started talking, but then a lady came in and asked to speak to Ben. He never returned and when she returned, she told me he was only a student and didn't have the answers for me and that I should leave.

Leave? This was the place where they were meant to have some answers to some of my sensory questions! I had waited years to be able to talk about this with people that knew what they were talking about. These people must have had hundreds of children pass through their doors all with sound sensory issues. The whole therapy was costing the Caudwell nearly £2,000 and us about £1,000, just to stay in London. I had travelled for hours on buses, trains and taxis just to get here – and they were fobbing me off? I was speechless but she was still showing me the door.

For all my asking – and I did go back – they couldn't give me definitive answers, but interestingly I later found them.

Following these ten days in London, we returned home and Erik and I noticed immediate changes. I say it best in an email I sent to the lovely student at the Sound Learning Centre a few days later:

> 'Hi Ben, We are getting some fantastic results – seriously! Erik and I are trying to be realistic with our hopes but we are quietly quite excited! I can now sing and hum a little when close to Tim at his bedside, while he is eating, in the car etc – unheard of before. Also, he is so much calmer and seems less muddled in his head. He seems to have lost a lot of his 'fight or flight' reflex which has dominated him for years. He seems a bit more patient and mature (someone else commented on that when I had said nothing) *and* he has been so much less controlling – I have had a fantastic two days with him – he is more relaxed and doesn't seem to switch off from us.
>
> Something else I have noticed is that I don't have to keep asking him to look at me – he looks at me easily and more frequently and also initiates loads of conversation – mostly logical and full of sense and opinion. It is like he is not having to work so hard to cope with just existing. Erik and I are still trying hard not to get our hopes up as we have a

> lot of experience of these changes being flashes in the pan, but it is *lovely* living with him at the moment. He even had two new children approach him to be friends at a play centre the other day. I can only put that down to him being more accessible

Interestingly we never lost any of these amazing changes. This therapy created a massive and permanent shift in Tim in all the areas I mentioned in the email.

Totally Go with Motivations

When we were at the Sound Learning Centre in London and hanging around in the flat between therapy sessions, Tim had suddenly said to me, 'I want to do a concert.' He was writing lists of the songs he wanted to sing and told me that he wanted a live band with drums, a keyboard and a guitar. His passion was evident and it filled his head with plans and ideas.

However, we were at the Sound Learning Centre *because* he hadn't so far been able to tolerate loud sounds around him and even quiet ones – even us whispering or singing in his ear would upset him, so I couldn't see how this would pan out, short of a miracle. The point was I didn't need to see it. We would go along with his motivation, show interest, talk about it and if it evolved more, we would be more than willing to make it happen. My own head filled with ideas – a concert, friends, invites, food, – all the things we could work on.

If I hadn't listened to Samahria Kaufman in the CD *Special Children Special Solutions* I wouldn't have put such value on these six quietly spoken words or known the power they held. I might have dismissed them but I had learnt to see the value in every single word and to act on it.

When we came back to regular lessons, Rachel came in and after a catch up, she started talking about ideas she had for Tim's session that morning. I told her that Tim had been talking keenly and incessantly about wanting to do a concert.

'Oh, we'll do that instead then,' Rachel said as it was something that was full-on in the forefront of Tim's mind. She could keep a lot of her learning goals the same as they were all based around thinking, talking and writing skills, but she would change the focus. We were so grateful for the freedom to be flexible! Between the three of us and the freedom we had, we could spontaneously have a massive impact on Tim's learning.

Progression Through Obsessions or Powerful Interests: Still Trusting the Process

I will call these powerful interests. That is what they are and the term 'obsession' can sound so negative. The Son-Rise Program use the term powerful interests and see the growth opportunities that sharing these with your child can bring. They recognise that these interests are a great way to connect to your child and can be used in multiple ways to help the child to communicate, learn and can create growth in every area.

In a recent autism qualification (NVQ level 2 in Understanding Autism) I undertook, purely to find out how the Government were explaining autism to people, they talk about setting limits on someone's time to talk about their powerful interest and I quote: 'limits might need to be set, such as, for example, two half-hour conversations a day. This should avoid the conversation being dominated by the specialist subject.'

In another autism book I read, someone recommends that children should be allowed ten minutes at a time to talk about their chosen subject, before being directed to move on to other subjects.

But the Son-Rise Program says the opposite – to really listen to the thoughts, desires and interests of our children and to use them to create a shared interest, and be close and promote learning. It's an incredible driving force and can help a child in every area of their development. They helped me to see the growth that going with Tim's powerful interests could bring.

Raun Kaufman made me laugh during his initial lecture in London when he said that if your child is interested in trains, you should become a train *freak*! I got the message immediately. I would become even more interested in Tim's powerful interests than he was and be one step ahead, making all these things happen and using them in every area of his development.

It seems that when adults are advised to limit children's powerful interests, it is because of a desire either for control, or to put social acceptability first rather than what will ultimately help the child's processing. Helping the child's processing first will ultimately help them to learn, grow and relate to people better, which in turn will lead to improved interactive ability, inevitably leading to better social acceptability in the long run from a willing child. This is the paradox of the Son-Rise Program approach, which made a lot of sense to me. My priority has always been – and still is – on Tim's social processing rather than his social acceptability, because the former ensures the latter occurs anyway.

I like the Son-Rise Program approach best as it seeks to delve inside the child's own thinking and to help them know that their thoughts are important and that they can talk for as long as they need on their chosen subject and can even have someone be excited about what they like with them. The great thing is, this leads ultimately to both goals being met. The child doesn't feel that who they really are is pushed out by social protocol, so will feel better about themselves and they also learn about reciprocity of conversation and being interested in someone else's thoughts and ideas through first having someone show interest in them. It just takes a long time. We knew this.

Even in the book, *I am special* which I quoted from earlier, it states: 'Conversations with people with autism should have a clear structure and should be directed towards a definite goal and preferably be conducted according to a set plan. It is best not to let the person with autism decide on the subject, the duration, the course of the conversation. In the hands of a person with autism the chances are it will turn into a never-ending purposeless and chaotic discussion (because of the associations they make). It will certainly not be very results-orientated. If you are talking with people with autism you should be directed... When the person with autism introduces a new topic because of certain concrete associations, this needs to be channelled. E.g., by saying 'we'll talk about that later because we have to finish this first' or 'I will take note of that and we'll come back to it next time'

I find this really disrespectful to the person on the autistic spectrum. Everyone wants people to listen to what they are really saying. How else is anyone going to know how you are feeling? Also, why pull someone into your agenda? What makes your agenda right and theirs wrong? If the issue is connecting and communicating, surely it should be the task of people who find these things easy to show interest. Why put on a time limit to something that is helpful? This is a way to connect. And what does The Son-Rise Program say? Connection is the foundation for all learning and growth. This was how I was viewing Tim's powerful and ever-changing interests – by understanding them and using them, though some were easier to use than others.

Making Radio Programmes

Through the first two years of Tim's part-time Son-Rise Program, he had wanted to dictate stories. Then he advanced on to wanting to write them. Next, he was moving on to something else – making radio programmes. This showed a real progression as it involved talking and being listened to. There is an audience for a radio programme and you expect that someone will be listening – so, for me, this opened up the perspective a lot. The dictations and stories had purely been for Tim's amusement but this was for an audience. He very much wanted other people to make the radio programmes with him and he would write scripts of what he wanted them to say. He also sometimes told jokes with other children as DJ's can do, then introduced songs etc. He could still be overwhelmingly controlling in this activity but we were working on his flexibility daily, and these radio programmes were excellent for spontaneous talking as he enjoyed making them so much.

In his lessons with Rachel, he always wanted her to do recordings with him and she often allowed him to do them in his 'choosing time' at the end of the sessions.

While Tim has moved through his varying powerful interests, he has had some which others could not easily relate to, such as the BBC World Service and subjects like Recycle on Demand (a story and concept of Tim's making), which I'm sure was brilliant, even though we didn't quite understand it, But when younger, one that was really helpful, was his enthusiasm for The Magic Key early reading books featuring Biff, Chip and Kipper when he was in infant school. Now, he was into another really helpful one – pop songs. In fact, this is a relatively common interest for most children and teenagers. Hooray – another meeting place for him and his friends!

He started to listen to and enjoy all the chart songs, getting to know the artists and bands. This meant he could then talk about them and listen to songs with his friends. It was a great way in for social conversations. It's like hitting the jackpot when your child's natural desires work with what they want to achieve socially.

What's the Plan?

Tim's awareness of time was interesting. He would constantly ask, 'How many minutes' as if he wanted everything he had to do to stop soon. When people were visiting, he would often ask how long they would be staying – in front of them. We thought this was because he found the whole social element hard, or that he was looking forward to what would happen when they left. He also had a high need to know 'the plan' at all times. In fact his first question of the day was, 'What's the *plan*?' Nothing could be left to chance in his world at this point – we couldn't just hang about and see what happened, and we couldn't have a day without a plan. If a friend was involved, the plan was just as important – Tim could never just spontaneously spend time with a friend as they had to be occupied doing something specific that interested him.

Reward Systems Working for the First Time

At this point, rewards, little presents, treats and surprises meant a lot to him. So we started giving him outward reward charts for when he had been specifically cooperative and willing to try something he found hard. I say 'outward' because since our involvement with ABA sessions, which are full of coercion and rewards, we had taken a step back from unrelated rewards in favour of intrinsic motivations. However, now that he became excited about gaining stars, winning money or prizes, we used this as a way to give him some control over his own rewards and success, which he loved.

The vital difference at this stage was that these reward charts were not used to fire up his intrinsic motivation – his motivational engine was already running – it was simply a method of celebrating his success in a way that he loved. In fact, he was particularly inspired to stretch himself in areas of self-help – washing his hands, brushing his teeth, eating – all things which he struggled with to varying degrees. We never docked reward points or threatened to do so as a way of coercing him, if he didn't do something, but would only use them for celebration.

We also included him in our goals for him. I would sometimes say, 'Wow – what you said just made total sense!'

And he would reply, 'We *must* tell Rachel!' as he knew it was his target and his rocket on the reward chart would take a step further towards the top. And the top meant prizes.

Learning to Think

One of my greatest desires at this point was to assist Tim's thinking. I was sure that if we could help Tim's inner thinking (which had been muddled from the beginning) the improvement would be evident in his talking, listening, writing – every element of his communication – and he would be able to express himself. So far, what he said and wrote was often incoherent to outsiders and I wasn't even sure he could make sense of it. His neurological processes seemed so complex.

These are examples of some of his written sentences at that time:

'Tim made a bakery outside a house with a table, phonic words and his both of things in his bags.'

'We sing a Demand theme but they sing that song to me. I call Michael to be the candidate 1 2 3 Go!'

'Oh wait, Alarm Musically Morris! My hamster, Tim Wagter, needs to be Santa Claus!'

'Tim Wagter's children in stories sat on the bed in Tim's, hug, hold hands, and lie down on Tim's bed, and they sung long and too much.'

While Tim's ability to write, spell and punctuate was impressive, the meaning was such an issue that I couldn't see the point in helping Tim to improve his speech or writing if we weren't addressing the real issue of where he was with his thoughts. It seemed obvious that's where his muddle stemmed from and it was all to do with his inner processing. I explained all this to Rachel and it turned out that she was just naturally brilliant at helping Tim with his inner thinking. She spoke to him about everything – they talked everything through. He would write something and they would read it together and she would start to question him about what made sense. Because of her many hours of fun and the trust she had built up with him, he was happy to talk with her in this way. Gradually over the next year, he began to correct himself. I wanted him to judge for himself if something made sense, without always relying on the other person to tell him. I believed that learning to make sense of his own thinking was surely the start of his independence.

Theory of Mind

I found the concept of Theory of Mind very interesting at this point and was beginning to learn more about it. I had been reluctant up to this stage to ask Tim the well-known Theory of Mind question, as I didn't think he'd understand it. One way to get the first element of Theory of Mind is to follow this story.

I go into the kitchen and put my keys in the usual spot and then walk out. Someone else comes in, takes my keys and puts them in the cupboard and walks out. When I come back in, where will I look for my keys? Well, of course it's obvious that I will look where I left them, but if somebody lacks Theory of Mind they will say that I will look in the cupboard because that's where they are.

This is literal, black and white thinking and I know it's common for children with autism to have this kind of thinking. Theory of Mind, as I understand it, is all about putting yourself in other people's shoes, being aware that people can think things about other people's thoughts and feelings and not everybody sees something in the same way. Key words for him to understand would be *know, think, believe, if, promise* and issues such as getting the difference between a lie and a joke or whether someone would smile even if they weren't happy. It seems that most typically-developing people have an innate Theory of Mind, but children with issues like Tim struggle with it, making meaningful social interactions difficult.

At this stage, Tim was not able to follow this series of events, let alone answer the question about where I would look for my keys, so I knew he wasn't ready for me to ask him this question. He also wasn't able yet to put himself in someone else's shoes. Temple Grandin, the famous autism author and speaker, calls it 'perspective taking' and she sees it as the most fundamental element of social skills. I knew Tim wasn't yet able to do this.

This is why we were constantly using The Son-Rise Program Social Curriculum stages with him. The quality time we were spending and our continuous nurturing interactions were enabling Tim to gradually see life through our eyes as well as his own and be aware of our feelings, which could then lead on to him caring about other people meaningfully and would gradually widen his views and his social thinking.

Interpreters Needed 24/7

At this stage, Tim always needed someone with him to act as an interpreter wherever he went – someone to understand what was going on around him and explain it to him in a way he could comprehend, then interpret what he said and wanted back to the other person in the outside world. As he developed, I envisaged a little man on his shoulder acting as his interpreter and helping us to be free and him to be more independent. Ideally, I wanted him to get to the point where he could be completely free without the need for any interpreter. This was my major goal.

From 'I Can't' To 'I'll Try'

When the pressure started to come off Tim – when he realised he was not going to be pushed beyond endurance and we were there, helping him with his processing, his ability to cooperate started surfacing. Instead of insisting, 'I can't, I can't' in a negative, agitated voice, he would say, 'I'll try'. What more could we ask for? This had the power to turn everything around.

Once when he was with two friends, running around at some local skate ramps, his friends were scrambling up one of the steepest ramps and managed to get to the top. He was complaining, 'I can't do it, I can't do it!' but then with encouragement and some reaching out of hands he managed to get up there and he stood triumphantly and turned his words around, *'I did it!'* His pleasure at his own achievements became a huge motivating factor for him and has continued to be so.

The Beano

In the first term of Tim's Son-Rise Program home/school experience, he started to love car boot sales. This was great as I loved car boot sales too. He wouldn't be too patient if I saw something I liked such as clothes or boots and wanted to linger, but he did love looking at all the books, CDs and DVDs. When browsing through a stall at some point, he happened across a *Beano Annual*. He was really interested, bought it and became instantly hooked. He loved the characters, the humour, the silliness and the fact that it was all done in comic style. He has loved them ever since and has built a huge collection. I loved this because it was fuelling his love of story, play on words, comedy, jokes and was something that most boys his age enjoyed and appreciated. He started to read them in his free time and would tell us about the stories. Erik and I bought him boxes full of second-hand *Beanos* on Ebay for his ninth birthday.

First Why Question

On 18th March 2011 when Tim was nine, on Red Nose Day, when Rachel and Tim were working on special projects, I was passing Tim's room and I heard him say to Rachel, 'Why is today so important?'.

I couldn't believe it. This was the first time he had ever asked a why question. It was relevant to the situation and was quite a conceptual leap. I was really excited. A while later, we saw exactly the same question in his *Beano* and though I felt a little disappointed that this actually wasn't his own thinking and questioning, I realised he had understood the question, interpreted it well and used it in exactly the right context.

Tim, to this point, had asked a few what and where questions, wanting to know concrete specifics about his day, but *why* questions use a different level of thinking. He actually wanted to know the answer, too, and seemed to understand the answer Rachel gave him. All progress!

Acknowledging Invisible Processing Issues

Everything we did with Tim put relationships first. It was about building his inner trust with us all, so he would feel safe enough to let go of his anxieties and start to want to do things with us. We welcomed every emotion and never asked him to be quiet or to stop any processing he felt was necessary. He responded to love, nurture and acceptance, apologies and reconciliation. What he didn't respond to was being forced to do things against his will, rules he didn't understand and having people insisting he react appropriately when his ability to process had broken down. He needed us to see and respond to the feelings and pressures he was under that most people couldn't see. Only because we acknowledged these aspects of where he was at this point could we proactively help him.

When Rachel could see a meltdown coming, she would say, 'If you want to cry and scream that's OK but I will be here for you as soon as you are ready to talk'. She had time for him to process his feelings and she had the strength to remain calm and loving with him throughout his panic and noise and she was ready and waiting when his 'green light' came back on and he was able to focus once more. Gradually, however, Tim had less need to meltdown.

My Commitment to Tim's Social Development

I had committed myself, when we took Tim out of school, to do something social with him every afternoon for as long as it took to help him feel comfortable with his emerging ability to relate to people. He needed to be with other children and he needed to have opportunities to develop his abilities to connect and be friends with other children in non-pressured, fun ways.

Friendships were very difficult for Tim at this time. He desperately wanted them, which I took as a brilliant sign, but he didn't yet have the skills to show interest in others or to mix and match in a group. Tim was very specific and controlling in what he wanted a friend to do. He would talk about things they weren't interested in, while not listening to anything they wanted to tell him. But instead of shying away from other children because of this, I felt it was all the more reason to be with children every day – to do fun things, so start to learn and show Tim how much fun relationships with other children could be.

He was able to be alongside other children doing things he liked. So that's where we would start. He liked going to car boot sales and second-hand shops to buy things – so did other children. He liked playing particular board games – as did others; he enjoyed trying to play table tennis – which other children also liked. So there were lots of starting points and meeting places already. I tried to arrange to see the same child or children each week on the same day to bring some continuity. A lot of children liked Tim, he just couldn't yet communicate with them easily – which made it hard for all concerned. It's not easy to spend time with someone who has unusual interests, is highly controlling without being intrinsically interested in you. So, I filled the gaps. I created opportunities every day for activities of mutual interest to happen – crazy golf, tennis, table tennis, shopping, and board games. Sometimes we went for walks to playparks or down to the beach.

It wasn't always easy but it was always exciting. I've recently read a book called *A Shot of Hope* by Zack Peter and I love the concept in the title – every single time Tim managed to say something to another child or respond to a joke or they ran off together, it felt just like that – a massive shot of hope. I had heaps of these 'hope shots' and they kept me going. They kept me going when Erik said to me one day, 'Do you realise that you do *all* the running? You take children out, pick them up, take them places, play with them, take them home. And no one ever reciprocates.'

I had my Son-Rise thinking to comfort me – which was 'if this is what it takes to help Tim relate to his friends, I will do it all day every day, because that is what I want to do and I can be incredibly grateful that these lovely children are happy to come with us and be part of it.' After all, I could see progress. I had my little 'shots of hope' to keep me going. Also, I hadn't become a teacher for nothing. I loved being with children.

Back in the Focus Room we could talk to Tim about what had happened the day before with particular friends and how he felt. It created continuity and we could see elements of social ease appearing.

Tim started to be able to cope in groups if I was there – just going with a group of home-educated children through the woods to the park. He could take turns at games of mini-golf and board games. His conversation was limited, but we could keep the fun and interest going and help him to initiate topics of conversation with friends.

At one point, Tim was given a scooter and we took him to the ramps with a friend. There was a lovely moment where one of the confident boys stopped to show him how to manoeuvre the first-level ramp on his scooter. Tim was scared. It was a kind of procedure where you had to take a risk and trust the process, as once you'd gone over the edge there was no going back. I stayed well back and watched as Tim was encouraged to do this. When he did it, he was overjoyed. He and his friend stayed there for hours – just queuing up and going over the ramps again and again.

Watching another child be kind to your child when they're not aware anyone is looking is an incredible feeling. On the flip side, I really worried what Tim would be saying as they all queued up. These boys were tough and street-wise and Tim had a tendency still to talk about himself in the first person – or he would say, 'I'm Master Tim Wagter' in a really unusual way. If you knew him, that would be par for the course, but someone who didn't know him might wonder what was going on. I tried not to intervene, caught between wanting to protect him from himself and wanting him to have freedom.

In the holidays I took every opportunity I could. We went out with friends to the park, boating, to the beach… It was one of those Easter holidays that felt like the middle of summer. We made the most of every single sun-drenched day. With Tim it was always about spending more time on practical activities and less time on specific moments where conversation was necessary. On a boating park at a large lake in a local town, I felt confident to trust Tim and a friend to go off on a boat and navigate independently, making decisions between themselves. I found I was increasingly able to do this for short periods of time, during specific activities. I could sit on the bank and enjoy the sun – if only for a moment or two.

If Tim was more comfortable being with other children and we were working all the time on his underlying ability to relate to others at home, he couldn't help but start to feel more natural in this area surely? There were many happy moments between Tim and his friends which helped him to feel good about it and gave me an opportunity to see just what was possible.

Ninth Birthday Concert – Motivation at Its Highest

If you recall, I mentioned at the Sound Learning Centre that Tim had shared his interest in doing a concert. Well, in the five months since then, his Son-Rise Program playroom sessions with Gel, who still came weekly to 'play' had turned into singing lessons. His motivation was so high that he was able to take elements of instruction in amidst his need to dictate and make radio shows. He had learnt five songs and at his request we had asked a home-educated friend, Roman, to play the drums, Kevin, who had created his playroom, to play the bass guitar and Gel to play the keyboard. He had his dream band. We had come together once with just Gel and Roman to play through the songs, but otherwise had done no other rehearsing. We were just grateful that Tim wanted to sing and have fun. We were aware that the process held a lot more worth than the outcome.

On the morning of the party, it was a lovely sunny day and we went to a beach café near our house. Tim was cycling along the promenade – a great feeling for us to watch him (as it had taken months, in increments, to teach him how to ride) and we sat down and decided we ought to start planning his party. The party was that night. Every day was so intensely filled up that it was really hard to organise anything properly in advance. We put our heads together and thought of some games the children could play following the concert that Tim was going to put on for his friends.

However, I shared with Erik my gut feeling that Tim could make a complete fool of himself – on stage – in front of twenty friends. Up to this point he had always been in the background as so much of what he said hadn't made sense to others and to put him on stage in one way seemed madness. But we were doing this because he had specifically asked for it. Erik and I reckoned we would just go with the flow, and maximise the potential for social fun and interaction, whatever happened. This was a great choice and I let myself breathe out. As always, I wanted things to go well and for Tim to be seen in a good light by others, but that wasn't the important thing here. Just interacting, seeing friends and trying new things were all great activities and could be nothing but good for him.

I asked Tim when we came back if he would practice the songs for the evening and he told me he wasn't singing them now but would sing them tonight. So he didn't appreciate the concept of practicing. I let it go, once more deciding to focus on the fun, whatever happened.

A New Motivation – the Highest Yet

When we arrived, Tim was so excited. He helped us set out the tables and put the decorations up. The band arrived early to practice and with Erik's help they set all the equipment up. Remembering how he had always cried in pain at loud noises, it was already a miracle that he could even be in this environment without becoming distressed. Erik and I could only put it down to the Sound Learning Centre and the many hours he spent in his Focus Room, away from pressure and impossible demands, where he was able to build up his strength and resilience.

I think I was helping in the kitchen when I first heard Tim singing into the microphone. I looked up and couldn't quite grasp what I saw. Tim was on the stage, with a kind of presence around him that I had never seen before. He was singing with an unusual amount of confidence – he enjoyed it and looked completely comfortable up there. I had never seen him so connected and confident. He held the microphone like a natural and walked around like he owned the stage. I just stood there, gaping.

When his friends turned up and Erik had introduced him on the stage, he held the microphone and said, 'Hello ladies and gentlemen, boys and girls, welcome to my concert, and now it is song time. The first one is 'You've Got a Friend in Me', the second one is 'Scooby Doo', the third one is 'Spiderman', the fourth one is 'This Little Light of Mine' and the fifth one is the happy birthday song. So, I'm starting with 'You've Got a Friend in Me' from the Walt Disney Pixar Film – okay!' and he started singing.

He sang all his songs for them and at one point they all stood up and started clapping along, while he was talking in between songs to them, full of confidence and charm – what was this? If I had been expecting anything, it wasn't *this*! I was gobsmacked! He was happy and excited while slap-bang in the midst of a social event with everyone's eyes on him. In true Tim-style he also sang, 'Happy birthday to me' at the end.

After the concert, Tim threw himself right in the midst of all the party games and opened loads of presents – very excited – and stayed connected right to the end, even helping to sweep up the floor when everyone had gone. The progress we had seen was momentous. It really was a defining moment. He was genuinely happy and this was the first time Erik and I had any idea of his love for performing on a stage. My teacher mind went off on one again. This was a massively high motivation that we would use a lot more. If I had not taken heed of Samahria Kaufman's words and taken active care of Tim's desire when he told me he had wanted to do a concert, this progress would never have happened. Another fun factor was that this motivation was particularly great for me, because I was in my comfort zone working with children, music and performing.

I had given away my piano while Erik had stopped worship leading and both of us had stopped singing around the house for the last *eight years* but now the spark that had died in us were lighting up in Tim. He was starting to do the things we had stopped doing because of his high sensory overload. Maybe this could start to bring an element of our own music back to us? It seemed so ironic that he was the one now making all the music, when he had been demanding that we stay quiet for the last eight years.

More Progress

Rachel was gradually introducing Tim to jokes – basic 'Knock knock' jokes, wordplay and puns, which he started to understand and find funny. When he started to tell them, he realised that jokes brought reactions, which made him even more keen. This was a great way to bridge gaps, when Tim struggled to initiate a conversation, we could say, 'Oh, why don't you tell Peter that joke you told me?' and it would break the ice and get some back and forth banter going.

We also realised that Tim was starting to gradually build a knowledge base, with the ability to retain more information and begin to follow instructions. Up until now, his written responses had followed his own track, however now he was beginning to be able to write with more coherence. Rachel was working with him on writing what actually happened or what he could actually see in a photograph etc and he started giving it a go. He would often go off on a tangent, but Rachel would gently guide him back to factual and reality thinking. We had to mix the two worlds – showing full respect to his interior world, while gradually expanding that to the world on the outside. Rachel and Tim played so many word games and made words so much fun. One exercise Rachel did with him would be taking a simple sentence and adding new words to make it more effective. A sentence that started out as 'James has a dog' turned into 'big, hairy, spooky, ghastly, sandy, green James the monster had a fat, greedy, enormous, brown, stupid dog!' Sometimes Rachel would give Tim a sentence for him to change on his own. He changed 'He stood on the beach' to 'Gulliver stood firm on the stony beach at Bognor'. He changed 'I fell over' to 'I fell over a stone while I was on my scooter, which is blue and grey' and he changed 'Mum used the phone' to 'My Mum, Sally talked for about 90 minutes on the phone in the corridor', which I found particularly amusing.

Sometimes Tim gave Rachel the words and she scribed to make the process quicker as Tim's brain worked much faster than his handwriting. However, Rachel did still focus a lot on Tim's handwriting as we knew this was a good learning process. Thinking and writing your thoughts is a great process and can often be how people learn and best take in information. We felt for him that it was an important part of linking his thoughts with his ability to communicate them.

If Rachel asked Tim to do a task, she would often do it too. Tim was never just left to process his thoughts alone. That was key and there was no judgement over his ability to complete a task. It was always done together in these early days.

Hazard and Hope

One day Rachel came up with a brilliant game. She drew out a board game and the spots each person landed on had either meant picking a fun card or a challenging one. She could change the challenges according to what Tim was working on. The great thing was that Tim could also write out tasks and challenges for Rachel so it was two-way. As one of Tim's major challenges was eating, some of his tasks were to put a piece of apple for a few seconds on his tongue, for example, but as Rachel hated cheese and onion crisps, Tim would give her the challenge to eat one. This game could grow and change with any subject and any personal challenge Tim was trying to overcome, being highly adaptable.

The Genius Idea of Making a Film

At around the time of Tim's ninth birthday, Rachel introduced the idea of making a film as Tim was buzzing with story ideas, but struggled to make sense of them. She decided to work with him on making a story board and turning it into a film, which would help clarify and order his ideas. They created a story called 'Pirate's Gold' and over the summer turned it into a storyboard, so it was clear what was happening in each scene.

I couldn't visualise how she would go about making a film or how she would be able to persuade Tim to learn lines in advance, but I could see the idea had potential. His friend, Peter, wanted to be part of it. So, we worked on costumes, found an old boat in a friend's garden and Rachel set to work making props with Tim. Halfway through the filming, I went along to watch and could suddenly see what Rachel was doing. She was telling Tim and Peter what to say and do in tiny increments – practicing it, then filming it then doing the same for the next scene. That was good. There were lots of tiny scenes, which could all be put together when editing. Clever! Tim was so excited to have the film edited that Erik worked out how to do it and between them they put together Tim's first ever film. We didn't know it at the time, but this would turn into another of Tim's major long-running passions – acting and film-making. Talk about doors opening up…

We gave Tim a small video camera and he started to film and create movies all the time. Wherever he went his camera went with him. He would record himself talking and ask us to film him and a friend. He would present to the camera as if he were making a documentary and he would then edit the whole thing together and add music, a menu and put it on a DVD for us to watch. He was still very quirky with his speech and his movements and even with his ideas but he loved the process and the process was what it was all about.

Performances at Every Opportunity

As Tim really rose to the experience of performing and could look forward to it for days, we were always on the look-out for opportunities to perform. He wasn't ready for mainstream groups, so it was up to us to create these opportunities. Soon after his ninth birthday party, some friends put on a festival and invited him to sing. He sang 'This Little Light of Mine' while Erik played guitar. The interesting thing was though, that he didn't just sing it – he performed with real connection and invited the audience to join in with him. A whole field of people were singing and clapping along with him. It was incredible to watch – and again, the spark lit up in him like he was coming into his own.

When he was young, we had had singing games parties for him and his friends but now we started to do 'performance parties'. At every birthday and Christmas we put on variety shows where all the children could perform what they liked. I would invite children to our house to practice and they would work on songs and dance routines with Tim in the weeks beforehand. These were the first opportunities where Tim's emerging ideas for such things could really be heard and adhered to in a larger setting. He would choose songs, decide what to perform, and gradually he began to understand and enjoy the concept of rehearsing and working with other people.

Suddenly Seeing Babies Everywhere

Now I know this is a weird leap and a total change of subject within the context of this book. But here, obviously, I am focusing on Tim's life, whereas in reality, Tim's journey was a large chunk of my life but not all of it. The idea of Erik and I having another child had been put on hold for so long that I had almost forgotten about it. I had largely blocked it from my mind. However, I suddenly found myself noticing babies and craving the intimacy, love and connection that mothers had with their newborns – the soft touch, the response, the bond.

When Erik, Tim and I were sitting in a café one day, I caught sight of this beautiful little baby and just couldn't take my eyes off her. I knew that I had it in me to love and nurture another child. Sometimes the concept of another child seemed ridiculous and sometimes it seemed within the bounds of possibility. All I knew was that I was suddenly seeing babies wherever I looked and it was triggering a repressed desire in me. Maybe for the last nine years I had put it on hold so much that I had begun to believe it would never happen,

From the very beginning, Erik and I had always wanted more than one child, but Tim had needed our undivided attention for so many years that we couldn't see how it could realistically happen. Friends of ours had been having second children around us, but we had had our vocation set out for us in helping Tim.

Now things were changing. Tim was happier. His skills were developing, his ability to learn was improving, his social skills were starting to take shape and life in our house was becoming easier. Whenever we had the conversation about another child Erik was more ready to take the risk. I knew about the statistics of siblings. Articles were everywhere stating that if you have one child on the autistic spectrum there's a 20% chance their siblings will be, too. I just didn't know if I had it in me to go through again what we had been through in the last nine years. But when I just couldn't decide, I asked myself whether I would rather go through the rest of our lives with another person alongside than not, I decided I would. Life is about relationships after all. The thing that tipped it finally for me was realising how good it would be for Tim to experience the process of having a sibling in his life and a relationship with someone else as well as us.

Spain Again

After Tim's ninth birthday, we all found ourselves in Spain again. Erik had surprised me by organising it as he knew how much I craved the sun and holiday feeling. This time Gel was going to join us for a few days so that Erik and I could have a few moments together. It was only two years since the last time, but Tim's behaviour was noticeably different. He loved sitting for hours writing and drawing. He loved playing in the pool and going bowling. He did still struggle with the beach though and could only handle it if we sat in the shade playing 'Old Maid' or 'Monopoly'. So, we spent many hours playing these games at the beach but I had my feet in the sand, palm trees above my head and could at least *see* the sea! He still liked to know what the day was going to hold, but he didn't have a need to meltdown if things didn't go his way. He had come a very long way in these two years.

It was on this holiday that I discovered I was pregnant with Sammy. I was excited and felt it opened a whole new chapter. While dreaming and making preparations and going for all the necessary check-ups in the months to come, I still stayed fully immersed in Tim's home programme with the same level of passion and excitement as I had always had.

Chapter Eleven – Breakthrough – a new love of learning

Sleep

When we came back from Spain something totally unexpected happened. Up until now, Tim had woken up every single night without fail and come into our bed. Erik always got out and went to Tim's bed and we all slept that way until the morning. We had decided to choose our battles and this wasn't one we were currently focusing on. However in Spain, Tim had slept in a room with Gel and at the point when he woke up, he quietly spoke to Gel. She reassured him of her presence and he went back to sleep, leaving Erik and I with a whole night of uninterrupted sleep! This set all sorts of ideas going in me – the idea of baby monitors, allowing Tim to speak to me for reassurance in the night before going back to sleep. However, when we got home, we all went to sleep as usual and were suddenly awakened in the night when Tim opened his door and went to the loo. Just as I was expecting him to walk into our room and for the bed-swapping madness to begin all over again, I heard him go back into his room and shut the door. Erik and I lay there, listening in shocked silence. Tim had actually returned to his room and gone back to sleep all on his own. He never looked back. He has slept every night in his own bed ever since. Erik and I have no idea why this switch happened but can only deduce that for some reason Tim felt ready. It was always in his time and when he felt ready.

The Ideas Man

At the very beginning of his interest in making films, Tim opened up. When he was highly motivated and really wanted to share, words poured out of him. I had never heard him talk so much and with such enthusiasm. He would tell me all his ideas for hours and I would listen with complete interest. We were always keen to listen and talk with him for however long he needed. This also had a massive impact on his writing. He knew we were interested in his ideas and he started to write ideas down constantly, then share them with us. It was almost like a creative dam bursting within him. I'm so glad we let him direct so much of his own learning in this way.

Then he would tell me he wanted us to film with real horses in the real desert, for example and I would find myself faced with a choice. Did I quash all his ideas and tell him he couldn't do that? Or would I carry on listening with interest, knowing that at some point he would realise for himself what was possible? I chose the latter. He spoke so passionately about his ideas and I loved to hear them and help him realise the ideas that were possible.

Only once did I tell him something wasn't possible. He went away and ripped up three pieces of paper he had written all his ideas out on. I felt mortified. I got the papers out of the bin and I told him to keep writing, because loads of things were possible and you never know what can happen. He was sharing with me his emerging thoughts and ideas that were so vital to his growing sense of self and I realised his ideas needed nurturing, not limiting. Whether something was possible or not wasn't the point. The point was Tim was brimming with creative ideas – it was my job to work with them. His written sentences became more structurally coherent and fluent. I really believe this happened because he had such a strong desire to communicate his ideas.

Grateful

I feel so grateful that we chose this route, because what emerged was the strongest motivator which carried Tim through most of his key social developmental milestones. In all Tim's years at infant and primary school he could never access music, drama, dance etc because of his high sensitivity to sound and his inability to follow instruction. I suppose that just because he couldn't cope didn't mean it wasn't something he longed to do – it's just that at school he didn't have the chance. Now I could see the power of it in every element of his learning, I had my feelers out constantly.

Temple Grandin also says in her book, *The Way I see It*, how vital it is to go with motivations and to big up every good thing a child with autism can do, rather than focus on deficits. She also says that often talents and gifts often only come to the surface once sensory overloads and behavioural difficulties have been largely overcome.

'Six Gun Sid'

On the back of his first film, Tim made his own plans to make another – this time by himself. He wanted to call it *Six Gun Sid*. He actually started writing the story and I could see that his story lines were starting to become clearer. He had specific ideas as to how he wanted the film to look. It was basically a Cowboy and Indian film which I was pleased about, as it was a storyline that others could easily relate to.

Lily and Albert, Tim's friend and her brother, wanted to be in the film and Tim had very clear ideas of who he wanted them to be and what he wanted them to do. Well, this created a great learning opportunity, as Lily and Albert wanted to be in the film but Lily did not want to be called Six-Gun Beryl and Albert wanted to be an Indian, instead of the cowboy that Tim had imagined as his character. Tim was taken aback and this time I did not intervene until later. When I had Tim to myself, I tested his flexibility by suggesting that it would possible to think of a different name for Lily's character and for Albert to be an Indian. Surely we could then think together about someone else to play the part of the cowboy? He was actually willing to agree – and furthermore allowed me to work with him on the next stage of the planning process.

I thought back to the dictation sessions where Tim had simply blanked all our ideas. Now, while working on his latest project which he was passionate about – not only was he was considering what I was saying, he was also willing to change his thinking. This was huge. Tim's need for control could extend to us and the people who worked with him specifically, but he could not control other children or their thoughts, ideas, needs, or wants. They were outside his control but he wanted them to be part of his film so he would have to relent (what a lovely word) and be flexible to *their* needs and wants. It was our job to help facilitate him to do this.

Emotional Connections – Seeing His Effect on Others

At one point, Tim felt he had been too bossy with Lily and upset her. He told me all about it and I agreed to help him write a letter to Lily to apologise, because he really wanted her to know he was sorry.

On another occasion, he and I went to his friend Ellie's house and on the way home he told me that he had 'done well – because he had not told Ellie what to do too much'.

On a different day, he and I were having a cuddle before bed and he was sharing his worries with me. He told me that he had been really controlling with his friend, Peter, and he wanted Peter to forgive him – he was really tense and stressed about it all and couldn't let it go. I suggested we phone Peter in the morning to say sorry or that he write a letter to him. He felt better knowing this was possible and then he asked me, 'Mum, do you think God will forgive me for being controlling?'

I told him that God would definitely forgive him for being controlling. He then asked me if God loved controlling people and I told him God *especially* loved controlling people. His body softened into mine and I could tell he felt relieved. He let go and fell into a peaceful sleep. This was the first time I had ever known Tim to share an awareness of his effect on other people or have any concept of needing to be loved or forgiven.

This was so huge I could barely get my head around it. Without this awareness, real friendships were not really possible, but with it possibilities of meaningful friendships opened up. It was just the start, yes. But it was a start. I had waited nine years to experience this level of emotional connection with Tim. It was there in him. It existed. The need. The connection. The communication. The socially connected side of me could now relate to the emerging socially connected side of him.

I had believed this could happen. We had been proactively working towards it on faith that it would happen – and here it was. The culmination of all our years of loving input.

Tim was at the beginning stages of understanding about human emotions – doing wrong, needing forgiveness, caring how people felt – the natural elements of each human being that seemed so incredibly complex in the world of autism. With theory of mind, perspective, an awareness of other people and his effect on them, it opened so many doorways into relationships with people and life, as the majority of people around him experienced it.

This was such a pivotal point in Tim's development. If he could start to think and care about others and was aware of his effect on them, this was a game-changer. In everything you read about autism, they talk about limited communication, limited social interaction and limited social imagination. But in all the therapies and programmes I had been introduced to, none had focused on the social elements as the core issue, like The Son-Rise Program® does. Yes, it had taken a long time, but it had been a process of putting lots of tiny building blocks in place. Tim's developing interactive ability was starting to bring him into the world of deeper relationships. This, I knew, was far more important than any academic progress. Social progress would ultimately give him the most independence and freedom.

Emergence Into a New World

So now the negative edge had been taken off Tim's social difficulties, leaving him newly aware of people's feelings and emotions and his place within the whole world of people and their social interactions. This was a new stage of my job – to now nurture him through this maelstrom of life, thoughts, concepts and people, while keeping him safe in his knowledge of himself and how loved he was.

For me, this was an emergence into an incredible new world. The thing was, he was very new at it at a much later stage in life than most other people. He was learning to talk to others and consider their feelings at the age of nine. He had very few cooperation issues now – only a willingness to learn. Therefore, it was also my job to work out where he really was in all his developmental levels. Now we could reach him, we could start to determine what he could do and where we needed to help him next. I no longer needed to say, 'I want to reach him' – we *had* reached him. And it was brilliant, however, it was hard to find anyone to relate to me in this situation. Also, most other people didn't know about Tim's increasing awareness of others, so still treated him with the 'does he take sugar?' mentality.

On one occasion, Tim had been invited to a swimming party from the class he had originally been in at his primary school. When I had spoken to him about the party, he immediately wanted to go, enthusing about the children he hadn't seen for such a long time and with his growing social imagination, I think he envisaged that everyone would be pleased to see him, so he could join in all the games. As we left for the party he was in a highly excited and expectant state, but when we arrived, every single child walked past as if he didn't exist and didn't once respond when he reached out to say hello to them. I sensed his visceral hurt – why didn't they want to talk to him?

I hated the rejection, the ostracization. It hurt me in places I didn't even know could hurt. I *ached* for him. It seemed there was a permanent barrier between him and others that just could not be penetrated. I felt desperate for change and for growth to happen and now that it was occurring, along with the excitement and progress of connecting with a friend, it also opened up opportunities for him to feel excluded. The hurt made me feel so disempowered because I couldn't control the environment around him sufficiently to protect him. I had been to this hurt place many times before, but this time around Tim was also there and could feel it, too.

I knew if I allowed the hurt to overwhelm me, I wouldn't be helping Tim at all. I decided to be fun and proactive trying to bridge the gaps as I knew all the other children well and had great relationships with them. The children all took notice of me and responded with great pleasure, but there was still no response to Tim whatsoever. It was as though I had to come to the party with an invisible child. I decided to take a shot at the direct approach. I asked John, the brother of one of the children Tim regularly saw, if he'd play with Tim. He willingly agreed, so relieved, I turned to talk to someone and when I turned back John had swum off, leaving Tim there with a different child, Ewan.

I still tried to remain breezy so I said, 'Would you play with Tim for a bit, Ewan? He looked at me blankly and said, 'But I don't know what he wants to do.'

'Ask him then!' I mentally screamed at him. However, instead I breezily let him off the hook and suggested gently and lovingly to Tim that he get out.

We chatted while he changed and I helped him to focus on all the moments that could have been seen as fun. I knew he felt hurt, but I didn't want to focus on the pain. Perhaps, if he could look to me and see I was OK, he would be able to follow suit.

I was trying to keep face in front of all the other parents and for Tim's sake, but inwardly I felt gut-wrenchingly rejected. I didn't want Tim to be aware of my feelings, so I tried to put them in a place, while chatting positively with him. As we left, the other children were running about, shouting, playing and laughing together, oblivious to the fact that we were leaving. Maybe they still saw him as the child he had been before where he always given the impression he had wanted to be left alone.

When I dropped him back home with Erik, I took myself off in the car and cried and cried and cried. Tim had worked so hard to get to this amazing stage, where he was increasingly aware of others. But what if this just set him up for a new layer of heartache? What if we weren't able to continue progressing him far enough along to get past this?

After thinking it all through really deeply, I realised if I was going to actually help Tim, I'd have to put this experience and my pity party in the background by using every ounce of on-the-spot forgiveness that I could muster and focus on being the person I needed to be. I also knew I needed to genuinely believe that on-going change was possible for him. I had to take my sense of urgency off myself with regard to his progress and decide to go through life at his pace and delight in his every achievement.

This was a conscious choice every day which became harder with negative comments and looks from others and people's negative prognoses over his life. It was also hard because I knew the level of care and attention I needed to give was way more than average. I was very tired so I ate as healthily as I could as I needed to summon up large amounts of strength every day and I didn't know for how long I would need to keep up this mindset. The more stressed I was, the more I looked after myself as I knew if I let myself go, I would lose the high level of mental, emotional and physical energy I needed every second.

On another occasion, we picked up one of Tim's friends to go to the beach, who spoke intelligently and fluently to me, before turning to Tim and talking to him as if he was three years old. I could feel my hackles rise, so I told myself that this was to be expected as she couldn't know how he had grown since she last saw him, so I continued talking and behaving positively.

As the afternoon wore on, they gradually began talking to each other independent of me, wading into the sea, running off to wash their feet and going off to buy ice creams together. (I let go my no dairy rule for that one!) This demonstrated that Tim could now relate successfully with a friend. Maybe groups were too much, but one-to-ones were possible. This gave me renewed hope and a sense of purpose, as I realised he now needed lots of opportunities to relate one-to-one with another child to help him to continue his social progression. Functioning with groups could come later.

Because I had clarity over Tim's social development and could see where he was in every area – I knew when progress was being made and also when he was regressing or sitting on the ledge for a while. This meant I could naturally celebrate when spontaneous leaps forward happened and I knew how to access my attitude of resolution and hope when Tim's development regressed. Without being able to identify and celebrate these leaps forward, or knowing how to re-group in the difficult times, I wouldn't have been able to sustain what we were doing. It wasn't Tim I had an issue with – he and I were on the same side – it was other people's belief systems and responses that now had the potential to hold him back.

I often needed Erik's help, but I often received strength from another source – Tim himself, who would talk and sing songs to me. One day I was sitting in the lounge, feeling a bit overwhelmed, when he came to me with his iPod and asked if he could sing to me. When he put on the backing track and started the song, I couldn't believe it when I heard when I heard the words: 'When you're down and troubled and you need a helping hand, and nothing, nothing is going right, close your eyes and think of me and soon I will be there to brighten up even your darkest night'...I sometimes wondered if he had a sixth sense as to what would touch my heart strings the most, but in actual fact he sang it because he loved it himself.

I knew I wasn't alone because even though I had no contact with the Son-Rise Program team, I knew I could get in touch if I needed to and that they were there rooting for all the families that were on this journey. So my belief, my knowledge, my clarity and my certainty sustained me and my knowledge that out of all the options this was the best.

Because I had built such a relationship with Tim, I wanted to be with him. I know the feeling of a demanding child pushing your buttons and you needing a break but I managed to overcome this feeling by getting back to my beliefs and choosing to want to dive into his world. When I was there with him, I saw the world from his point of view and I actually began thinking and feeling life through his eyes most of the time which gave me a higher sensitivity to how life was for him. While I felt his pain, I also genuinely delighted in all the things that made him happy and celebrated when he felt successful and good about himself. These instances really did create shots of hope for both of us.

Throughout this time, some people would still sometimes speak to me about him in front of him as if he wasn't there and other people would speak directly to him. In order for him to continue to grow in independent communication, it was vital for people to communicate with him as if he had his own thoughts and ideas, which of course he did – but this was out of my hands. That's what the Son-Rise Program know – and why they advocate *being* the person your child needs you to be, by creating and being the environment around your child, thus giving him the encouragement and sense of self-worth that he deserves. I was relieved that I didn't have to rely on others to do this and that I was already able to create the optimal environment myself. This also protected Tim from the people who didn't know how to talk to him or proactively help him with his development. In this way, I knew we were giving Tim the best chance at self-belief, being who he was and accessing learning and relationships.

My Friend Nina

A major mind-opening experience for me came when talking to my friend, Nina. It was Nina's children who had taken part in Tim's film, *Six-Gun Sid*. I had, to this point, felt that everyone whose child could look at them, talk to them and get on fine in school, were insanely lucky and that they all sailed through life on a different level to me. Lily, Nina's daughter was the epitome of a happy, pretty, fully-functioning child. She was always right in the centre of any group, laughing and joking. She had been to all Tim's parties and she and Tim had moments of fun. In fact they got on well together and I felt that Lily actually enjoyed his company and wasn't just being kind. I asked Nina if I could pop round sometimes and she was really pleased to see me and Tim. Albert often had friends round and Nina was always organising outings and sleepovers. Her house was full of life and laughter and happenings.

But through many talks, Nina confided in me her fears and hopes for her children and the level of passion with which she spoke suddenly convinced me that she felt the total same level of passion for her children that I felt for Tim. It dawned on me the similar levels of concern other people have for their children even without specific issues, which was a new thought for me. I had assumed if your child didn't have autism your life was easy. A bit simplistic I know, but these weren't conscious feelings, more subconscious beliefs. I never viewed other children and parents in the same way after that – I realised I wasn't in a bracket on my own but one of many parents all who care about their children, issues or no issues. My parenting journey had been side-tracked before it had scarcely got underway and that was what I had based my experience on. Maybe as a parent I wasn't so different. One of the main reasons I was drawn to Nina was her passion for her children and their development. We spoke about this for hours and because I had taught her two children, we always had lots to say.

The First Time Tim was Invited Somewhere without Me! (aged nine)

One day I rang Nina to ask her if Tim and I could pop over as we had no afternoon plans and she told me she was going to the pictures with a whole group of children. She then asked if Tim would like to go with them to give me a break as my pregnancy was making me quite tired.

This may seem like a very normal question – but it was actually the first time anyone had ever offered to take Tim out without me. I thought that he would probably cope whereas Nina was adamant – 'he'll be *fine*!' Tim went, thoroughly enjoyed it and came back buzzing! Nina told me he was totally cooperative and he really enjoyed it. Tim told me all about the film, which inspired him with ideas for his own films more too.

This was just the start. It was both exciting and normal at the same time. While for so many children, going out with a group of friends was just a normal activity – this was something I couldn't have imagined for Tim only a few short years before. Normal was exciting to me – very!

Later Nina told me that one of the parents had told her she was brave having Tim round and taking him out. I suppose that was fair enough as he'd had so many meltdowns at school – but they were such a thing of the past now. Instead, cooperation, willingness and an interest in life and people were the new name of the game. People didn't need to be brave to take him out, just to be aware of his vulnerabilities. I had to pinch myself sometimes that we had come to this stage. I also had to be bigger than these comments and realise that other people wouldn't know how much Tim had changed. He should be congratulated with the biggest trophy and cheered by the whole world, in my opinion.

Another reason for my friendship with Nina was her totally accepting attitude. She genuinely saw nothing different in Tim. She spoke to him easily, adamant that he was a lovely boy. She loved him and saw only the best in him and supported Tim and Lily's friendship all the way through. Tim was always invited around to her house, to parties and even to stay the night. Nina saw nothing different in having Tim to stay than any other child. Sometimes I would be round there and Tim would disappear off running about and playing silly games for hours with the others, while Nina and I sat in the kitchen talking. Even *this* had been one of my dreams. Nina was total gold to me and I don't think she had any idea at the time just how much her friendship meant. She accepted Tim and I, not out of kindness but out of genuine love and interest. When I tell her this, she says I'm silly to even think about such a thing. Acceptance is just a normal part of her thinking.

Goodbye Meltdowns, Hello Easy Cooperation

The more Tim enjoyed life and could be certain of his trust with us, he found he had less to fight against. We would ask Tim to do something and he would jump up and say 'sure' and when he had gone Erik and I would ask ourselves if that had just really happened! It was like watching a miracle happen in front of our eyes.

I started to be able to go to friends' houses with Tim just to hang out without an agenda. He and his friend would decide together what they wanted to do, all very naturally. It was a gradual realisation that Tim was much happier, more confident and increasingly able to follow someone else's agenda. Elements of flexibility had started to appear in his social thinking.

Dancing Lessons

I had read at one point that dancing can be really good for children on the autistic spectrum as it helps with all levels of coordination, balance, left-right brain links etc and I decided to look into it. I had seen Tim work on dance routines with friends and thought that it would be something he might be interested in. I asked about a local dance class and Tim was happy to go along and check it out.

Before we arrived, I told him he only needed to watch, he didn't have to join in, so we sat at the back together. This was the way he always coped with new things, watching first. We saw lots of his friends from school – all girls. And after a while, they called him over, encouraging him to join them. Sometimes I felt so grateful for the children who knew Tim. He watched and joined in and when the teacher stopped him, just as she did with all the other children, to demonstrate how to improve the dance move, he took the instruction and attempted the move again, taking note of the teacher's comments.

She had no idea that this was the first time I'd actually seen him do this in such a social environment. I hadn't been able to speak to her beforehand so she hadn't even adapted her teaching style. Tim was mirroring. Mimicking. Copying. Taking instruction. Learning. Trying again. Watching what she was doing and doing it himself because he wanted to amidst a hall full of children and with loud, thumping music all around him. I thought back to what I had learned about mirror neurons, which were sparking massively here as he was taking in what he was learning, registering it and remembering. It felt like a miracle.

The children were taking turns and the moves were challenging – but he was right up there with the best of them. These developmental leaps were almost too huge for me to grasp. I sat quietly at the back hugging my knees to my chest in excitement, silently thanking God and The Son-Rise Program for this amazing present.

Following this, he agreed to do the class. The class was once a week for an hour on a Saturday. There was a big heavy door between the reception and the dance studio, with the unspoken rule being that parents weren't to go in. My gut feeling told me that I could – and should – take a risk, to trust him that he could handle it and just let him take part. Lily was in his class, which added a dimension of security for him. Week after week, Erik and I dropped him off and watched him go in then come back out an hour later saying he'd had a good time. Just for once, I chose not to be part of it. This was something I now had to get used to.

Changing our Attitudes to Help Tim's Learning

Erik and I talked continuously about what we could do next to support Tim's learning. We'd meet with Rachel and when necessary, we could make changes and implement them immediately.

One example is that Tim went through a long stage of finding it really hard to lose in games – he really couldn't deal with it. Rachel had originally interested Tim in games with her brilliantly silly reactions to winning and losing and it had created high motivation in him. But when games started to matter to him, the outcomes became far too important. We decided to change our attitudes immediately – in that from now on we wouldn't be pleased if we won or disappointed if we lost. We would put all our energies into enjoying the games. His own reactions calmed down in just a couple of weeks. I thought back to the school system. There would have been no way we could have ever spoken to his teaching assistants about their attitudes with him. We would have had to have long meetings about all this, then wait weeks for them to alter their approach – probably with some following the new mindset and others not doing so. Here we could all change our attitudes at the drop of a hat if we were convinced it would help – brilliant!

On one occasion, when Tim did struggle once with losing a game at a friend's house, he became so cross that he cried for an hour and didn't want to say goodbye to his friend's mum at the door. When we came home, I talked it all through with him and suggested that he phone his friend's mum to say sorry for his reaction. This was all part of the continued journey of his awareness of how he affected other people. He willingly phoned and said sorry and this mother was fine with him, but I felt it was all part of the process of gradually being part of wider humanity. Life wasn't one-sided anymore – there were other people on the receiving end of his behaviour. I always made sure he knew he was allowed to respond in the way he felt he needed to, but I also helped him to see it had consequences.

Elements of Echolalia

Tim still had traces of echolalia, repeating what he'd read or heard, thinking he had understood it or it was appropriate when it didn't make sense in the context of the situation. For example, in one of his *Beano* stories, one character was chasing another shouting, 'You're for it!' Tim later said with a similar sense of gusto, 'I'm going to for it'.

However as well as this, his own thoughts were increasingly emerging. What was fun was that he was more than willing for us to tell him something he'd said hadn't made sense and he would laugh about the silliness of him saying things and not realising they didn't make sense! This was the beginning of an amazing self-awareness, which has gone on steadily developing ever since – and also demonstrates his keen sense of humour. Sometimes he would tell me jokes he had just enjoyed or show me stories he found funny. I was delighted he wanted to share what he was enjoying, without being prompted.

Because of the heavy echolalia in his early years, whenever an idea or thought came from his own thinking, we welcomed it and metaphorically watered the ground for it to grow. It was his *own* thinking I wanted to know and share so I was delighted when I realised that the stories in his head were increasingly his own, even though they were sometimes muddled. The best way through was to work with him on his talking, thinking and making sense on a 24/7 basis through our responses and interactions with him, constantly encouraging his own thinking to come to the fore. I remembered back to the days of speech therapy where only half an hour a week was allocated to actual talking and making himself understood – that wasn't even a drop in the ocean.

This 24/7 approach was such a huge commitment that sometimes Erik and I were completely exhausted. By this time, I was about four months' pregnant so was even more tired than usual and it was often hard to see steps of progress. But every so often we would realise things Tim could now do, or we would meet someone who hadn't seen him for ages and they would exclaim about the remarkable change in him. It's hard to see progress when you are right in the midst of something and can't see the wood for the trees.

Teaching Elements of Friendship

We were now regularly attempting to encourage Tim to be more aware of how he came across with friends and others. This was mostly still through all the underlying techniques of The Son-Rise Program Social Curriculum, but sometimes we would now also talk directly to him about specific friendship issues, not with any judgement and always at a time when he was calm and in a good state to listen and take things on board.

We always knew when the best moments were because we could feel them. We could never offer explanations or talk things through when he was stressed, but in quiet reflective moments we could ask him a few basic questions about how he felt and how he thought a session with a friend had gone. This could lead to interesting talks that could last as long as his attention span would allow. He would then switch off and want to do something else. We could elongate these sessions with little bits of role play at times, again, to the level his comprehension would allow.

Conversations and talks about feelings were still at their embryonic stage but I still loved that they were happening and that they helped him. He *wanted* to get on with his friends so by doing this, we were helping him achieve one of his own goals.

In fact it was all about that. He started to make his own goals clear and we helped him to achieve them, passing many developmental milestones in the process. We were going with him, not against him, at every step and he was showing the way.

Kindness

Tim was amazingly kind during my pregnancy when I had a bad back and found walking difficult.

One evening when Erik was away, I suddenly realised I needed to get to the chemist by 6.30. It was 6.15 and already dark. Tim had just settled down to his much longed-for half an hour on the telly (he was still on a daily half-an-hour treat) but I desperately needed to get some pain relief for my back. I went in and said, 'Tim, I'm so sorry but I need to get to the chemist right now and I'm going to have to ask you to come with me'.

He looked up and immediately agreed – no ounce of resistance. I apologised and handed him his shoes.

As I hobbled out to the car in the cold and the dark with Tim beside me, I called out to him, 'You know, I should call you my flexible friend!' then immediately realised what I'd said. In the car I turned to him and said, 'I'm sorry about this.'

And he said kindly, 'You don't need to be sorry, Mum.'

He was so kind, so companionable, so much fun. He was totally happy to be my side and to give and take with me.

I thought back to all the hours where we had consciously worked on his ability to think flexibly as one of his main social development goals. To hear him say this was like finding water in a desert.

At one point I was consigned to a wheelchair because of the severity of my sciatica and when Erik went away on work commitments, in the later stages of my pregnancy, I could ask Tim to pass me things and to do particular jobs. He was always very willing and helpful. He had also never put himself to bed at this point, but one night I had to explain I actually couldn't walk to his bedroom to do his night-time routine with him and he told me he was fine with that.

With these growing connections, something began to release in me. I had what I wanted. My grief could start to subside. Tim and I had an easy companionship. I know I was his mum but he was also like a friend to me. There might still be lots of other issues to work on but this was the thing my parent-heart had wanted most – a feeling of friendship with my child, a place where the two of us could relax and feel happy together. A meeting of minds where we could share our lives and feelings.

Audio-Visual Passion

With his much-beloved camera, Tim would make films of everyday events then put them on the computer and edit them – all independently. When anything remotely interesting happened he wanted to film it. He seemed to feel more comfortable when he had a camera. It gave him something to do – a purpose when other people were around, to the extent that whenever any willing adult gave him quality time, this was his favourite activity. He also filmed Rachel playing games, asking her to present the programme he wanted to create.

When he had a sleepover with Lily, they filmed little adverts together. When he played mini-golf with Peter he filmed them, made commentaries, then edited them, added music and put it all on a DVD. In this way, we encouraged this activity as most of his friends loved taking part in these mini-projects of his, which helped in his on-going socialisation.

When out with friends they would create stories and he would film them. He and Susannah would also spend ages in the garden under the apple tree creating stories with various toys and filming them. His friends loved watching themselves back on the computer once Tim had edited what he had filmed. He also loved his radio programmes which he called 'Lily and Tim on Air' or 'Hot on Air'. He would write scripts for his friends to speak throughout the programmes and was delighted when they were happy to take part.

He also filled up the voice memos on his iPod with all sorts of recordings of rehearsals, performances, conversations, songs etc. It was very obvious that he had a keen interest in all things audio and visual. He loved watching and listening back as much as he loved creating these projects and making the memories.

Before and After the Beginnings of Theory of Mind

In hindsight, I would say everything before Tim's initial awareness of other people as separate entities, was difficult, painful, heavy and highly dependent. Everything after his realisation was lighter, more fun, more hopeful and relationships were increasingly possible. As far as I understand, the whole essence of Theory of Mind is something that can't easily be taught. It's more something that develops gradually within you if the environment and intention is conducive. I knew that Tim's ability to have people around him had gradually opened up since we took him out of a crowded, one-size-fits-all environment.

This was because he had more space to develop in a way that was natural to him, instead of one that was decided on in advance by others. I also knew this process couldn't happen quickly. The building blocks of the last five years putting relationships first had gradually seeped in. The decision to take him out of school had been the right one. It had been a tough call but now it was constantly paying off in many ways.

Tim was starting to be aware of me and my feelings, too. He would come to me and say, 'How are you doing, Mum?'. It was an incredible awakening for both of us.

We also sometimes had conversations about his past, in small increments when he showed interest and we were in some such discussion one day when he said, 'Well, you've got the *proper* me now.' This was massive – he was showing an awareness of his own emerging personality and reflecting on what was happening to him.

Friends

Tim now had friends. He was collaborating in projects, working in groups, writing and talking more easily. This could not have come about through any form of coercion – it was all about helping him to get to a state where the processes to learn could begin and stay nurtured. I thought back to the time he had only had volunteers as friends. Now he can make his own friends. Friends visited and the children played collaboratively together, out of choice. No one was with him as a favour. They were with him because they wanted to be. This was something I had always yearned for him.

That infamous gap we'd been warned about wasn't getting wider – on the contrary, Tim was getting closer to being able to relate to his peers, not further away. He was heading towards his teenage years which, for the first time tentatively looked like they might work. Yes, he still needed help with lots of practical things, conceptual thinking, etc but all this could now be taught. It wasn't the end of the world and it was all possible.

A Whole New Trajectory

With social pathways opening up, the neural pathways to cognitive thinking and learning started to open up, too, and Tim started to enjoy fiddling about with melodies on the piano completely independently.

Since starting the Son-Rise Program approach full-time, Tim had not been pulled kicking and screaming anywhere. The occasional frustrations and Tim getting emotions out of his system, I didn't consider to be meltdowns. They were just a normal part of development and life. And we could always find a resolution after stressful moments, helping him to process his own thoughts and feelings. I felt like I was seeing the whole process of neuroplasticity unfolding in front of my eyes, as I was having to constantly adapt to Tim's ever-changing brain.

However, I don't believe any of this just happened. This transformation occurred *because* of the thousands of hours of one-to-one relationship-focused quality time. Four years of giving control had led to Tim never needing to be controlling again – to the extent that he began to go out of his way to be helpful and mindful of our needs and wants. We worked *with* his grain not against it and we respected every emotion. We saw reasons behind every behaviour and helped to solve them rather than ever trying to change his behaviour.

Rushing

Tim found rushing really hard. He couldn't hurry! It stressed him too much and we kept having to say, 'It's OK, you don't need to hurry, just *remember* to eat' etc! If we used the word hurry with regards to his eating it stressed him – even though it used to take him an hour to eat a bowl of soup but if we asked him to *remember* to eat it was OK! He even wrote a soup-eating song with Rachel and listened while he ate – with the song reminding him every so often to take a spoon. We were constantly using motivations to reach his goals in all areas.

Using our Attitude to Help Tim With his Anxiety

Tim was also very concerned about making mistakes and would become very stressed over this issue. The way we knew to help him with this was to constantly be happy with him, make sure he felt no judgement and if he felt he had made a mistake calmly help him through his feelings.

For years we had been really calm with Tim if he had made mistakes or got anything wrong or had accidents of any description. This was vital as Tim's default place had, for so long, been a feeling of inadequacy. He seemed to naturally feel wrong about himself and so it was important that when he made mistakes our attitudes didn't confirm this.

One day I went into the bathroom while he was in the bath and saw he had put his video camera underwater. He was simply curious about whether he could film things underwater and aged ten, didn't realise that his camera wasn't a waterproof model. It was obvious his beloved camera would never work again. I had a choice here as always. I knew there was no point in being angry or disappointed as that would have only made Tim highly anxious and he would have to deal with my emotions, as well as realising his camera was broken. All Tim needed was for me to explain really calmly that most electronic things will not work once they have been under water. The consequence was natural. He couldn't use it anymore. The last thing he needed was for me to be cross about it. This was also a great moment to emphasise the very real danger of water and electricity which he had never been able to grasp as a young child – this was one of the more dramatic examples of the knowledge gaps we had to start filling in, due to his development delay.

Another time he was in a shop at Christmas looking at all the decorations. He happened to be holding a small glass decoration in his hand when it dropped to the floor and smashed. Immediately I knew it didn't matter – that it just needed to be cleared up and paid for. I was always quick to walk through consequences mentally myself and feel OK so that I could lead the way for him emotionally. Fortunately this was only £2.99 but even if it had been £299 it would have been important to keep my attitude the same, whatever the consequence for us. Tim hadn't done it on purpose and was already mortified. My job was to keep him level emotionally so he didn't start feeling guilty, which he had a tendency to do. In this case, Tim came with me to the counter while I explained and the lady didn't mind at all. She was lovely, saying 'accidents happen' and refused to take any payment. I love it when people confirm what I am trying to model to Tim, that such things *aren't* the end of the world.

Coverage

We taught Tim academic subjects in a bespoke way at this point. We had no programmes or books to follow but had to really work out what he knew, what he didn't know, what he needed and then take it from there. This was not about coverage (teachers ticking boxes to show they have covered a certain subject), it was all about teaching something until Tim had understood it enough to be secure to use it in his own work.

When Rachel broached topics like telling the time, she could clearly see that Tim wasn't ready, so she would let it go and then try again a few months later – then a few months later – then when he was ready, he 'got it'. She taught verbs for two full weeks every day – not just once, then a few weeks later, as schools might – but they did verbs in all sorts of fun and motivating ways until he completely understood them.

I was amazed one day that he could take a piece of writing and underline all the nouns, verbs and adjectives in different colours independently. He had really understood these things.

A Baby Brother

So, while all this amazing learning and development was going on, our baby's birth was fast approaching. Tim's birth had been so horrible for me that I was really scared about going through that again. In fact, because of my fear I had a doula, Caroline, who had become a great friend and ally through all of the aches, pains, fears and excitements of my pregnancy. I was sure that she would be with me through the birth and she and I had talked through all the possible options. I had originally wanted a C-Section as I couldn't erase the pain from before but knowing how much I needed to carry on with life afterwards, I wanted to try and overcome my fear and have a natural birth again as I would recover faster. I thought maybe the answer was to have an epidural so I could have a natural childbirth but with less pain. I saw a couple of specialist doctors to make sure this would be in place for me as I needed the reassurance.

The afternoon before Tim's brother was born, he'd had two friends round and they'd been playing in the garden. We had plans that when the time came, whatever time of day or night it was, Tim could go to our neighbour, Rick, and stay with him until Rachel came to take over.

Things started kicking off in the early hours of the following morning and we gradually realised it was serious as the pain escalated. When Caroline arrived, she tried to encourage me to have my baby then and there, but I had no intention of having my baby at home, preferring to have the security of a hospital and my promised epidural. So we called Rick, who collected Tim and got in the car – Erik driving and Caroline helping me deal with my labour pains in the back seat.

I always think it's a bit surreal that you see people going into hospital looking averagely normal and you see them come out a few hours or days later all relaxed and with a baby in their arms. What you rarely see is the bit in between which, when you are going through it, feels interminable.

I did manage to have the epidural but it didn't totally take the pain away. The contractions brought unbearable pain but having Erik on one side of me and Caroline on the other really helped. At 11am my beautiful baby, Sammy, was born and, as with Tim, I was immediately overcome with wonder at the emergence of this new little person into our lives. I spent that first day gazing at him sleeping and re-familiarising myself with feeding and nappy changing.

When Erik brought Tim to see us the next morning, he took the experience in his stride, pleased to meet Sammy and also keen to tell me all that had been happening with him since he last saw me. There were a lot of visitors to the house throughout the next days and weeks. Lots of my friends and family were delighted to meet Sammy.

I resolved to give Sammy as much security as possible, proactively feeding love and certainty into him from the very beginning. I was determined he wouldn't feel as insecure as Tim had done in the first few years of his life and wanted to input as much love and connection as I could. Sammy, from the beginning, seemed contented, peaceful, happy. He had a steadiness about him and quickly became very responsive to us. I found it incredible now being a mother of two. I had always wanted to be able to say 'my children' instead of 'my child' and now I could.

Regrouping the Social Connection

A couple of months after Sammy's birth in March 2012, I started to see that Tim was becoming more moody, irrational and less communicative. This could have been a direct result of having a baby in the family and a massive chunk of attention going in a new direction. I decided to take action and made a decision that Tim and I would spend a quality hour together every morning – to get the day into perspective, to sort our expectations out, and to warm up his communication muscles.

I would sit up in bed feeding Sammy and encourage Tim to come and join me with his breakfast. Tim didn't want to do this to start with, but soon warmed to the idea when he realised he felt better through talking to me. He even started telling me his problems. He saw that Erik was reading a *How to...* book and he said to me, 'I need a book on how not to be bored.' So we started a little book, writing down all the things he could do so as not to be bored.

Also, every evening, Tim, Erik and I would meet and we'd discuss what Tim had felt had gone well that day, what he had found hard, and what he was most proud of. Then Erik and I would add our contributions. This was a great rebonding activity and I really felt it held Tim together that summer.

During this period, I realised just how much talking and connection he needed in order to feel secure and happy. I could increasingly see that whatever else was going on around him, Tim required vast quantities of love, connection, rebonding, planning for the day ahead, then thinking and reflecting on his achievements and regrouping. Tim had a strong desire to connect with people but was still needing help to build on his emerging skills and to feel more secure in this area. Emotional support was vital. I couldn't let go. In fact, I needed to increase this level of emotional support as he went on developing in these areas.

These social skills were just emerging and as Raun says in *Autism Breakthrough* these skills are like weak muscles that need to be worked. They were just coming into existence. It was our job to nurture them and work all Tim's 'weak muscles' in an enjoyable and encouraging way.

Whenever I explained him to other people I would always say, 'More talking and involvement is always better than less' as Tim yearned to be talked to and be involved in activities around him, even though his initiative was still limited and people might have drawn the conclusion that he was stepping back because he wasn't interested.

Interestingly, I know lots of people believe that children on the autistic spectrum have all these problems with communication and social interaction as a 'done deal' and there's nothing to be done to improve their difficulties – and worse still, don't need or care about socially interacting with people around them. We have learnt that nothing could be further from the truth. I have experienced in Tim's case the total opposite was true – for as long as he was able to communicate, he has always shown that he cared about people and being part of a social group. Not everything is final and set in stone. The brain is pliable.

Can Others Allow Us to Move On?

In the midst of all this amazing success, we still had to deal with people who had known Tim throughout his life and witnessed his full-blown meltdown days. Some still saw him that way, despite his progress, though I was relieved that others would see him after a long period of time, be surprised with how far he'd come and alter their perceptions and responses accordingly.

We were in an unusual half-way house. Tim didn't have many of his sensory overloads or behavioural issues anymore, but he was only at the beginning stages of learning enough social skills to be part of the wider social world. I didn't know any other mums at this point who had been doing the Son-Rise Program with their children – there was no Facebook community yet, like there is now.

In the summer, when Tim was ten, we met up with an old school friend of his and went out to a park. They had a wonderful time laughing, chatting and going off on bumper car rides and her mum and I drank tea and talked in the sunshine. I was revelling in the freedom of this situation – I never took these easy situations for granted. And as I had been thinking a lot about Tim's developing motivations, I asked if she knew of any clubs in the local area that Tim might like to join, thinking of music, drama, filming and a way to meet new children etc. She told me that she knew of a club for children with disabilities and behavioural problems which might be good for him. Oh my goodness, it had happened again!

Right in the middle of my excitement, someone had brought in their belief that obviously no progress was possible and thrown in a negative comment again. Hadn't she seen him all afternoon? He'd been happy, talking, laughing, playing – was it the label that made her say that? Was it her memory that prevented her from being able to see further? Couldn't she believe and see that Tim was moving on from his deeply complex behaviours and that there was more to him than his label?

I thought back to the time I had never wanted Tim to have a label at all. In my world, he didn't have a label – he was a person who I adored and totally respected, who had a few issues that I was helping him with. I was *beyond blessed* to have him. He was *gorgeous.*

Why would someone keep on harping back to disabilities and behaviour problems? He hardly had any behaviour issues anymore and he was really overcoming much of the complexity of his processing and communicating.

On another occasion, a mother of one of Tim's friends (who had never spent any time with Tim) phoned me up and told me she felt really sorry for me and that she knew how I felt because she had a 'retarded' sister. I didn't even get a chance to get a word in edgeways about the 'retarded' issue but I realised I hated dealing with so many misconceptions. Yes, *life* was challenging, but Tim wasn't 'retarded'. Again, the two worlds – who Tim really was and people's conceptions of the label attached to him just didn't seem to fit.

On a different day, at a friend's house when Tim was playing really easily and happily with her three children in their garden and I was starting to feel relaxed, she blurted, 'It's really good for my children to know someone like Tim'.

Someone like Tim? For goodness sake, can she not hear how that sounds to me?

Nina helped me so much here because she didn't see any of this. In fact, she laughed at it all with me. She knew Tim was emerging as she could talk to him, related to him and liked him very much. She was a real ally on this journey, full of the belief and positivity that I needed. Nevertheless, I felt I was between two worlds.

Powerful Processes

Sometimes Tim's processes were really full on and powerful – talk about an engine you couldn't turn it off. 'Mum I've written a song, come and hear it, Mum, I've got a brilliant idea for this scene, Mum, I've found a piece of music that would be perfect for this act, Mum, can you edit this song for me?' I could see that creativity really drove Tim. His thinking was highly creative. He believed all things were possible, something we must have somehow instilled subconsciously in him after all these years of loving and responding to him. Therefore he had ideas that were highly complex and improbable but he had a solid belief that he could do them!

Tim still needed to pace around at times and would talk his overloaded ideas out under his breath. It was as though everything he experienced just built up inside him and needed an outlet. Sometimes it was almost as if he were acting out scenes and scenarios. The difference was, was that when he was doing this in his intensive inner world, I would call out, 'Tim, are you OK?' and he would reply 'I'm fine' and then go back to it. If I asked him to come and do something he would either immediately respond or he would call out, 'two minutes'. So he wasn't cut off from us when he was doing this – he just still needed to process in this way. At this stage, he needed to do this for about an hour altogether in a day.

The interesting thing now, though, was that he never paced or muttered in front of other people, showing that he was aware it was an unusual thing to do. Once, on a beautifully sunny day, he was in the front garden, pacing around and talking ideas out. I popped out to ask him if he was OK and then, as if reading my thoughts, he said, 'Don't worry Mum – when other people come, I stop.'

Another time when the neighbour's fence was down, he wanted to go in the garden to pace and I said, 'Go on, they'll like to see you' and he replied, 'If they see me, they might think it's weird'.

He clearly had an awareness of what other people might think and that awareness was the bit I liked the most – what incredible progress – and thinking about what other people think of him. But I also found it interesting that there was still something so complex in his neurological system that he needed to do this.

I must admit, this did still make me feel insecure on occasions. I would hear his feet landing on the wobbly paving stones outside the back door as he leapt from one to the other and a part of me would panic. My logic knew he needed to do this but emotionally I felt a pang of fear and wanted it to stop. I knew his desperation to keep his friends and I felt if his friends were to see him do this, it would ostracise him. My gut reaction was still sometimes to jump up and stop him, but I knew better than to actually do that. If I just couldn't stand my own insecurity anymore, I would sometimes go out into the garden and talk to him. He would stop immediately and talk back to me and I would be filled with relief. Sometimes I would ask for a hug. I think this stimming of his could still sometimes return me to a place where fear, separation and grief had been a reality. I needed assurance that I hadn't lost him, that he was still with me. He was.

Active Listening: Just Talk and I Will Listen

Sometimes, when I had had a long day with Sammy, I would have to psyche myself up for active listening sessions, but I knew their importance as we were using this experience as a way to help Tim be more aware of who he was talking to and how he might come across. We were working on turning his one-way conversations into natural two-way conversations.

We never ever stopped him talking to us. By default, because of his past, we always fully welcomed *any* communication for however long he needed to talk and if he had big ideas and wanted to talk to us about them, then we would actively listen out of genuine interest. Sometimes though, one of us would have just settled for a long-awaited ten minutes to ourselves to read or write an email and Tim would come up to us and without warning, launch into telling us all about his new ideas.

There were times when Erik and I would share moments of amusement when this happened – particularly if it happened to the other person. Once I actually fell asleep while listening. I couldn't believe I did it but I was so incredibly tired and Tim needed to talk so much. You know how you feel yourself going and your head suddenly jerks forward, which wakes you up. I felt mortified, but he forgave me.

Another thing we noticed was that if Tim wanted to talk, he couldn't wait. Sometimes he would come into the room and start talking avidly to us when Erik and I were in the midst of a conversation ourselves. We knew he wasn't being rude and the focus at this point wasn't about being polite and waiting his turn. At this point, he genuinely found it hard to retain sentences in his head. If we *did* ask him to wait before talking, he would pace about telling us that if he didn't speak now he would forget what he wanted to say. Therefore Erik and I couldn't carry on anyway. At this stage of his development, we were aware his desire to talk was more important than our need to teach him to be polite. That would come in time.

Each time I listened actively, responded excitedly and asked questions to make him think further. I was constantly aware of how much of a miracle it was that he could talk and that he wanted to share his ideas with me. Then I realised I could use these ideas of his to ask further questions and to think more deeply and conceptually. I would ask him details about a character he was envisaging, or about what the room looked like that the scene happened in. In this way he started to add more context to his ideas.

We were encouraging him to speak *to* us, being aware of our feelings and reactions, rather than speak *at* us, which he tended to do when his mind was full of creative ideas and he was on his own track-thinking.

I was just so keen to let him talk, even if he went on and on, so I kept thinking 'keep talking, keep talking,' as I loved to hear his voice and his zest for life.

Chapter Twelve – Discovering Tim and his talents

Dance Show

At the beginning of summer, Tim's dance school put on a show at a local theatre. I had been going along with the process, organising costumes, taking Tim to extra rehearsals etc and still had seen nothing of the dances, or what he was actually doing. It felt great. His teacher kept telling me he was doing fine and I would wonder, fine for *him*, considering his issues? Or genuinely fine in the way the other children were fine? I couldn't keep asking these things, as I felt it would make me look paranoid – and what if he actually *was* coping and I just went on and on about it?

When the time came for the show, Erik and I went to the theatre, right down by the beach and hung about outside. I wasn't planning to watch the whole show as I couldn't be away from Sammy too long, but I was planning to get a programme and sneak in for the dances that Tim was in. When I went in, the theatre was dark and the plush red curtains were pulled across. There was a heavy air of expectation among the murmuring audience. I felt sick, then I felt butterflies, then I felt excited. Then I panicked – what if Tim couldn't do this and would explode into a meltdown on stage? Think of all the people, all the expectation, all the cooperation, all the social activity around him – and I wasn't there to help him. Could he process it all? How was he feeling? He had never been in such a big theatre before. What if they had given him a mascot part, because he couldn't follow instructions in the same way as the others?

The curtains opened to a sea of children all dressed in black and white costumes. Some were sitting on the floor, some were in circles, all part of a carefully choreographed stage. The introduction to the song 'London is London' from the musical *Good-bye Mr Chips* started filling the theatre.

I scanned the group looking for Tim. Oh my goodness – there he was – looking so handsome with his black cap, waistcoat and matching trousers. Just like all the other children, he was sitting on the floor among a group of perfect young dancers. As I watched, my panic turned to elation. He was dancing just like the other children – creating circles and skipping around, marching across the stage, listening out for cues in the music to join other groups… And he looked so confident and happy up there! No one could have picked him out as having any special difficulties at all.

My goodness. Two years ago, he was considered so uncooperative that he had to have four teaching assistants a week. Here, he just had the normal support network that all the children had. He took the instruction, did as he was told, learnt the moves and enjoyed it! I also couldn't believe he could cope with the loud music, along with all the other sensory bombardments. Things were really changing and I was witnessing it first-hand.

Progressing to Summer Schools

It was around this time, because of Tim's love for all things involving drama and music, I had a gut feeling that he might – just might – be able to cope with a drama summer school that summer. I had seen an advert at the theatre where the dance show was and felt really excited about it. Rachel told me she thought I was pushing it and he wouldn't be ready, but I just so much wanted to give it a try. I knew how much Tim came into his own with drama, dance and music and that he found social connections so much easier because of it. Erik and I decided to sign him up for it but to keep a Son-Rise Program® mindset about the whole thing. If he couldn't cope, that would be fine and we would just accept that he wasn't sufficiently ready yet. Anything he *could* manage, we would celebrate. Just for once, I felt frustrated about this – why did I always have to be careful and not get excited? I *was* excited. Actually I had a really *good* feeling about it and I wanted to enjoy that, but I needed to protect my feelings if it all went wrong.

The tutor, Andrew, was an excellent theatre studies tutor from the local university and when I phoned him he was instantly keen for Tim to come along. He told me his Mum worked with people on the autistic spectrum, so he was used to some of the issues. I explained about Tim's situation and he asked me to write down some useful pointers for himself and his staff. He agreed that Tim could meet him a few days beforehand, on his own.

When we went into the theatre to meet him, the first thing he did was greet Tim and talk to him, leaving me pretty much out of the equation! If I could put into words how much that meant to me, I would, but I can't find the words to do it justice. I was so used to the 'does he take sugar?' mentality that this bloke just blew me away. Tim might not be perfect in his communication but this lovely chap was giving him a chance. He had so much respect for Tim and interest in what he had to say.

Tim knew that they were going to do part of the show *Hairspray* and he had watched it and learnt some of the songs. They discussed all this and at no point did Andrew talk to me about Tim's difficulties in front of him. What respect! We left there happily, looking forward to the summer school.

Now this summer school could either be seen as a risk or an adventure – five full days with a group of children Tim had never met before and a performance on stage in the theatre at the end of it. I knew that Tim might be in his element there, but I also knew that he may well fall apart and need to come home. Which way would it go? I chose to see it as an adventure and to be comfortable with whatever the outcome was.

We prepared Tim as much as we could. As he still needed support in eating, I told him I would pick him up every lunch time and take him to the car to eat – (I knew he needed his protein in order to keep up his energy, so to me this was the best option). Otherwise, he had his snacks. Details of food, how to ask if he needed the toilet, where to wash his face (which he always wanted to do after eating) all had to be discussed with him. We encouraged him to be interested in and respond to the other children as best he could. He was already very keen on the musical *Hairspray* and couldn't wait to take part. I knew he had the capacity to enjoy it and I hoped so much he would cope.

DAY ONE – WILL HE MANAGE?: On the first day I took him there, the buzz of children met us at the door. It reminded me of the 'wall of sound' he'd so often ran away from when he was little. I took a deep breath and sent him in.

Oh my goodness, what had I done? Would he have enough skills to cope? When I went to pick him up at lunchtime, I saw a group of chatty, confident children in the foyer, all hanging around and looking like they belonged together. Tim was brought out to me by an adult.

This was a shame, because I knew how chatty and confident he could also be, but I sat in the car with him and asked him how it was. He told me that he didn't find it that good. He said there was a lot of boring listening and the dancing was too hard. He was very tired and distracted. On taking him back, Andrew said he'd been fine and joined in everything, that at one point he'd wanted to tell a joke but Andrew had asked him to wait until break – which had made him a little negative. He also mentioned that when asking the whole group the question 'what's important in acting?' Tim had put his hand up to say he knew all the characters in *Hairspray*. At one point, apparently he had told Andrew he was tired and Andrew let him lie down on some chairs at the front.

I asked him if the other children were laughing at Tim and he told me 'no, but they were looking at me as if to say what's all this about?'. He told me he had spoken to the group about treating each other equally and working as a team and said he thinks that they read between the lines and realised he was talking about the struggles that Tim was having. I always cringed with being told things like this – but I still had full trust in Tim. I knew he had it in him, once he started to feel comfortable, to relax sufficiently to enjoy the experience.

So, what could I glean from the first day? Tim was not altogether aware of the situation and was quite disconnected, still sometimes coping more with his own thought processes than able to respond to the moment – and saying the talk was boring probably meant he couldn't understand or relate to what was said. But given there were lots of new people and he only knew one adult, he did brilliantly with lots of instructions and it was a very long day – five hours of concentration, especially considering he was used to just one hour and then a break. In addition, he was expecting the day to be based around the show *Hairspray*, today hadn't included anything relating to the musical at all.

Under this type of pressure Tim's best side couldn't emerge – not yet anyway. While he wasn't unhappy, neither was he happy. And yet he was willing to continue attending. At the end of the first day, Andrew said the most we could hope for was a few instances of interaction throughout the week, clearly preparing us not to expect anything too much.

DAY TWO: This was a much better day. Tim enjoyed the dances and the tour of the theatre. He had a chance to sing a solo in a microphone with headphones on – which everyone clapped to – and in the afternoon they read scripts. He had a chance to read some parts on his own which he was pleased about. I knew that Tim needed specific tasks – things to do, songs to sing, dance steps, words to say etc and that he didn't cope well yet with anything less structured.

Tim enjoyed this day far more as he felt he'd had a chance to prove what he could do and always liked performing.

DAY THREE: We woke up to an email from Andrew, telling us that Tim was doing really well, had connected a lot more on the second day and did we think he would manage some lines in the play?

Wow! Fantastic! Of course! We knew that he would cope with this brilliantly but to people who only met him at face value, they probably wouldn't realise all this. Yay! Andrew wrote in a part for Tim in the play which was peripheral so that if for some reason Tim was unable to face performing, the play could still go ahead. That was OK. We felt sure that Tim would rise to the occasion but it was reasonable for other people to still wonder.

When I walked in at lunchtime, I saw a group of children talking animatedly in the foyer again and I braced myself to wait for Tim to be brought out to me. Then I looked closer. One of the children *was* Tim – with no adult in sight. He was chatty, happy, involved… I watched him and my heart filled with so much love and gratitude. I was experiencing another dream that I had longed for since his initial diagnosis.

It was such a shame to pull him away from such a moment. When in the car, I could see he needed to switch off and get some soup inside him, but I also sensed he really wanted to return to the theatre, so I asked if he'd like to take the rest of his food back in there and join the others and he said yes. He then said he could go in by himself, from the car park. Just to be safe, I drove him to the entrance and watched him walk in. Just inside there was a girl, laughing with a few others. I wondered how he'd be with her. He walked right up to her, was involved in a chat for a while, then moved on, mixed with a couple of others, then walked into the studio. It all seemed so straightforward.

DAY FOUR: On the fourth day Tim ate really quickly in the car with me as he wanted to get back and when I said I wanted to come into the studio and talk to Andrew about clothes, he really didn't want me to, saying, 'This isn't a place for mums'.

Clearly embarrassed he was adamant he didn't want me to even be seen. I let him go in and walked out of the theatre hugging Sammy tight. I'd ask Andrew about his costume another time. Tim didn't need me! He could handle this! What a brilliant feeling!

At the end I was told he'd done well – all very normal. In Andrew's words, 'No major shakes.'

DAY FIVE – SHOW TIME: On the final day, Tim went in very happily and at lunchtime he wanted to eat really quickly again as he said two of the girls had promised they'd share their chips with him if he was back in time.

As we drove back to the theatre he said, 'I'd better unbuckle my seatbelt and get back where I belong'. He was so excited...

In the morning Andrew said Tim had asked if he'd done OK and Andrew said he'd done brilliantly, then asked the other children how they thought Tim had done and they all put their thumbs up, clapped and cheered. Andrew said the look on Tim's face was a picture. When Tim told me the story he said it 'made his dreams come true'.

When Erik, Gel and I arrived at the theatre to see the show, we were a mixture of excitement and apprehension. It was the same theatre that the dance show had been in with its plush red curtains, anticipatory buzz from the audience, high ceilings and gilded decor. All those familiar feelings came back to me – a mixture of excitement and nerves. What if he doesn't know what to do? What if it all gets too much for him and he needs to escape? Where can he escape to? Who's specially looking after him? No one was specially looking after him. He was just part of a general group.

When the curtains pulled back, we saw him on stage as part of a large opening number, completely confident, fully involved and not appearing in the least like he needed any looking after at all. He was in the middle of a group of children, acting, miming, singing, and dancing. We couldn't believe how much he had been able to take in. Dance moves, what to say, how to respond, where to be on the stage. It was an amazing feeling to watch him interacting animatedly and being a part of it all, fully involved and loving every second. He delivered all his lines brilliantly and took part in five dances.

He came out on a high, feeling so pleased with himself with white hairspray zig-zagged through his cropped hair. Others were pleased with him as well. He had hugs with some of the children and they all danced and celebrated in their post-show high together.

It turned out that the grandmother of one of the girls was Gel's friend. A few days later they talked and her friend said that her granddaughter missed Tim and gave Gel her number in case the children wanted to get together. We also took the numbers of other children who wanted to stay in touch.

How much more proof did I need that this was Tim's highest motivation and the very best way to help him access friendships? Erik and I were every bit as excited as Tim and we all went home on a high.

A Goal of Normality

Normality can be construed as a neurotypical mother just wanting her son to be neurotypical and not accepting his autism. The thing was, normality to me just meant lack of distress and for Tim to be *able* to do the things he liked with the people he wanted to be with. I like the word normal. I would sometimes comment to friends that my ultimate goal in life was just to live an average life. I had no great desire for Tim to gain University degrees, high level jobs, or other things that many people considered to be the epitome of success – unless Tim wanted these himself, of course. I just wanted him to relate to other people. It had been a goal for Tim for so long that now I just wanted to enjoy every single second that he wasn't struggling and that he seemed happy with his world. What I especially loved was the fact that the side I had seen of him when he felt comfortable at home was now starting to be visible in the outside world.

County Assessments

It was at this time that we had a visit from County. They wanted to do a yearly home education assessment to see what we were teaching Tim and how he was doing. This assessment was extremely positive. Andrew from the summer school had written a report for us about how well Tim did, which was read by County and we were able to provide evidence of Tim's achievements and developmental shifts. At the same time, aged ten, he also had a full Educational Psychology assessment, accompanied by a report which was also very positive. By now Tim's development was clearly visible for all to see.

In light of this, Erik emailed County to ask whether, as we had such clear evidence now of how our system was working, they would take over the payment of this education for Tim – therefore relieving my Dad. Unbelievably, County agreed! They evidently appreciated that we had provided records throughout and we could fully explain the correlation between our approach and Tim's progress. It was wonderful and empowering to be recognised in this way and for County to be able to trust us and also to see that our way of educating him was the answer.

However, there was a catch. They wanted Tim to go back into the system at Secondary level – which was nine months away – and wrote in an email: 'we can meet Tim's needs in a West Sussex County Council maintained provision. If you wish to express a preference for a non-maintained or independent school this will need further consideration at the Special Educational Needs Panel.'

But what we were doing was working. I wanted to keep it going. The whole issue of schools and panels struck fear into my heart, given that my life and Tim's development would be at their mercy again. County would only pay for this education for the next nine months and my Dad had told us, understandably, that he couldn't continue to fund this education for Tim at Secondary level. We had a choice of course – we could home educate him all through his teenage years and try to do the Son-Rise Program ourselves, but I knew that would be hard because we would both have to work and I didn't want to rely on volunteers for this level of his education. Also, without Rachel or other highly specialised tutors, I wouldn't be able to give him the opportunities I knew he needed.

We would have to at least look at schools. I was thrown back to the 'out of control' feeling that despite having struck gold with the Son-Rise Program and with such proof that he was growing, we would need to try him in the educational system again. In the past this had made him feel anxious, rushed, nervous, misunderstood and very unhappy. I desperately needed to protect him from this. With how we were treating him at home he was developing confidence, he knew he was safe to make mistakes, that he would never be laughed at or judged, and he was in a place to *enjoy* learning and relationships with peers. This was invaluable.

But part of me was also slightly curious as to how Tim would cope in school now that he was so much more social and able to learn. I knew he was growing because of what we had put in place but maybe the changes in him were secure enough that he could take who he now was into a classroom setting and still be able to grow there. Then his life and learning could open up again to yet a new level. I thought about the summer school and this gave me hope. I then remembered the swimming party and I wasn't sure. But we had nine more months left of the beautiful Son-Rise Program environment that was working so well for him and we would make the most of this while trying to prepare him for the change.

Searching for the Next Stage

Armed with the knowledge we had, Rachel, Erik and I started looking at schools. We knew that Tim was still in need of nurture and support in his development. A mainstream school would probably be a bit too fast-paced with typical deficit thinking and expectations which could bring back anxiety, while limiting his learning. The ideal setting would be a private, mainstream-type school with small classes that understood Tim's autism like we did and be sufficiently aware of his processes to open up doors for his motivations. We also needed an establishment that would be willing to form a real relationship with us as parents. The lack of willingness to talk about Tim at his last school was still very raw for me. We needed a level of togetherness that I knew most schools wouldn't make time for.

In the search, we came across schools which had X-boxes in their quiet rooms, used the Wii instead of PE lessons and had massive screens in every room. Most focused entirely on behaviour management in order to gain cooperation. In some I observed lots of troubleshooting but couldn't see any proactive approaches being used.

We were no longer focusing on behaviour – and if Tim did struggle at any time we would understand, immediately listen and help him, knowing that there was always a good reason. A focus on behaviour, especially in a one-size-fits-all capacity did not work for Tim. He already knew he needed to listen and follow instructions and most of the time he could manage this. But I knew he still had a lot of complexities and sensitivities in the way he perceived life. If he became stressed or anxious and his response was perceived as 'naughty behaviour' this had the potential to send him back to his 'there's something wrong with me' mentality which we were working so hard to assuage.

Yet again, there was so much focus on screens, as if it was the only way children on the spectrum could learn. We knew the opposite – that removing screens and focusing on human interaction was the most helpful thing for Tim's growth and learning. Would there be anywhere out there that would respect this?

In one unit in a Secondary school, the lady who showed us round just wanted to show off their amazing new facilities and didn't once ask us about Tim. This was a deciding factor for me against sending him there. I didn't care about all the hi-tech facilities. I cared about the relationships and approach they would use. She seemed flummoxed when I asked her about this and had no real answer for me.

In the end there was only one school out of the selection we found that I felt, if Tim had to go somewhere, might be the best option. It was just twenty minutes from our house – a large country mansion overlooking the beautiful countryside with small classes that promised a range of creative subjects. It wasn't a mainstream school and neither was it a special school. They considered themselves to be a small school that supported boys with particular learning needs. Their slogan was 'believe, inspire, succeed' and the secretary, when showing me round, told me that the boys were virtually given medals for breathing. I took this that they noticed everything the children could do well and acknowledged it, which seemed promising. The atmosphere initially seemed full of kindness in amidst the structure.

When Tim and I went to visit, I was really proud of how he talked to one of the teachers and answered questions about himself. We saw a beautiful music studio and were told all about the concerts and recording possibilities that would be there for him. They also had a well-equipped photographic studio. It all seemed inspiring. We decided to give it a try.

Of course it wasn't as simple as that. Because this was an independent school, there was no guarantee of a place. We had to put our reasons in writing and wait for a decision from that lovely panel again.

I remembered back to when the faceless panel had not listened to us before and how hard we'd had to fight, often being dismissed. I could not afford to be dismissed again. Tim in his emergence was too important. I could not bear to think of him being discussed like just one case on a conveyer belt of invisible children. We were faced with home education with no money, a fast-paced one-size-fits-all secondary school with thousands of students or this particular private school that looked like it might hold some good opportunities for him. How could they know what would work for him or be best for him? They really couldn't.

I wrote a letter to Olivia Stone, who was our contact at County and oversaw Tim's progress, and said 'As they will be discussing the future of our child and we have been responsible for every element of his education for the last two years with great success, I think it makes sense if we are part of the discussion process that makes decisions about his life. It will be vital for us to know the thought processes that take the panel to their decision if it is a different one to our own'.

I always had to be so careful in how I worded everything, staying polite and reasonable and having all the evidence and facts at my fingertips. It was unprecedented that Olivia actually agreed to this. She thought it was a good idea, too. We would actually be the first family ever to go to the panel meeting to put forward in person what we thought would be best for our child.

Erik, myself and Sammy attended the meeting in January, with just seven months left before Tim would need to start at this school if he got a place. My voice was trembling as I explained in detail Tim's progress and our reasons for wanting this school. I always became shaky when having to speak about something so important to me and especially when the outcome was so vital. I spoke passionately about the environment that had shut him down and what was vital in an environment that gave him a chance.

As we left, one of the panel members rushed out to thank us. He said that it had made a huge difference having us there and that he thought more families should be able to put across their requests in person.

We soon received a letter to say Tim had a place at Fielding College and he was due to start the following September. Although we had pushed for it and were pleased, I still reserved judgement.

'Mum, I Want to Do a Pantomime!'

Now elements of Tim's relationships and abilities were developing so well, I wondered what our next goal would be. I would wait for Tim's lead as I had learnt very well to take my cues from him and it didn't take long for me to find out.

One day, soon after the summer school, Sammy was asleep and I was sitting in the lounge when Tim came up to me and said, 'Mum, I want to do a pantomime'.

'Really?' I said, thinking through all the implications of this. It flashed through my mind, all the hard work involved with regular practices, asking parents to give their children lifts, hiring halls, costumes, stage design etc and then I thought about all the opportunities for interaction, the relationships he could form, the direction he would need to take... 'OK.' I said. 'We can do that. Tell me what you want to do…'

'I've written the story,' he said.

I did the Son-Rise Program technique of active listening which I often did with Tim when he wanted to tell me about his ideas. He hardly took a breath and talked non-stop for forty-five minutes. It turned out that Tim had seen a film of *Cinderella* and he wanted to put it on as a stage performance.

I listened and responded actively as if everything he was telling me was new and fascinating – which actually, it was. I knew the story but it was totally a new thing hearing it from him. He now appreciated the types of jokes and banter between the actors and the audience that he had seen in pantomimes and wanted to incorporate similar humour in his own production.

Later he brought his story to me and we sat together turning it into a script. We talked about who of his friends might like to join us and discussed what parts might be available. Tim said he would like to be the Prince. I mentally ran through a list in my head of whose parents might be willing to bring their children to this project. We could probably find children who would love to play the other characters.

I decided I would type if Tim dictated the dialogue for each character, which would be quicker and easier on Tim and his creative thinking could flow more easily.

He knew exactly what he wanted each character to say and what he wanted to happen. I could see quite quickly that he had a clear vision for it. He was dictating to me, like he used to when he was little and I did have to sometimes question him about things people said and make suggestions, but this time around he was willing to listen to all my questions and make changes.

I was aware that there was an actual audience for this script and that it was a great opportunity for Tim to share his ideas with others. I needed to be quite tactful, in that some of the material that he found hilarious would not translate to a wider audience, so we needed to discuss and adapt some of his ideas. We had great conversations about this. He was keen to bring in lots of jokes and change words in songs he knew to make them relevant to the story. What a great way to bring in the learning of language and meanings, fuelled by his passion to put his vision on a stage. This led to Tim writing his first ever song, 'We are the ugly stepsisters'. Little did we know this would be another of his major passions – song-writing.

The Beginning of Piano Playing

A few months earlier, because Tim had shown an interest in fiddling about on our keyboard, my Dad had given him an old keyboard of his which had been gathering dust in the loft and he had started to pick out melodies on it. If you recall, I'd got rid of my own piano some years earlier when he couldn't tolerate the sound.

Anyway, now that his love of music was developing, he enjoyed sitting at the keyboard trying to re-create melodies of songs he loved. He started by taking known melodies and changing the words and then started creating his own tunes and words. He adored this process and he and I spent hours listening to the melodies he was writing and playing around with words that worked best. I jumped right into this creative process with him and it was fun. I had written a bit of music back in my degree days but had always found it a really difficult process. He was running with it and loving it. No written music – just all by ear.

The Tuesday Group

We started a regular Tuesday drama group which became known as the 'Tuesday Group' where we worked on the pantomime. Since the dance show and the summer school, Tim became interested in acting on the stage. He was comfortable with the concept of rehearsing now and would happily practice scenes repeatedly with the others. He was able to take instruction well and contribute lots of his own ideas.

I decided to let all the children contribute. They changed words to songs, tweaked their scripts, worked out costumes, had lots of laughs together and really bonded. It was a highly creative experience for everyone with a lot of spontaneity, which I particularly loved. This also created some great friendships. They would go to the cinema, the beach and come over at other times just to hang out.

Sammy and I led the rehearsals together. More often than not, he was awake in my arms and seemed to thoroughly enjoy watching the children laughing, singing and having fun.

If Tim behaved in an unusual or intense way, which he could still do at times, I would acknowledge it and respond naturally to him as always. The others took my lead and did the same and soon all Tim's personality, talents and contributions were noticed and valued far more than his occasional unusual behaviour. However, he wasn't yet able to speak up for himself in the way the others were, so I would have to ensure Tim had his turn to share his ideas, in amongst the others.

Just a week before the show was happening, I had a great opportunity to work on my own and Tim's flexibility. One of the mothers realised she had double-booked her child, who wouldn't be able to attend the performance after all – with everyone's expectations high, one week to go and after months of rehearsing. I felt gutted, considering how excited the children were and how hard they had worked, but Erik asked me the ultimate question – what do you want the outcome to be? I said I wanted to still ask this girl to be part of our shows and to stay friendly with her mum.

'Well', he said, 'keep that attitude and we'll work on finding a solution when that's done'. I did that. I told her it was alright and that we would work something out and not to worry. We then racked our brains and found another lovely girl who we knew loved acting and she was excited at the chance. She volunteered to rehearse throughout the following week. She performed brilliantly in the show, in the process becoming a new friend and was in a lot of our subsequent shows. What a great result. Tim was fine about the whole thing. It was a great opportunity to teach him about using a positive attitude and flexibility, with a good outcome.

The pantomime was a huge success. In front of a hall full of people Tim and his friends acted, sang and danced away, telling the story with evident enjoyment. There were a few mini-stresses behind the scenes but nothing unresolvable. At one point he danced a beautiful waltz with Cinderella. I had arranged specific lessons for this and it was lovely to see how he had recalled the steps and was able to perform it with such conviction and confidence. In fact, throughout the show, Tim demonstrated his ability to act, sing and dance with no difficulty whatsoever. This was a milestone for him, because it was the first time he was able to bring his own ideas and version of a story onto a stage with a live audience – quite a feat in a way for a ten-year-old.

We were to learn that this beginning was just that – Tim now was highly motivated to continue to work on writing scripts and went to write yet another script, but this time, completely independently. He had an amazing focus and ability to apply himself, which was now expressing itself in his creativity, song-writing, composing music and writing scripts.

Cinderella was filmed, which of course meant that editing it would be the next project on the agenda. Tim was able to produce a

DVD totally unaided, complete with background music, menu and credits, as over the last few months he had taught himself new aspects of this process independently – more proof that his neurological pathways were opening up.

Hoodwinked – A Stage Play about Robin Hood

After this, Tim was hooked on the stage and wanted to start working on the next performance. This time we decided on a ready-made Robin Hood play, recruited more people in our group and started all over again. There was so much social interaction in the process and this was playing to Tim's strengths – a brilliant combination. Our house was often filled with friends and music, transforming it into a social and open place to be. Liveliness, banter, laughter and silliness were the name of the game and elements of it felt very natural. I could use a lot of my Son-Rise Program skills, alongside my teaching ability with these lovely children by celebrating them, putting relationships first and bringing out the best of their talents. And it worked as everyone grew in their relationships and confidence in their own ideas.

Madacts

We also found a local, low-key children's drama group which Tim could take part in. Some of his friends went too, though there were many children he didn't know. I stayed to support Tim along a little, as in, 'why don't you talk to so and so' or, 'why don't you tell so and so what you did on Saturday?' etc as he still had a hesitant social engine and a level of anxiety in large group situations where he didn't know many people. For this, he needed kindness and a can-do attitude behind him, which helped decrease his sense of isolation and improved his feelings of confidence, helping him to be able to reach out more naturally.

I also knew he wanted to feel more comfortable in this area. He actually said to me one day, 'Mum, I need a book on how to make friends'. If no one prompted him, he could stand awkwardly around, feeling miserable. What could happen then was that he would hate being there and eventually not want to go. I realised that, without support, he could very easily end up socially isolated in larger groups.

Taking instructions, however, was not an issue. He was the first to take on board what he was being asked of him and try really hard to get it right. Games posed a bigger problem in that he sometimes didn't immediately understand the rules and sometimes his responses were a little behind the others and he found himself quickly losing. So long as he didn't feel bad, that was OK – I just needed to encourage him to ask if he needed help. In one game I was impressed by his ability to respond to the instructions. The leader called out 'jump' and they had to squat down as every instruction needed an opposite response – and he cottoned on immediately. Excellent!

Developing Friendships

When my friend Sarah had stopped looking after Tim when he was a baby, it was because she had a new granddaughter, Alex. She'd had to stop caring for Tim as at the age of three, Tim had not been able to cope with Sarah dividing her attention. However by this stage, Alex and Tim had become firm friends. Alex had always been drawn to Tim's creativity and fun and they had always just clicked. She was very chatty, full of imagination and stories and when she and Tim had got together when they were younger, they would disappear into his room and come out in a great variety of different costumes wanting to show us plays they had made up. At the time, Alex could be brilliantly bossy and when she told Tim what to do, he did it willingly as he loved her ideas and was happy to go along with whatever she said. This had seriously helped him in his 'high need to control' days. Now they made comedy videos together and were always laughing and inspiring each other with stories and ideas, many of which were genuinely funny and madcap.

Another friend Tim had made was Susannah, who was also very creative. She was an amazing dancer and singer and immediately she and Tim would immerse themselves in creative projects. Later, she would play Marian to his Robin Hood in three different plays and films.

Tim's creative drive was inspiring friendships with other children with similar needs to be creative. If they were working on mutual projects, such as making a film where they were in basic agreement over the idea, they could just get on with it for hours. These were instances where Tim could show great interaction, flexibility and friendship qualities and continually exercise his social muscles – the more so because he was getting so much enjoyment and happiness from these relationships.

At one point during this time, Tim had two friends round who we knew from church – brothers, Miles and Lee. They shared experiences through being in rehearsals together for Tim's Robin Hood play and through a band they had started to create. They were here for three hours, amusing themselves, playing in the garden, making films, going down to the woods nearby, popping in and out of the house, making themselves drinks etc and they didn't need me at all. In fact, I felt I cramped their style.

Once Tim and Lee were rushing round the house so much so that they pulled a whole set of curtains off the wall – I didn't care about the curtains but I *did* care that he was playing with others and didn't need me.

One day when Susannah was coming over, I thought I'd better ask Tim what he was planning for them to do. In the past he'd had very high hopes when a friend came that they would do exactly what he had been planning and preparing for them. These days it was usually radio shows or films, but sometimes his friends didn't want to do these activities and he would come crashing down emotionally as if it was the end of the world whenever this happened. His hopes and expectations were always so high and I felt for his friends in these situations, but I wanted to protect him too.

Therefore there was a lot of thought behind my casual question to Tim, 'What are you going to do when Susannah comes?'

He said, 'I'll see what Susannah wants to do and we'll do that first. Then maybe we can do what I want to do.' And he meant it.

I have never forgotten this because it was such a significant milestone. He was willing to put his own plans and needs behind those of his friend, in order that she would have a good time. This was the beginning of his ongoing thoughtfulness for his friends that has since characterised all his relationships.

Chapter Thirteen– Reflection and where next

Celebration

When we had first withdrawn Tim from the school system at the age of eight, it had often taken him up to an hour to go through a meltdown and come out the other side. Two and half years later, if there was something he didn't like or something changed, we had a brief chat with him and he could cope. He could reason on nearly all levels, progressing from a one-hour process full of emotion and complexity to a two-minute chat. Even when he had been looking forward to something and we couldn't do it anymore, he would be flexible, calm and open for change. Life became easy and enjoyable with him – something unthinkable only a few short years ago.

Clarity of social ease

At this point, I checked where Tim was on the Son-Rise Program® Social Curriculum. At age six he had been on Stage 1 for eye contact, flexibility and interactive attention span and stage 2 for communication. Now, at the age of eleven he had virtually achieved Stage 4 for all these things. Some of the things in the Stage 4 Son-Rise Program Social Curriculum that Tim had achieved were as follows:

He was now able to ask and answer questions and make statements about past and future events. He was able to answer simple why questions on what he had just experienced/observed and ask his own why questions. He could have conversations with over 5 loops or more. He could speak using nouns, verbs, adjectives, prepositions, pronouns, conjunctives and articles. He was gradually understanding and using basic social cues (facial expressions, tones of voice, body language), could share lots of joint attention and take turns listening and talking. He could occasionally initiate conversations. He was generally polite and respectful, would comfort someone if they were hurt or upset and he was largely able to interact appropriately with a peer.

Tim still needed to develop further in the areas of giving his opinion, being genuinely interested in others in a deeper way, initiating conversations more easily, participating in others' activities etc – but these skills were all developing. He was also learning to postpone an immediate payoff for a longer-term payoff, being OK with the fact that everyone is different, that if people are unkind it's often about them and not about him. These are the perspectives encouraged in Stage 4 Son-Rise Program Social Curriculum. He could participate in small group activities, follow a timetable in his focus room, listen to and follow instructions. He had proved conclusively that he could spend hours rehearsing performances, working collaboratively and creatively with peers and also enjoy meaningful friendships on a one-to-one basis.

This social curriculum stated that if your child is able to maintain 75% of the skills required in Stage 4 for about two hours a day, they are ready for a school setting. This gave me confidence when thinking about the next stage of his life. I love the fact there is so much clarity within the Social Curriculum, so instead of just relying on my gut feeling, I knew exactly that progress was happening and where.

We knew we still had some of Stage 4 and all of Stage 5 of the Son-Rise Program Social Curriculum to work on, but it was obvious to us that he was growing in all these areas. I couldn't wait to get to the next stages and see where Tim's progress would take him.

With all of Tim's stage shows and friendships, it wasn't only me, Erik and Rachel who had to believe against all the odds any more. Other people could now see Tim's progress too. His motivations were growing, the outside world was opening up to him and I felt excited about all the possibilities for his future and incredibly chuffed that we had chosen the Son-Rise Program approach to help him. He was only eleven and still had plenty of time to grow and discover his path in life.

From all I had learnt, I knew it would be vital that we still kept a close eye on how Tim was feeling, wherever he was being educated, to ensure that he continued to grow and progress. All I cared about was that the bond we had worked so hard to achieve with him, would be honoured and allowed to continue to grow. My nightmare was that he would regress and stop communicating in the natural lovely way he now was with us.

We would always put relationship first – trusting his words, his feelings, his processes. No one would be making decisions for him without his input. We would continue to give him autonomy, kindness and respect. We knew that wherever his future took him, these factors would always remain most important to every aspect of his development and our relationship with him and would be the biggest determining factor on where his future would take him.

I would love to share with you now what happened between the ages of eleven and seventeen, but this book is already long enough. And if you think what we went through to the age of eleven has been a roller-coaster, the next six years also tested us to the limit as a family. But it was totally worth it! I have charted all our experiences – good and bad – in *Miracle in Slow Motion Part 2*.

However, as I am writing this right now, Tim is seventeen and I really can't resist sharing some good news about him. He just found out the other day that he passed his level 2 Music Diploma at Chichester College with distinction. Just before his sixteenth birthday he made the front page of a local newspaper after writing, performing in and editing a two-and-a-half-hour musical film. He has also passed exams and earnt money playing the piano at various events. I think he has around 120 songs in his current repertoire, which he can play by ear. He loves the feeling of independence and the other day went on a bus ride over two hours away just for a sense of adventure. He has some lovely long-term friends, who he regularly goes out with.

To me, he is amazing and turning into a really caring, responsible young adult. He goes out independently and also likes being home alone. He willingly helps me with the housework and he has recently taken to looking after Sammy for me so I can pop out. He is nothing short of a miracle to me and I have every confidence he will find a way to make the great vision he has for his future a reality.

Testimonials

Over the past 10 years many professionals have worked with Tim. Here are some testimonials of their experiences.

Gel Allchurch, Teacher – 'When I first started working with Tim, he was completely controlling and absorbed in his own world. Two weeks ago I gave him a music lesson and he gave me his full cooperation for 2 hours. He is taking his grade 2 singing in 3 weeks time'

Tracy Morgan, Community Nursery Nurse – 'Tim was a shy, isolated, withdrawn child with minimal communication skills. He has grown into an articulate, motivated, social, happy young man who appears to be thriving, happy, content and confident in himself and his abilities'

Maria Griffiths, Nutritional Therapist – 'Tim would be like a distressed wild animal at times. He would cry hysterically and didn't want to be part of anything – totally untouchable – unreachable. Now he's conversational, polite, responsive and cultured'

Sarah Higbee, English specialist teacher – 'Tim used to be rigid with fear – he was very controlling, very inflexible and uncooperative. He would also tip into tantrums very easily – it broke my heart. Now I am his English teacher and for 2 hours on a 1-1 he remains 100% enthusiastic, responsive and willing – resistance and defensiveness is long gone'

Katie Strong – Sally and I were friends in our twenties when we attended the same church but we somehow lost touch with each other for a few years before Tim was born. One day we bumped into each other again whilst out shopping in our local town Son-Rise Program®. My son would have been around six or seven and

Tim a couple of years younger, although Sally was on her own on this occasion. We went for a drink together in a coffee shop where Sally explained that Tim was autistic making it impossible to take him shopping. She said that he couldn't understand why he shouldn't take anything he wanted from a shop and that he would get very upset when Sally tried to prevent him. She said that he was easier to manage in a home situation and we invited them to our house so that the boys could play together and we could have a cup of tea and chat. Having no knowledge or experience of autism at the time I imagined a child with mild behavioural problems having a tantrum in a shop as many children would.

When I first met Tim I realised straight away that this wasn't a case of mild behavioural problems. I greeted him and Sally encouraged him to respond but he seemed to be in his own little world, very distant and unaware of my words. Sometimes when prompted he would repeat something, maybe hello or thank you, but there was no connection with him. When he was a little older he would say a greeting or a thank you unprompted, sometimes even a complete sentence, but it was spoken as if recited or read from a book rather than a spontaneous interaction.

When Tim played together with my son, Sally would delight in the smallest of achievements. If they spent a few minutes looking at a book together she would view this as a wonderful step forward. Even if for the rest of the playtime Tim played on his own shunning any attempts to persuade him to join in, Sally would treasure those few moments of social interaction and say that it was a huge encouragement for her. She had a level of patience that I have not seen in any other mum. If Tim had a tantrum about something, she didn't mind how long it took her to calmly explain until eventually he understood enough to calm down a little.

On arrival at our house Sally had to look around for dangers such as making sure that the front door and garden gate were securely closed to stop Tim from getting out and wandering off as might be necessary with a toddler rather than an older child.

When the time came to leave there were always problems. Tim would have become attached to a particular toy or video and would want to take it home with him. He would have a tantrum which would last a very long time. My natural reaction was to say that he could borrow the toy and take it with him but Sally warned that it wasn't the right thing to do and would make things more difficult in future. She was determined to get him to understand no matter how long it took so would often spend a good twenty minutes calmly explaining the reasons why he couldn't take someone else's toy whilst Tim would fuss and cry. Eventually he would calm down enough to leave without the toy.

On one occasion when Tim came to play he took a large toy lorry onto our trampoline. He was playing on his own, jumping with the lorry on the trampoline. When I asked him to take the lorry off of the trampoline in case he hurt himself it was as if he didn't hear me. It was as if he was in his own world and unaware of anything around him.

On another occasion when Tim came round to play we had two other children visiting at the same time and they became loud and boisterous, laughing and teasing each other and pulling each other around the floor. Tim couldn't cope with this and became very distressed. It was probably the worst meltdown I witnessed from him and it seemed to me that he was panicking and scared. Sally took him into another room and it took a long time for her to calm him down. I often noticed that moderately loud noises bothered him. He would cover his ears and said that it hurt. After he went for specialist noise therapy there was a noticeable improvement, so much so that Tim was able to enjoy a birthday party where people did musical performances and he was able to sing into a microphone. He obviously has musical talent and it must have been hard for Sally to be unable to include him in some of her music projects, especially the DVD filming, because although he may have managed the tasks, he would not have managed the necessary social interactions with the other children or the demands of filming, In hindsight I can see that the Tim at the musical birthday party was already quite a different child from the Tim I had met a few years earlier who would never have coped with such an occasion.

Not long after Sally began to home-educate Tim we didn't see each other again for a couple of years. By the time we met up again Tim was approaching Secondary school age. When I greeted Tim I was surprised not to get the usual recited reply lacking in any feeling, but instead he immediately engaged in conversation. It was as if his words came from his own mind rather than being read from a book. I watched amazed at how he interacted with my son, how they played and chatted together, how he was happy and helpful becoming excited at the prospect of a particular game he liked. After a while I turned to Sally and told her that the difference in him seemed miraculous and that I wouldn't have even guessed he was autistic had I not already known. Whenever I have seen him since I have experienced the same awe at the transformation. He now seems to really enjoy social interaction with both children and adults but it is more than that, he hears, he understands, he responds, he engages. I can't see any reason why he shouldn't follow whatever path he wishes in life and only a few short years ago that would have seemed impossible.

Steve Kitt – I think the greatest compliment I can pay in all this is that it is almost as if there are two Tims; the one that I know now and the one that I've been reading about in the first draft of Sally's book. Yes – I was around back then, but he has come so far that it feels like it was a totally different child that I was trying to help. The Tim of today is so courteous, well-spoken, communicative and comfortable with people – certainly with me, anyway. Autism in him is difficult to detect; I'm not sure that I would have guessed if I didn't know the background.

I've known Sally through a few stages of her life. In the 1990s, when she was in her 20s, we were part of a really nice group of friends, all of us young, free and single at the time. We did a lot of things together and had a lot of fun. She was noteworthy for being "all-embracing" to people who might be seen as 'misfits' by others. Then along came Erik, who was absolutely perfect for her; she was very 'hyper', and Erik brought a calm stability into her life. Attending her wedding was just fantastic – one of my greatest friends marrying her ideal soul-mate. We were all thrilled to bits to hear she was having a child, and that remained the case for the first year or so. Then I saw her devastated by the medical report, absolutely heartbroken. Trying things that simply didn't work for Tim and which were going against all Sally's natural instincts must have been agonising for her, but she was willing to try if there was any way it was going to bring about a positive change. I suppose it needed a person who had come through autism himself (Raun K. Kaufman) to really understand how a person with autism functions and what is needed to bring them through. Sally and Erik have absolutely devoted themselves to Tim, and the 'end-product' is way beyond expectations – how many adults can compere shows, write imaginative film scripts, as well as write their own songs and perform them?

Sally, Erik and Tim…we salute you!

The End

Glossary

Applied Behavioural Analysis (ABA) Applied Behavioural Analysis is a way of teaching complex tasks by breaking them down into small pieces. Rewards (or reinforcers) are given for correct responses or behaviours, and inappropriate responses are corrected, ignored or redirected. It targets many skills such as attention, imitation, language, self-help skills and academic skills as well as behaviour. The aim is to increase useful behaviours and decrease behaviours that may cause harm or interfere with learning.

Auditory Integration Therapy is a therapy that was developed as a technique for improving abnormal sound sensitivity in individuals. It involves listening to music modified by filtering and modulation with the aim to create better pathways between the ear and the brain, resulting in less sensitivity and better auditory processing.

Candida is a fungal infection caused by a yeast called Candida. Some species can cross the blood brain barrier and aggravate brain cells, causing brain dysfunction. If this occurs in a very young baby or child, the normal developmental growth may be seriously affected.

Dr. Natasha Campbell-McBride MD, M.MedSci (neurology), M.MedSci (nutrition) is a doctor who wrote the book *Gut and Psychology Syndrome*, which helps struggling parents with the health of their children with ASD.

Echolalia is a stage of learning to talk where the person repeats what someone or something had just said to them. Phrases they remember that they have heard and repeat, such as favourite TV programmes is known as delayed echolalia. Often phrases are repeated over and over from favourite TV programmes (see Scripting). It can be part of the developmental process of learning to talk, but some individuals do not move on from this stage.

ISM is the term that the Son-Rise Program use instead of 'Stimming' – see my more detailed explanation in Chapter Six.

Joining is a term used by the Son-Rise Program to describe a technique of entering into your child's world in order to connect and build relationships.

Jonathon Tommey is a Nutritional Therapist, who studied nutrition to help his autistic son, and with his wife Polly, created a magazine called *The Autism File* containing helpful advice about healing and managing autism.

Leaky gut is also called 'increased intestinal permeability', is a digestive condition in which bacteria and toxins are able to leak through the intestinal wall, and possibly cause disturbance in brain cells, thus contributing to conditions such as ASD.

Live Blood Analysis is a simple test from a single drop of your blood, put under a microscope and magnified 1000 times or more. Any unhealthy blood cells can be detected, which can indicate an unhealthy digestive system, due to diet and stress activity.

NVQ Level 2 Understanding Autism is a National Vocational Qualification I did out of interest to see whether the way they were explaining autism matched up to how my son experienced it and what helped us to help him.

Occupational Therapy This is the use of assessment and intervention to help individuals gain the strength and skills, in order to take part in the everyday activities necessary to be independent.

Oxidative Stress is an imbalance between free radicals (the bad guys) and antioxidants (the good guys). Free radicals are an unbalanced form of oxygen, which lead to an unhealthy chain reaction in the body causing inflammation. If this happens within the brain, normal development in a young child can be affected. Antioxidants are the antidote to this inflammation and we all need them for our health.

Pathological Demand Avoidance (PDA) is a proposed sub-type of ASD, where the person has an innate need to avoid what other people ask of them, in order to be in control.

PECS/PECS Cards The Picture Exchange Communication System is a form of alternative communication in which a child is taught to communicate what they want with an adult, by giving them a card with the relevant picture on it, in exchange for an item or activity he wants.

Portage is a home-visiting educational service for pre-school children with Special Educational Needs and their families. For us, it involved one hour a week for a few months followed by Portage Plus which involved a support worker helping us for 10 hours a week for a year and a term.

Powerful interest is a phrase used by the Son-Rise Program instead of the term *obsession* which is used a lot to describe the high-level interests of people with ASD.

Scripting is the repetition of words, phrases, intonation, or sounds of the speech of others, sometimes taken from movies, but also sometimes taken from other sources such as favourite books or something someone else has said. People with ASD often display scripting in the process of learning to talk.

Self-stimulatory behaviour (also known as *stimming*) is when the person engages in repetitive body movements or repetitive movement of objects, such as rocking back and forth, or pacing around. Some view it as a behaviour to be prevented but others see it as a way that the person regulates and looks after themselves.

This behaviour becomes more apparent when the person is stressed, or excited.

SENCO stands for Special Educational Needs Co-ordinator and is the teacher in every school, who is responsible for assessing, planning and monitoring the progress of children with special educational needs/SEN.

Sensory overload These are sensory differences which can be extreme for a person with autism such as hearing all sounds around you at the same level, a brief touch feeling like pain, or being afraid of the unpleasant sensation of food in the mouth. Some individuals with ASD experience extreme (hyper) or low (hypo) sensory overload issues. As you can imagine, these really affect an individual's ability to process the world around them.

Speech and Language Therapists provide treatment, support and care for children and adults who have difficulties with communication, or with eating, drinking and swallowing. They are allied health professionals.

Statement This is a document which sets out a child's Special Educational Needs and any additional help that the child should receive. The aim of the Statement is to make sure that the child gets the right support to enable them to make progress in school. The term Statements changed to the newly formatted Education, Health and Care Plans (EHCPs) in 2014.

Temple Grandin Boston, Massachusetts, U.S. Mary **Temple Grandin** (born August 29, 1947) is an American professor of animal science at Colorado State University, consultant to the livestock industry on animal behaviour, and autism spokesperson. She also invented the "Hug Box" device to calm those on the autism spectrum.

The Autism File is a magazine created by Jonathan and Polly Tommey to give health and therapeutic advice to help people with ASD.

The Son-Rise Program is a home-based program for children and adults with ASD and other developmental issues, which was developed by Barry Neil Kaufman and Samahria Lyte Kaufman for their autistic son, Raun, who is claimed to have fully emerged from his condition. This program is child-centred and sees the parent as the expert of their child.

Thera-play This, for us, was a playgroup with autism specialist teachers who played with the children. From these sessions they also took the children out to OT and SaLT sessions. It was a place to watch the children's behaviour over a long period as part of the diagnostic process.

Transition is a difficulty that individuals with ASD can have during changes in or disruptions to activities, settings, or routines. Transitions can bring on meltdowns as coping with changes can be highly stressful.

Triad of impairments are the three key elements that are seen as the main difficulties for people with ASD. They can vary, but I have understood them to be social communication, social interaction and social imagination and this is what I mean when I refer to this phrase in my book.

Bibliography – In the order they appear in the book

The Reason I Jump: one boy's voice from the silence of autism by Naoki Higashida, Foreword by David Mitchell, Random House, 24 Apr 2014

'What is Autism?' article by Dr. Nick Walker on Neurodiversity, found on his website www.neurocosmopolitanism.com, 1 Mar 2014

Gut and Psychology Syndrome: Natural Treatment for Autism, Dyspraxia, A.D.D., Dyslexia, A.D.H.D., Depression, Schizophrenia, by Dr Natasha Campbell-McBride, Medinform Publishing, 1 Sept 2004

Let Me Hear Your Voice: a family's triumph over autism by Catherine Maurice, Alfred A. Knopf, 8 June 1993

A Life To Rescue: the true story of a child freed from the bonds of autism by Karen Michelle Graham, Innovo Publishing LLC, 5 May 2010

Facing Autism: Giving Parents Reason for Hope and Guidance for Help by Lynn M. Hamilton, Foreword by Bernard Rimland, Waterbrook Press, 14 Mar 2000

The Thinking Moms' Revolution: Autism beyond the Spectrum: Inspiring True Stories from Parents Fighting to Rescue Their Children
Foreword by Robert W. Sears, by Helen Conroy(Compiler), Lisa Joyce Goes(Compiler) Skyhorse Publishing, 9 Apr 2013

I am Special: Introducing Children and Young People to their Autistic Spectrum Disorder by Peter Vermeulen, Jessica Kingsley, 28 Nov 2008

Autism Breakthrough: The ground-breaking method that has helped families all over the world by Raun K. Kaufman, Vermilion,15 May 2014

Son-Rise: the Miracle Continues by Barry Neil Kaufman, Hj Kramer, 1st Jan 1994

How Children Learn: 50th Anniversary Edition by John Holt, Hachette audio, 2017

Acknowledgements

I would like to thank Raun K. Kaufman for giving the lecture I attended in London when Tim was just five years old. Your presentation, your energy, your knowledge and the hope you offered was the beginning of life-long change for us and has totally changed the trajectory of Tim's and therefore our lives forever. There are no words to thank for you for sparking that hope and possibility in my mind and understanding. Thank you too for our two-year correspondence when I first wrote to tell you how excited I was about Tim's progress and told you I was thinking of writing a book. And a final major thank you for writing the Foreword and truly understanding what this journey means to us and also for other parents and children.

Thank you to Bears Kaufman and Samahria Kaufman for creating the Son-Rise Program® in the first place, for not believing the naysayers and for forging your own paths and for then sharing your knowledge and passion with the world. If it weren't for your journey, Tim wouldn't be where he is now and for that I will forever be grateful.

I would like to thank John Caudwell and the charity Caudwell Children. Without you we would likely never have done our Son-Rise training, received the level of nutritional support we needed or had the auditory integration therapy, all of which were fundamental to all the changes that happened in Tim's life. Thank you from the bottom of my heart.

I would like to thank Kevin Peskett, who out of the blue, offered to build Tim's Son-Rise playroom the moment he could see we needed it. You worked for other clients and instead of asking them to pay you, you asked them to provide the materials for Tim's playroom. You then gave us your time for free. You have no idea how much we appreciate you and all you did for us. Thank you, Kevin.

I would like to thank Rachel Morris – without whom Tim would not be where he is. Rachel, who spent over 2000 one-to-one hours with Tim over a three-year period, who loved him and gave of her highly creative, inventive and playful self while gradually instilling discipline and a love of learning. Rachel, we are forever indebted to you.

I would like to thank Steve, who for many months cycled 15 miles weekly to play with Tim, jump into his world, follow his lead and share his energy and zest for life with him. Steve, you are one of our very best friends and we love you totally!

I would like to thank Cathy, who could have chosen to sit back in her retirement but instead chose to join the team and played with Tim regularly for months, working with him, following his lead and committing to weekly sessions. Thank you, Cathy.

I would like to thank Janina, who committed to playing regularly with Tim the moment she knew we needed help. Her dedication and willingness to learn to see through Tim's eyes and be led by him was exceptional and we are eternally grateful for her hours of care, connection and creativity with Tim. Thank you, Janina.

I would like to thank Rosie, who's bright, sparkly personality lit up the room with an all-consuming love and acceptance. Thank you, Rosie, for your fun, your silliness, your willingness to connect to Tim in any way he needed and for your creativity. We love you!

I would like to thank Dani. There's something about you Dani that children just adore and Tim was no exception. Your ability to connect so beautifully to him, to emotionally attune to him just puts you in his top list of favourite people and I thank you for being that for him.

I would like to thank Siobhan. Now, what can I say? Siobhan, you came at a time when I was in despair and you saw no deficiency, you saw no disability. You saw no deficit. You only saw a beautiful child who needed a playmate and you became the best ever playmate for Tim and the best ever babysitter for us. We felt seriously blessed to have you in our lives for so long and will always appreciate your major part in Tim's life.

I would like to thank Maria Griffiths who supported Tim nutritionally from the age of six with tests, supplements, incredible knowledge and emotional encouragement. Thank you so much, Maria.

I would like to thank Tania, who regularly printed out multiple copies of this book on her printer to enable me to give it to others to read and edit. Thank you for your work and time, Tania - I literally couldn't have done it without you!

I would like to thank Nina Flinders, who accepted Tim and I for who we were and genuinely loved us! Thank you for having Tim and I at a moment's notice and for inviting him for so many playdates, sleepovers and cinema trips! You are a total star!

I would like to thank Gel for volunteering to play with Tim in his Son-Rise playroom every week (and sometimes twice a week) since the age of six. It would be hard to find someone more devoted, consistent, kind and willing to give all of herself to Tim, despite having many grandchildren of her own. It was Gel who ultimately led him into a life of music. There are no words to express our sincere and profound gratitude to you, Gel.

I would like to thank Sarah for being one of my very best friends and my saving grace when Tim was just three months old. Thank you for loving him as much as you did, for being on the inside circle all the way through and walking through the whole journey of grief and hope with me. Who better to have as my editor than you, not only a friend and comrade on this journey but a professional writer, too. Thank you for going through this whole thing with me. I love you totally.

I would like to thank Riet (Oma) and Piet (Opa) for their consistent love, prayers and encouragement, total non-judgemental acceptance and love for all of us as a family.

I would like to thank my Mum, who has spent so many hours researching, gaining nutritional knowledge and cooking regularly for literally ten years in order to keep Tim in the healthiest state possible – for all her emotional support to me and for being the best Nana ever to Tim and Sammy.

I would like to thank my Dad for all our talks, shared decision-making, financial support and unconditional emotional encouragement – for being willing to always work as a team to do everything we can to support Tim in every way.

I would like to take this opportunity to thank my amazing husband, Erik, who has been my best friend and 100% with me on this journey. For sharing the pain, the sadness, the battles and the hope. For supporting me when I lost my confidence and building up my strength again for each step of the way. For the father you have been and still are to Tim and Sammy and the anchor of foundational support you are to all of us.

Finally, a big thank you to all my friends and wider family for your emotional and practical support through our journey. You know who you are and we love you very much.

About the author

I'm a free spirit – I love to travel, get out and meet people, experience new challenges, love studying and gaining new knowledge and be open to amazing, spontaneous happenings. I have travelled extensively in Australia and Africa and spent four years training to be a teacher, before marrying a kind, handsome Dutchman and settling down to work.

Our lives before our first child were busy and very sociable. I was so excited at the thought of being a mother. And when Tim was born, I instantly fell in love with him. So when he was diagnosed with autism, aged two, I embarked on the steepest learning curve of my life – and it has continued daily, ever since.

I have never accepted any form of hopeless prognosis – and there were far too many of those, especially in the early days. Watching Tim's struggles tore at my heart and I knew I would never give up finding ways to help him. This journey has taken me on a remarkable path. I want to share it with you, because I believe that what I have discovered and learnt could also help others, who are also facing confusion and heartbreak.

I now have two children and have been a qualified teacher for twenty-four years. My husband, Erik, is a social worker who trains social workers in the Solution-Focused approach. Currently, I am helping Tim embark on his musical career, bringing up his younger brother, and have started a consultancy to help families, whose children have similar diagnoses.

If you'd like to see where Tim is now, you can visit http://www.timwagter.com/ and if you'd like to contact me, I can be found at http://www.autismdevelopmentconsultancy.com and http://www.releasingmychildspotential.com.

Printed in Great Britain
by Amazon

44737679R00192